THE DISCOVERY OF ABUNDANCE

Simon N. Patten and the Transformation of Social Theory

Published under the direction of the American Historical Association from the income of the Albert J. Beveridge Memorial Fund.

For their zeal and beneficence in creating this fund the Association is indebted to many citizens of Indiana who desired to honor in this way the memory of a statesman and historian.

THE DISCOVERY OF
ABUNDANCE

Simon N. Patten and the
Transformation of Social Theory

By DANIEL M. FOX

PUBLISHED FOR THE

American Historical Association

CORNELL UNIVERSITY PRESS

ITHACA, NEW YORK

First published 1967

Library of Congress Catalog Card Number: 67–22192

PRINTED IN THE UNITED STATES OF AMERICA
BY THE COLONIAL PRESS INC,

Acknowledgments

I have incurred many obligations in the course of preparing this book. Some of them relate mainly to my efforts to understand the life of Simon Patten and the concept of abundance. Other obligations are to those men who had the generosity to teach the historian's craft to, and discipline the feelings of, a young man impatient for the life of a social activist. Finally, there are a number of other personal debts reflected in the manuscript.

This book could not have been written without the cooperation and interest of Patten's surviving students and friends and of those who are preserving the archival remains of his contemporaries. I have listed in "A Note on Sources" the names of these people and the various institutions where valuable papers are preserved. I feel a special obligation to the individuals who have died since they made their contribution to this book: Miss Frances Perkins, Solomon S. Huebner, J. Russell Smith, and William H. Allen.

My teachers deserve special thanks. Howard Mumford Jones generously helped me to understand the limitations of earlier drafts of the manuscript. William G. Perry, Kiyo Morimoto, and Frank J. Jones, though not historians, listened through several versions and helped me to understand and measure the importance of hearing the feelings behind the most sophisticated intellectual schemes. Most important, Donald H. Fleming inspired me to continue thinking and writing long after I wished the job was over and gave me the benefit of his superb historical craftsmanship on numerous occasions.

Two grants from Harvard University made possible the research on which this book is based.

The War on Poverty requires an ambivalent acknowledgment: without Title II of the Economic Opportunity Act of 1964, this book would have been finished much sooner—but with considerably less conviction about the relevance to contemporary life of the ideas I discuss.

I have a special obligation to my wife, Carol, who heard the book from its beginnings, compensated for my inattention to mechanical detail, and encouraged me to keep thinking about abundance despite our immersion in the scarcity of the Appalachian South.

D. M. F.

Boston, Massachusetts
January 1967

A Note on the
Author's Assumptions

The theme of this book is the emergence of a new concept, or frame of reference, for perceiving the social and economic activities of Western man: there is, or soon will be, enough material wealth to provide every individual with the requisites for survival. Simon Patten is the central figure of this story because he was the first man to devote his life to examining the implications of an idea which only within the past decade has attained central importance in the debate over social means and ends.

The terms "economy of abundance," "pleasure economy," and "affluent society" cannot be defined precisely, since their meanings all ultimately rest on personal answers to the question, "How much is enough?" Yet when such terms are used by professional economists—men who, in J. M. Keynes's phrase, are trustees of the "possibility of civilization"—they signify rather more than utopian fantasies. In order to maintain their professional existence, economists must base their abstractions on data which laymen perceive in their own lives. To put it another way, the overriding assumption of this book is the statistically verifiable proposition that, throughout the nineteenth century in Western Europe and the United States, real wages, national wealth, and the supply of goods and services above what was needed to prevent general starvation increased. That this increase was neither uniform nor unilinear is not relevant to this study—although it is true that the irregularity of economic growth provides an effective argument in the analyses of men who contend that there is not "enough" wealth available to justify any substantial transformation of traditional assumptions about social means and ends.[1]

It would be naïve, however, to suggest that "reality" in the West changed over the last century and that a few forward-looking men perceived this change, while most of their fellows remained comfortably or uncomfortably blind to it. No group of social scientists has had a corner on the perception of reality during the past century. No social theorist worth writing about has deliberately or stupidly refused to acknowledge the existence of data which have come to his attention. The problem is contained in the word "attention." Why do men of comparable intelligence, education, and dedication to science "pay attention" to different facts? This question has had many answers: economic or psychological determinism, chance, "proof" that the scientists were not equal in intelligence or dedication, for example.

For the purposes of this book, it is assumed that the answer lies in the problems posed by the conflicting pressures to retain and modify the frames of reference by means of which men organize their perceptions and order their lives. Since history is the art of purposeful question-begging, it is convenient to begin with an assertion that will do just that: Within "commonsense" limits, "reality" is what men say it is. Human beings perceive events in the external world in terms of assumptions or frames of reference which order their perceptions in a satisfying way. These assumptions, acquired in childhood and reinforced by repetition and the pressure of communal commitment to them, generally persist throughout an individual's life. For many centuries, men suffered no hardship because they believed the sun traveled around the earth. Similarly, a man who is not poor, but who wants to help those who are, will not necessarily be discomforted by the assumption that poverty is an inevitable result of moral deficiency.

Nevertheless, there are times when a frame of reference becomes inadequate. This is not to say that it fails to encompass "reality"—but rather, that living with a particular set of assumptions produces discomfort, an awareness of paradox, or an annoying need to regard certain events as "exceptions" to the operation of general principles. When this discomfort occurs, men have three choices. Most often, they decide, consciously or unconsciously, to keep the frame they are accustomed to and live with occasional discomfort or uncertainty about a choice of action. Less often, men construct fantasies which they treat as perceptions and which fit quite well into a particular frame of reference: ideology and schizophrenia provide similar, if not equivalent, comforts. Finally, some men set out to modify their inherited frame of reference so that the paradoxes and exceptions are transformed into aspects of a coherent whole. The history of social change is the story of the process by which the modified frame of reference of a minority becomes the viewpoint of a majority.

A modification in a frame of reference cannot be examined for truth or error in the usual sense of these words. Although a frame can be tested for intellectual strength by examining its coherence and correspondence with "reality," such tests will not explain why a particular set of assumptions proved useful to a significant group of people. The ultimate test of the validity of a frame of reference is not intellectual but social and emotional. If a modification in a man's assumptions enables him to live in greater comfort, as he defines the word, the modification can be accepted as useful and true.

The development of religious toleration in England during the sixteenth and seventeenth centuries illustrates these points. At the beginning of the sixteenth century, most Englishmen believed that anyone who disagreed with Catholic views on any substantial point of doctrine or dogma and continued to disagree in the face of all persuasion was a dangerous heretic who must be cut off from society. When the Church of England rejected the authority of Rome, most men saw no need to modify their traditional assumptions about heresy. But it soon became evident to some men that, once there was more than one church in Western Europe, the number of possible variations in doctrine and dogma was infinite. In late sixteenth-century and early seventeenth-century England, the traditional frame of reference for dealing with differences of religious opinion produced discomfort and paradox. Moreover, the exigencies of foreign and domestic policy made it necessary to create exceptions to the traditional concept.[2]

Most Englishmen were anxious to maintain the traditional frame, despite the fact that occasional exceptions had to be made. The official view, promoted by Queen Elizabeth and Richard Hooker for example, was that certain matters of doctrine and ritual were "things indifferent," although heresy was still what it had always been. Others, particularly among the Puritans, saw heresy as a vast social problem, became convinced of the sinfulness of most of the nation, and sought to exercise social control in terms of their own assumptions. A few men, whose number increased during the civil struggles of the seventeenth century, tried to modify the traditional frame of reference. In their view, the growing equivalence in social power among groups in Europe which held different opinions made the traditional assumptions about heresy obsolete. These men introduced the new concept of religious toleration.

Although the debate over heresy was mainly the concern of intellectuals and public figures, its effects were felt throughout English society. The general public seems to have lost its appetite for witch hunting and burning by the second decade of the seventeenth century. By the end of the century, when the concept of toleration was embodied in public law, most Englishmen had already modified their assumptions about heresy. A new frame of reference—toleration for everyone who accepted certain Christian principles—had become the viewpoint of the majority. Those Englishmen who could not accept the new assumptions about heresy either remained quiet or emigrated to the New World.

Simon Patten tried to modify men's assumptions about the permanence of poverty, the effects of a more equal distribution of wealth, and the possibility of substantial improvements in their standard of living. Whether Patten was right or wrong, coherent or confused, is a secondary issue. In the last generation, an increasing number of men have found challenge, utility, and intellectual comfort in the concept of Western economic development which Patten stated clearly for the first time. It remains to be seen whether this concept of abundance—the assumption that man, harnessing nature, can create enough material goods to go around and can generate ideas to improve the quality of life—will exert an influence comparable to that of the acceptance of religious toleration as the first principle of an open society.

Contents

THE DISCOVERY OF ABUNDANCE

Simon N. Patten and the Transformation of Social Theory

The Context of Scarcity,
1750–1880

Simon Nelson Patten, an American economist and social theorist born in 1852, was the first man to base a lifetime of economic analysis and of proposals for social reform on the opinion
that the West was entering the period of what we now call the
"affluent society." The credit for a convincing argument that
an age of plenty could result from the wise application of the
wealth, skill, and technology that men have inherited and increased belongs to Patten. But the intellectual anguish, and struggle for cogency and consistency that enabled Patten to enunciate
his thesis, has a long history.

Patten did much more than point out that the myth of a
golden age of plenty had become a potential reality. The impending realization of the myth had been a central theme in the
writings of such men as the Marquis de Condorcet, William
Godwin, W. Winwood Reade, and Edward Bellamy in the
eighteenth and nineteenth centuries. Unlike these writers, Patten
was concerned with the achievement of abundance and with
the limits or restraints men would set on human desire in their
adjustment to new economic conditions. Patten sought answers
to specific economic, political, and moral problems that were

arising during the transition from the long age of scarcity to the new era of abundance. In his search for approximate answers to insoluble problems, he blended economic theory with Christian morality and the implications of biological and behavioral science. For his perception of the complexity of these problems, he was indebted to the tradition of reasoned dispute in scientific inquiry and to his experiences as an American born in a pioneer cabin and educated by dedicated Protestants and German professors, who was living in the period when the United States became the greatest economic power in history.

An image of America as a land of potential plenty emerged in the sixteenth century from European longing for a utopian golden age. But there was also an anti-image, a picture of America as a land of scarcity, misery, and hardship. For the next two centuries in Europe and America, supporters of the image, on the one hand, and of the anti-image, on the other, argued against each other's claims. This debate had little to do with men's thoughts about social and economic policy until the end of the eighteenth century, when economics—the analysis of the production, distribution, and consumption of wealth—was separated from philosophy and moralization. The Industrial Revolution and the development of rules and methods for the study of economic relationships by François Quesnay in France and Adam Smith in Scotland put the problems of scarcity and abundance in a new context. Was it possible to produce enough goods to enable everyone to survive and to distribute them in a way that would continually stimulate production? The future shape of Western society depended on the answers to this question.[1]

For more than a century after the publication of Smith's *Wealth of Nations* in 1776, most economists assumed that scarcity was the normal human condition.* Most descriptions

* Scarcity has several definitions in economic and social theory. It frequently refers to an economic situation in which, since all the conceivable wants of the participants cannot be satisfied, they are forced to choose among "scarce" resources. In this book, unless otherwise indicated in the text, scarcity means either the existence of mass poverty or the inability

of the economies of nineteenth-century nations and most predictions of future economic events assumed that a scarcity of goods and resources and the desire of men to obtain what they could from a limited stockpile were the central factors in, and major motives for, economic activity. A gain for one man usually meant a loss for another. There was no danger of an insufficient demand for goods, since it was impossible to produce enough to satisfy men's desires. Moreover, scarcity prodded men, by nature indolent, into the activity necessary for progress.[2]

Since Adam Smith, however, economists have struggled with the problems of scarcity and abundance. The environmental changes due to the Industrial Revolution prevented sophisticated men from remaining satisfied with an unquestioning assumption of eternal scarcity. The unprecedented growth of urban population, for example, could only have been the result of an unprecedented surplus of agricultural goods. If new farming methods could produce more bread and new machinery increase the output of manufactured goods per worker beyond the wildest dreams of any prophets of a golden age, might it not be possible to produce enough to guarantee every man at least the requisites for survival? Men of the intelligence of Adam Smith, Thomas Malthus, David Ricardo, J. B. Say, John Stuart Mill, and Karl Marx could not ignore this question.

The leading economists of the nineteenth century are sometimes divided by historians into optimists and pessimists. Frédéric Bastiat, the French philosopher who wrote of beneficent economic harmonies, and Henry Carey, an American inspired by his nation's rapid economic growth, are often considered to have been at the opposite pole from the dismal scientists of English classical political economy. According to this classification, Adam Smith was a pessimist who made some optimistic gestures under the influence of the French Enlightenment. Malthus, Ricardo, and the two Mills, however, amputated Smith's

---

of a society to produce enough goods and services to guarantee everyone a standard of living which will support a healthy, productive life.

invisible gesturing hand and condemned economic man, a rationalistic maximizer of satisfactions, to an eternal struggle for the means of subsistence.[3]

Recent students of the history of economic thought do not accept this interpretation, which derives from the yearning of men like Thomas Carlyle and John Ruskin for a simpler and better world. Only a fool is an unequivocal optimist or pessimist —and men with the intelligence necessary for economic analysis are rarely foolish. Classical economists were more concerned about the conditions under which either optimism or pessimism about the future was possible than with the ends of social action. Like most thoughtful men, they hedged most of their bets. Like other intellectuals who have risen above the anonymity to which history relegates most men, they preferred ambiguity to that painless consistency which comes from ignoring paradoxes in data and values.[4]

A strong case can be made for the claim that the classical economists believed there was no escape from perpetual scarcity. Adam Smith conjectured that some nations were condemned by their laws, institutions, and inadequate resources to a condition of low wages and scanty profits. Thomas Malthus' doctrine that population increases faster than the means of subsistence seems to imply an unending struggle for the requisites for survival and the impossibility of successfully extirpating poverty. David Ricardo based his system of economics on the frustrations produced by the interaction between an expanding population and scarce natural resources.[5]

In an age fascinated by concepts of progress, perfectibility, and the potentialities of science, however, most of these men could not be content with grim cynicism about the future welfare of the human race. Adam Smith was convinced that an increased division of labor, which caused productivity to rise, must lead to an increase in economic returns. Malthus, just a few years after condemning the perfectionism of Godwin and Condorcet, admitted that his law of population might be compatible with gradual improvements in the standard of living.

Moreover, in the later editions of his *Essay on Population*, Malthus claimed that, if technology and social engineering could create enough wealth to abolish poverty, "even at the expense of three-fourths of the fortunes of the rich," he would be the "last person" to oppose "making the degree of distress alone the measure of our bounty." [6]

Admissions that scarcity might not be eternal were more than mere rhetorical devices. The economists were trying to adjust their assumptions about human nature, and the inexorably logical conclusions which followed from them, to the rapidly shifting reality on which they relied for data. The most striking aspect of the new reality was the prosperity of Western Europe since the middle of the eighteenth century. The Industrial Revolution did not create poverty. Industrialization made poverty visible, and economic growth raised questions about the necessity of having the poor always with us. Poverty was the result, not of exploitation, but of the pressure of population on the means of production. If this pressure could be relieved by the application of science to production and of self-restraint to reproduction and by the infusion of raw materials from the American continents, the human condition might be radically changed. [7]

Yet it seemed futile to envision such possibilities, since human nature, as economists thought they saw it in the market place, was such poor stuff. According to Malthus, men were "inert, sluggish, and averse from labor." For James Mill and Ricardo, each man desired, as Mill put it, to "possess himself of the objects of desire at the cost of another." In 1715, Bernard Mandeville had demonstrated that private vices were public virtues—that the tastes of the rich created employment for the poor and that this situation provided a rationale for maintaining a rigid class structure. Smith, Malthus, Mill, and Ricardo rejected Mandeville's callousness. They preferred to praise selfishness only in the cause of virtue. [8]

Human nature, the economists believed, acquired undesirable characteristics because nature was niggardly. The fact that, within the lifetimes of the classical economists, men had made nature yield more goods did not necessarily destroy the assumption of scarcity. Only dreamers like Condorcet and Godwin argued that there were no limits to nature's yield. Tough-minded men like Malthus and Ricardo, however, were certain that limited natural resources and men's desire to maximize satisfaction made it inevitable that all human activities would reach a point of diminishing returns.

The economists, borrowing concepts from Newtonian physics, predicted that progress would terminate in a condition of equilibrium, a "stationary state." The idea of a stationary state was an opinion about what was possible rather than a vision of the future. In twentieth-century language, it was a model, a simplified picture of actual events, which economists believed had sufficient correspondence with reality to be useful to men of affairs. A half-century of biting analysis of the role of value judgments in scientific choice has, however, created a healthy suspicion of social scientists who hide behind allegedly colorless constructs. Although a model of the future is not necessarily a prediction of the "end" of development, the word tendency, as used by builders of such models, can mask a great deal of selective perception of the present. Since economists' models are abstracted from the reality around them and filtered through their own assumptions about the world, we can expect to observe gradual changes in these models which reflect changes in historical circumstances.[9]

The concept of the stationary state was modified during the nineteenth century as the prosperity of Western Europe and the United States increasingly threatened the assumption that there would never be enough goods produced to guarantee to every man subsistence and some improvement in his standard of living. From Adam Smith to John Stuart Mill and Karl Marx, the picture of the stationary state gradually became more pleasant. With Simon Patten and his successors, the pessimistic nineteenth-century models gave way to concepts of a pleasure economy, an affluent society, an age of abundance, or an era of high mass consumption.

The term stationary state was introduced by Adam Smith and made more precise in meaning by David Ricardo. In Smith's stationary state, wages and profits were low, and the further increase of wealth was limited by the niggardliness of nature. Ricardo's concept was based on his law of rent—the assertion that the major share of the wealth of an economy was gradually absorbed by the owners of land. As the point of diminishing agricultural returns was reached, rents would rise, profits would fall to the minimum necessary to stimulate men to bother taking economic risks, and wages would remain fixed at the level necessary for subsistence. Because resources were limited, the economy would reach equilibrium at a point considerably below that of Condorcet's expectation for his Tenth Epoch.[10]

John Stuart Mill, whose major work on economics was written and revised during the years of greatest prosperity in the nineteenth century, looked forward to more happiness in the stationary state than any of his predecessors had hoped for. Mill refused to look toward the point of equilibrium with aversion. He hoped men would pause to enjoy the beauties of nature and the altruistic pleasures of participating in moral and social reform before they strove for the upper limit of economic growth. Men, he believed, could afford to "be content to be stationary." [11]

Yet Mill could not discard the assumptions of scarcity he had accepted from his father, a friend and disciple of David Ricardo. Although he believed that the "problem of production" had been solved and that men would henceforth be concerned mainly with the distribution of wealth, he realized that, for most of the world, there was not enough to go around, by anyone's definition of adequacy. Moreover, Mill restored Malthus' pessimistic law of population, which had come under attack among economists in the 1830's and 1840's, to a central position in economic theory. For Mill, the assumption of perpetual scarcity existed in uneasy ambivalence with a sense of the possibility of abundance. With each new edition of the *Principles*, Mill seemed closer to a break with the depressing doctrines of economic orthodoxy.[12]

The prestige of the physical sciences in England in the first half of the nineteenth century was a limiting factor in economic theory. Because Ricardo and Mill assumed the existence of a point of equilibrium, they were forced to set rigid limits to the tendencies they perceived. The pressure to project a limit for economic development could be relieved only by men who started with the assumption that human institutions and values were in constant flux, that the complexity of the past obviated the need for precise statements about the future. This relief was provided by German thought. The basis for a new vision of economic and social change was laid by Fichte and Hegel in philosophy, Alexander Humboldt and Friedrich Carl Niebuhr in history, and Barthold Georg Savigny in jurisprudence. By mid-century, when historical economics began to challenge some of the assumptions of classical theory, biology provided analogies which gave increasing support to critics of the concept of a stationary state. Wilhelm Roscher, the dean of German economists, for instance, preferred to describe societies as "declining" or "flourishing" rather than as static or dynamic.[13]

Karl Marx, who tried to combine the historical and metaphysical sophistication of his German teachers with the analytical precision of classical economists, had a paradoxical attitude toward the problem of the stationary state. Marx's economics was based on the English assumptions of scarcity. His projections of future events, grounded on German historical and philosophical doctrines, anticipated an age of abundance. Accepting the classical doctrines of a wage fund independent of workers' actions and the Malthusian law, Marx argued that, under capitalism, workers' living standards could not rise above the level of a subsistence minimum. Nevertheless, he looked forward to a classless society in which "all the springs of cooperative" wealth would "flow more abundantly" and in which work would no longer be a harsh struggle against scarcity.[14]

Marx would have had no trouble explaining the contradiction apparent here. He claimed he was writing a "natural history" of economic and social change. For him, Ricardo was useful because he provided a framework of theory to explain the "antagonism of class-interests, of wages and profits, of profits and rents" in a "bourgeois economy." Ricardo was, however, naïve in assuming that his theories reflected "laws of nature." These laws could be brought to light only by examining the data of change in the context of a vision compounded of metaphysical and historical insights. Marx, however, has been justly accused of ignoring, despite his dedication to history, the increase in the real wages of labor during the nineteenth century. Although he admitted that the Malthusian and Ricardian laws, the doctrines of population and rent, could not operate in the abundance economy of the classless society, he did not use his historical tools to learn that capitalist society was also changing, from a basis in scarcity to a basis in potential abundance. If Marx had suspected that Ricardo's projection of a stationary state was valid only for the aftermath of the Napoleonic Wars, he would have had to replace his vision of impending revolution with the evolutionary doctrines of those German historical economists whom he dismissed as time-serving "bureaucrats." [15]

Both Marx and John Stuart Mill were forced by the circumstances of the economic growth around them to consider the possibility of abundance, even though their economics was based on scarcity. Malthus and Ricardo had discussed the possibility of abundance as unlikely and had then passed on to more immediate concerns. Mill and Marx developed uneasy compromises between the concept of scarcity and speculations about the effects of technological transformation, of the increasing availability of natural resources, and of the growing managerial competence of the men who carried out the Industrial Revolution.

In the 1850's and 1860's, when Simon Patten was growing up on a prosperous farm in De Kalb County, Illinois, the conditions of life posed new challenges to economists who had already come of age. During these years, there was a substantial increase in the populations of Europe and the United States and, in contradiction of classical economic theory, a rise in standards of living. Reality was threatening the assumption of perpetual scarcity, and the leading economists adjusted their theories to take some account of new conditions. John Elliot Cairnes, the most prominent of Mill's immediate successors, maintained, in the tradition of Ricardo and Mill, that the working of economic laws required the rich to become richer and the poor to remain poor. But Cairnes contradicted himself on the validity of the Malthusian law of population and implicitly called into question economic theory based on the assumption of scarcity. Cairnes, like Mill, claimed to agree with Malthus. Yet he demonstrated that the alleged pressure of population upon the means of subsistence was separate from the wages-population mechanism. The rate of production of children was determined by cultural forces rather than by a pecuniary calculus. Cairnes did not push his insight further. His commitment to the assumption of scarcity prevented him from suggesting that changing cultural forces, combined with increased production, might transform the basis of economic life from scarcity to potential abundance.[16]

William Stanley Jevons in England and Karl Menger in Austria began with the assumption of scarcity but, working independently of each other, created analytical tools which later economists would use to examine the implications of potential abundance. By shifting the focus of economic analysis from the production to the consumption of wealth, Jevons and Menger, along with Léon Walras in France, provided a means for examining the ways in which individuals sought to "maximize the utility" they derived from the goods and services available in a particular economy. Jevons formulated the central problem of economic theory in terms which, in other hands, could be used to undermine the "principle" of scarcity: "Given a certain population, with various needs and powers of production, in possession of certain lands and other sources of material; required, the mode of employing their labor which will maximize the utility of the produce." [17]

Although Jevons and Menger provided a theoretical framework which enabled economists to examine the way men balanced the pains and pleasures of existence, their conclusion that, in economic affairs, the sum of pains would always be greater than the sum of pleasures could not be challenged by theory alone. Only the examination of new data could dispute the validity of this calculation. By the 1870's, economists could draw on an unprecedented amount of historical and sociological data. Most of the new information about the evolution of economic relations and of the techniques of production was gathered and systematized in Germany by men who called themselves historical economists. A great deal of challenging data was available in the United States, where abundant natural resources and the absence of a large "rent class" of landlords had long been regarded by some men as an indication of potential plenty.[18]

The handful of American students, Simon Patten among them, who in the 1870's sought in Germany higher education in the social sciences were in a unique position. Many of them had participated in their own families' transition from the scarcity and hardship of pioneer days to comparative affluence as the family land yielded an increasing surplus because of hard work, new technology, and expanding markets. Even if they had not studied intensively the English economists, whose ideas were embedded in American textbooks on political economy, they at least had the linguistic tools to read them with ease. At the same time, they were willing converts to the sophisticated historicism of their German teachers. Unlike the Germans, however, who had a patriotic impetus to defend the superiority of history to theory, the Americans could freely integrate the ideas that flowed from Berlin, London, and Vienna. These men of the New World were in a position to challenge the assumptions of the Old World about the conditions and prospects of economic society.

Yet most of the German-educated American social scientists never challenged the traditional assumptions of European economic thought. Simon Patten was almost alone in his effort to replace the assumption of scarcity with an assumption of potential abundance. Prophecy is not a recognized profession in the modern world. Most men who have tried to predict the future can be dismissed as dreamers or solitary geniuses. But when a man like Patten, with a professional reputation to up-hold, becomes a prophet in the course of his daily work, it is likely that he has perceived a significant change in the spirit of his age. In the generation after Patten's death in 1922, an increasing number of social scientists, including John Maynard Keynes, the most important economist of the period, developed ideas similar to Patten's. This book is an effort to explain Patten's uniqueness, his lonely dedication to the problems of adjustment to affluence, and his legacy to social theorists of our own time.

CHAPTER I

Illinois and Germany,

1852–1885

In 1852, when Simon Patten was born, the hard-working Presbyterian farmers of Sandwich, Illinois, a hundred miles west of Chicago, were reaching the end of a decade of scarcity. Joining manpower and equipment, they had filled the stagnant ponds on their land to check the threat of malaria and had broken the prairie sod to enable wheat to grow. Under the leadership of William Patten, the most adventurous farmer in the county, who was a representative to the state legislature, a secretary of the county temperance society, and a church elder, the men of Sandwich had persuaded the Illinois Central Railroad to lay tracks between their town and Chicago.[1]

Twenty-four years later, when Simon Patten set out for Germany, Sandwich was a prosperous town, providing food for the expanding Chicago market and increasing its output by taking advantage of new developments in agricultural technology. The farmers' standard of living had risen markedly. Frame and shingle houses had replaced the original log cabins. The sons of the original settlers were sent to nearby Aurora for their secondary education and then on to Chicago for college, before returning to the farms or entering a profession. The town took pride in its morality and its Republican politics. Methodist revivalism had softened Presbyterian severity, but the townsmen were committed to temperance, hard work, and Christian charity. Although most of the farmers had been staunch Democrats in the 1840's, they had organized a station on the underground railway in 1850. As Abraham Lincoln cut his ties to the aristocratic traditions of the Whig Party, the farmers of Sandwich, led by William Patten, gradually came to admire him as a man who expressed their aspirations.[2]

When Simon Patten arrived in Hamburg in 1876, en route to Halle in Saxony, where he would attend the university, he was confronted with a society as prosperous and proud as the one in which he had grown up. Unlike the Germans he met, however, who were sons of farmers, merchants, and civil servants, Patten had lived among men who had struggled against a threatening environment. The Germans respected order and discipline more than the Presbyterian farmers of Illinois did. Consulting their history as a nation, the Germans viewed the past as a gradual approach to the present. They had no experience of the wrenching and uprooting of men and the environment familiar to an American farmer one generation away from the frontier. Germany had become the intellectual and economic pacesetter for Europe. Its rate of intellectual and economic growth, together with its recent experience of civil war, provided similarities to American experiences and aspirations, which made the young Patten more comfortable than he would have been in any other foreign country.[3]

Illinois and Germany were the major formative influences on Patten's career as an economist and social theorist concerned with adjustment to an age of abundance. From Illinois, he derived a vision of man's capacity to realize his aspirations, a respect for hard work and moral restraint, and a high regard for such institutions as the Republican Party and the Presbyterian Church as instruments for social change. From Germany, he obtained a vision of an orderly society that increased its wealth while it maintained active concern for those who suffered in the process of social change, an introduction to ideas and tools with which to analyze the world around him, friends who shared his enthusiasms and encouraged his work, and credentials as a professional economist.

Patten's German experience, of three years in a lifetime of seventy, cannot, however, be understood without a more detailed exploration of the experiences and assumptions he brought with him to Halle. His family, his upbringing on his father's farm, his religion and schooling created in him the receptivity which made Germany meaningful to him. The set of attitudes now called the Protestant ethic, which Patten assimilated as a boy, developed in him a commitment to practical affairs, to his calling as an economist, and to the need to avoid self-destructive temptation. These attitudes prevented Patten from becoming a utopian. They also interfered with his acceptance of some of the implications of abundance. Later, when he replaced God by science as the sanction for behavior consistent with the Protestant ethic, he was uncertain about the meaning of such virtues as sobriety, frugality, and thrift in an age when the production and consumption of wealth were constantly expanding. In an age of transition, however, in a time when the frame of reference for ordering social and economic life is changing, the struggles of the ambivalent man are more interesting than the certitudes of converts to a belief in a particular prophecy.

The Protestant ethic was very much alive in nineteenth-century America. Many men who accepted the doctrine of calling, the exhortation to energy and conscientiousness in a particular occupation, were concerned about a dilemma which had been built into the ethic in the seventeenth century. Although they believed that the moral Christian would prosper, they feared the corrupting influence of wealth. Affluence "might lead one into the City of Destruction, from whose sloth, negligence, chambering, wantonness, and vainglory Bunyan directed the Christian to flee." The rapid economic development of the United States made it necessary to reconcile economic expansion with virtue, opportunity with calling. The seventeenth-century doctrine of stewardship, by which the affluent discharged their Christian obligation to the deserving poor, had to be adjusted to fit a situation in which economic crises often prevented willing men from obtaining the work which was the emblem of deservingness. Conversely, some Americans looked forward to a time when everyone would be so affluent that no stewardship of wealth would be necessary, since there would be no poor. Would corruption then set in? Could the ethic be modified to imply stewardship in the cause of improving the "higher and better part of our nature"? Most Americans, whatever their feelings, adopted the language of compromise when dealing with these issues. The leading author of textbooks on economics in the decade before the Civil War asserted that happiness consists "in the gratification of our desires within the limits assigned to them by the Creator." Presumably Francis Wayland's Creator would redraw the limits as the Industrial Revolution modified the desires of moral men.[4]

These issues, whatever their interest to historians, did not concern William Patten, Simon's father, when, in 1843, he left his bride of a few months at his family's home in upstate New York and set out for Illinois. William, a shrewd, strong man, with no education past primary school, was more concerned with avoiding the corruption of others than with his own prospective sinfulness. He was impressed by the potential fertility of the land he had bought for a dollar and twenty-five cents an acre and determined to keep out of the way of local swindlers who understood the "ways of lying and cheating" as well as did their eastern counterparts. William was committed to hard work and "regularity" in his daily life. When, in order to obtain capital to improve his farm, he joined the California gold rush, he remained uncorrupted by, and rather above and apart from, the greed and vice around him.[5]

The Lord frequently tested the faith of William and Elizabeth Patten in their early years in Illinois. Their first two sons died in early childhood. Four years after Simon's birth, Elizabeth herself passed away. William did not waste much time grieving for his wife. Six months after her death, he returned to New York to marry another woman, who bore him five children during the next decade. The entire family worked on the farm. Young Simon, who at fourteen was a gangling six feet two inches, was, according to legend, frequently berated for laziness by his father. Simon may have preferred reading to rail-splitting.[6]

William, when his livelihood was secured, also turned from the daily grind to other activities. As a public servant, William was less concerned with the ambiguities of stewardship than with the creation of opportunities for other men to become successful. In the Illinois House of Representatives during the 1850's, he voted to petition Congress to maintain a liberal policy toward the admission of immigrants and supported efforts to remove legal restrictions on Illinois Negroes and to provide public education for their children. Yet William, in the tradition of the Protestant ethic, split the difference between absolute moral injunctions and practical considerations. He supported his town's underground-railway station and at the same time opposed "further agitation in the Congress of the United States upon the subject of slavery." [7]

Like such Illinois contemporaries as Jane Addams, the founder of Hull House, Simon Patten was proud of having come from the same environment as Abraham Lincoln. According to Patten's later interpretation of this pride, Lincoln was not a mystical hero. Rather, Lincoln had been transformed, in a short period of time, from a failure and a skeptic into a spokesman for the aspiration to affluence, restrained by the sanctions of the Protestant ethic. Lincoln's transformation was a result of his identification with men like William Patten. According to Simon, men like William forced Lincoln to renounce the aristocratic skepticism of Whiggery and change from a "scoffer into a believer." Between 1854 and 1858, Lincoln learned that, by sharing the aspirations and the restraints of Illinois farmers, he gained the "ability to pass over his emotions to people." [8]

Simon Patten believed that Lincoln, like the prairie farmers, had moved from a Calvinist to a Methodist approach to life, from loneliness to a sense of community, from the isolation of special grace to the warmer humanity of free grace and free atonement. The sanction for this freedom to participate in the emotional life of a community was the moral restraint of the Protestant ethic. Lincoln, like William Patten, had changed his focus from the individual to the community without losing his concern for individual salvation. It is impossible to know at what age William's son decided to devote his life to extending this transformation from the community to the nation. In a sense, Simon's movement from a Presbyterian home and elementary school to a Methodist secondary school and college followed the pattern of his father's evolution from a belief in rugged individualism to a dedication to community service.[9]

Simon's formal education began at the age of nine, in a log-cabin district school. As in most American rural schools of the period, the teachers were more transient than the pupils. Only one of them made a lasting impression on Simon. A young New England woman with a distaste for the flatness and philistinism of Illinois threatened Simon's pride of place and sense of sin. He responded by developing an animus against "bright colors, curved lines, fancy dress, and pretty faces" which was never, he later admitted, "thoroughly eradicated." [10]

Between 1870 and 1873, Simon attended Jennings Seminary in Aurora, Illinois, where he studied Latin, Greek, physics, geography, history, algebra, and geometry. Religion was an important part of education at Jennings. Itinerant preachers conducted frequent revivals, and visitors noted that "many conversions to God" occurred. In the autumn of 1874, he enrolled at Northwestern University, where he remained for a year and a half and studied the classics, physiology, botany, and German. Although he received excellent grades as a freshman, he appears to have lost interest in every course except German in his sophomore year.[11]

Two contradictory legends later grew up about the young Patten: on the one hand, that he was a bookish, shy black sheep, who incurred his father's wrath and was condemned by him for laziness—on the other hand, that William Patten, noting his son's interest in learning, directed him toward a career in law. The second story is more credible. Simon seems to have been less an intellectually inclined rail splitter than a hard-working, awkward lad who was given all the help toward achieving success that could be provided by the most prominent man in a prosperous Illinois county. The legends about Patten's difficulties with writing and about his lack of broad culture stemmed from the image of himself as an eccentric plowboy which he cultivated for personal and pedagogical reasons, and from his students' propensity to view him as a self-made man in an era when Americans had a high regard for the mythology of the dream of success. Patten never claimed that he was self-made. His writing difficulties, when regarded without Lincolnesque heroics, seem very similar to those encountered by numerous men who were educated at famous secondary schools and tradition-laden colleges.[12]

Although Patten's experience of the world was limited, he was dissatisfied with the ideas and attitudes he had grown up with when he left Northwestern in 1876 to go to Germany at the urging of a friend who had been there for a year. If his later recollections are to be credited—and they are the only data available—he was impatient with the political and intellectual standards of Illinois and uncomfortable with the restrained solemnity of the Protestant ethic. He was "tired of American politics and traditional religion" and "disliked classical studies." Although he had "little notion" of what he would find in Germany, he was "lured" there by a "craving for a broader view." [13]

Other young Americans in the 1870's regarded a trip to Germany as an opportunity for moral and intellectual adventure. G. Stanley Hall, later a noted psychologist and university president, relished the freedom to dissipate in Germany—the joys of experimenting with new vices at a cost to himself only, and not to his standing in the community. Richard T. Ely and Henry

Carter Adams, future professional colleagues of Patten, reacted against the sterility of American education in the social sciences by going to German schools.[14]

German universities had a special appeal for Americans which may have been more important than the students' revulsion against American education. Unlike American colleges, German universities did not prescribe a rigid curriculum. Students sat for examinations when they decided that they had mastered a particular subject. The German universities, moreover, were inexpensive and, unlike those in England, had no religious tests for admission. French universities restricted foreign enrollment. In addition, Paris had a reputation for vice which may have repelled American parents.[15]

The Americans were remarkably successful in Germany. They had been drawn there because they had greater vision, ambition, and ability than the average American college student. These qualities made them stand out from German students, most of whom were more concerned with passing state examinations for particular professions than with acquiring academic degrees. Moreover, German students had a tradition of dissipation and elegant negligence. No matter how eager some of the Americans may have been to indulge in vice, men like Patten, Hall, and Ely, who had been trained in restraint by American Protestantism, had no flair for immorality. Patten, for example, refused even to smoke or drink while he was in Germany.[16]

Like other Americans, Patten was seeking something new in Germany. His thoughts "ran wild" in the exhilaration of his discovery of the potentialities of social and natural science.[17] He had left home in full adolescent revolt, seeking a new basis for religion and politics. When he returned to the United States three years later, he still adhered to the imperatives of the Protestant ethic. German society and the study of economics had, however, given the ethic a new sanction—one based on science, rather than on God's will. It would still be necessary to restrain his base instincts, but God no longer provided the motive for restraint, and worship had become inadequate as a means of implementing moral imperatives.

The man who had the greatest influence on Patten's thought was Johannes Conrad, professor of political economy at Halle. Conrad's background and point of view were particularly suited to excite the young man from Illinois. Stocky, vigorous, just under forty years of age, Conrad had spent his youth on his family's large, efficient farm and was passionately interested in the techniques of agriculture. He had studied agronomy and chemistry before turning to economics. A Darwinian and a close friend of Ernst Haeckel, the leading German exponent of scientific materialism, Conrad used statistics and ecology in his economics research. Although Conrad later declared that Patten's mature work taught him more about economic theory than the writings of any other man, his own theorizing stimulated the thinking of the young Patten.[18]

In 1864, Conrad, then a *Privatdocent* at Jena, earned his professional reputation with a book which foreshadowed the ideas and echoed the personal experience of Simon Patten. Justus von Liebig, the foremost chemist of the first half of the nineteenth century, had asserted that, because of the working of the Malthusian law and because of the exhaustion of fertilizing chemicals in the soil, men must look forward to a future of scarcity and hardship. Conrad, combining data from both human and natural history, demonstrated that the long-term trend was toward abundance rather than scarcity. For him, the fertility of men and of soil was as much a social as a natural phenomenon. Birth control, the diversification of crops, the discovery of new sources of nutrition, the education of farmers in new methods of cultivation, the growth of world markets, and advances in industrial technology created a hopeful outlook for the future. Conrad was convinced that when a particular natural resource was exhausted, men would be able to devise substitutes to take its place. Simon Patten, who had observed the transition from scarcity to abundance on the Illinois prairie, must have been fascinated by Conrad's optimism. In Conrad's seminar he found a rational explanation for his father's commitment to agricultural experimentation, to education, and to the restraints of the Protestant ethic.[19]

Conrad was a member of a group of economists called the younger historical school. At Halle, Berlin, Heidelberg, and other German universities, men of his generation were producing an impressive body of work which took issue with the methods and conclusions of classical economics. These scholars, who came of age during Germany's industrial and political revolutions, were suspicious of the grandiose generalizations of the first generation of historical economists, who had begun to write in the 1840's, and were committed to using their knowledge to solve current social problems.[20]

Although they were deeply influenced by Hegelian concepts of the historical process and had been carefully trained in the research methods pioneered by such men as the historian Leopold von Ranke and the economists Gustav Schmoller and Adolf Wagner, Conrad and his colleagues were receptive to the theoretical economics emanating from London and Vienna. Only in the 1880's, after Patten had returned to the United States, did national and scholarly pride result in the *Methodenstreit*, a dispute between German and Austrian economists which destroyed the fruitful combination of empiricism and theory and pushed German economics out of the mainstream of professional development.[21]

Despite their interest in English economic theories, the Germans' assumptions about human nature and social change contradicted those of Ricardo and Mill. In general, the Englishmen regarded men as rational maximizers of satisfactions and society as nothing more than the sum of the human atoms within a particular geographical area. For the Germans, industrialization had not erased the assumptions of a long tradition of statist thought, capped by the insights of romanticism. They assumed that society was an organism which was more than the sum of its parts, that man's natural mode of action was collective rather than individualistic, and that traditions, feelings, and dimly perceived longings were the motives for human action. Unlike the classical economists, the Germans emphasized the creative potentialities of individuals and institutions and argued that men and society could best be understood in the context of their historical development. Simon Patten, who had internalized the individualistic assumptions of the English-speaking world, rejected organicism and was suspicious of historicism. Under the influence of Conrad, however, he accepted the historical economists' emphasis on the complexity of human nature and became sympathetic to their views about collectivism.[22]

The members of the younger historical school were personally involved in the formulation of German economic and social policy. Their historical approach to the study of social science convinced them that economic and social life was in a constant state of flux and that informed men could influence the direction of change. In their work, the line between knowledge for its own sake and knowledge as a tool of public policy was often blurred. Although traditionalists and doctrinaire liberals attacked them as "socialists of the chair," they never contemplated disloyalty to Bismarck's *Reich*. Much of the most telling criticism of socialist economics was first formulated by the historical economists.[23]

The historical economists, committed to ethical relativism by their methodology, sought a middle course between extreme individualism and extreme organicism. As consultants and administrators, and as members of a scholarly pressure group, the Verein für Sozialpolitik, German social scientists inspired government action in three areas: legislation recognizing labor unions and sanctioning strikes, the regulation of working hours and labor conditions, and social insurance. Although the historical economists' loyalty to the state enabled them to participate in the formulation of public policy, it blinded them to the necessity for thoroughgoing analysis of the German political system. They were open to the charge of social irresponsibility which Julien Benda later leveled at French *clercs*. Nevertheless, a great deal of human suffering was mitigated through their direct influence on social legislation, and their American students viewed them as models of the scholar in action.[24]

The German economists inspired their American students with zeal for social reform and with optimism about the prospects for success of planned change. But the historical economists did not regard state action as the only tool for social policy. The emphasis of Patten and other Americans on voluntary action was consistent with their German education. German social policy was less the expression of a new ideology than a new method for realizing, within the institutional context of any society, the traditional ethical goals of Judaeo-Christian morality. To some men, including Simon Patten, the reforms inspired by the Germans and, later, by the American Progressives, were the first installments of a much broader scheme of reform. But that broader scheme was never fully developed. Social policy, as conceived by German and American scholars, included no concept of a utopia against which to measure present conditions.

Conrad's lectures during Patten's years at Halle reflected the varied concerns of the younger historical school. Between 1876 and 1879, Patten heard his mentor expound national economy, the problems of public finance, statistics, the history of economic thought, the course of economic development, socialism, and the causes and remedies of poverty. Although Patten's thoughts ran wild, his doctoral dissertation, on local taxation in America, was a modest essay of sixty pages with a bibliography of only twenty items. Nevertheless, the dissertation showed that Patten merited the professional credentials bestowed on him in Halle. He explored the historical reasons for the primacy of property taxes in the United States, presented a statistical analysis of the sources of state and federal income in Illinois, and related his study to current German interest in tax reform. More important, he explored the possibility of financing public expenditures by a tax on surplus profits—a scheme which he later elaborated in a proposal to tax the fruits of abundance.[25]

Patten returned to America in 1879 with considerably more

than a doctor's degree. He was an angry man of twenty-seven, "in open revolt against the traditional concepts of our race." After the intellectual and social freedom of Germany, he "found the narrow, self-satisfied attitude of the American very trying." He had left home with vague feelings of dissatisfaction with American assumptions about politics and religion. He returned to Illinois with the equipment to transform his rebellion into social philosophy.[26]

It was six years before Patten issued his initial challenge to the economics of scarcity. In the interval, he experienced considerable personal and professional frustration. Although he was a trained economist, his German orthodoxy was heresy in America. If such an aggressive man as Richard Ely contemplated suicide because of his failure to obtain a university post, it is not surprising that the milder Patten, deterred by the lack of opportunities, did not try very hard to find academic employment.[27]

William Patten had strong ideas about his son's future. A few months after his return from Germany, Simon entered Chicago Law School. After only six weeks of legal study, his eyesight failed, and he returned in disgrace to the farm, unable to work or to read for almost three years. It is not known what was wrong with his eyes. The Patten legend implied that his blindness was a symptom of hysterical neurosis—perhaps a product of guilt about rejecting organized religion and perhaps related to his lifelong distaste for sexuality. Even the extent of his blindness is, however, unknown. The eye trouble was corrected by a specialist in Philadelphia in the spring of 1882.[28]

Between 1882 and 1887, Patten held a succession of elementary- and high-school teaching jobs in Illinois and Iowa. He kept in contact with the professional friends he had made in Germany, helping Richard Ely investigate living conditions in Pullman, Illinois, a "model" company town, and participating with Ely and Edmund James in the creation of the American Economic Association. In 1885, he published, at his own expense, a book he claimed he had conceived while he was blind, in the "compulsory darkness of a milkhouse" on his father's farm.[29]

In retrospect, *The Premises of Political Economy* can be seen as the first hesitant statement of a cautious and conscientious scholar who had begun to perceive the revolutionary consequences of rejecting the assumption on which more than a century of economic thought had been built. Patten appears to have realized that he was threatening the concept of scarcity, challenging the claim that men could never produce enough goods and services to guarantee everyone minimum security against want, disease, ignorance, squalor, and idleness. Although his German training reinforced his desire for a new frame of reference, the heritage of the Protestant ethic and his study of English economists made him hesitant to formulate one. Just as John Stuart Mill added more "exceptions" to Ricardian theories in each edition of *The Principles of Political Economy* and J. E. Cairnes couched his attack on Malthus as a "revision" of Mill, Patten claimed that his book was a "comment on certain positions of Mill similar to the comments of Mill on Adam Smith." Patten's confusing arguments and muddy style camouflaged his break with the past for his readers and perhaps, to some extent, for himself. Nevertheless, the book launched his public career and foreshadowed the future.[30]

Like Johannes Conrad, Patten refuted the doctrine of the niggardliness of nature which lay at the heart of classical economics. Pointing out the conflict between the pessimistic doctrines of classical economics and the evidence of America's expanding economy, Patten argued that human intelligence applied to the use of natural resources could produce abundance. Scarcity was a result of men's preferring "those forms of wealth of which nature is least productive." If people would modify their diet and consume the great variety of goods which could be produced in America—and in most other countries—everyone would prosper.[31]

Drawing upon his boyhood experience in Illinois, Patten questioned the universal validity of Ricardo's law of rent, the doctrine that differences in the fertility of various parcels of land accounted for the tendency of the price of food to rise. Working beside his father, he had learned that poor land could be made productive by hard work and the application of new scientific techniques, that these techniques enabled poor land to increase in fertility more rapidly than rich land, that fertility was a function of the variety of crops produced on a piece of land, and that most farmers were unwilling to let marginal land go out of cultivation, despite the law of rent.[32]

According to economists from Malthus to Mill, however, the potential abundance that might be created by the application of new techniques would not materialize, because of a constantly increasing population. Charles Darwin, whose theory of natural selection was influenced by Malthus' *Essay on Population*, seemed to reinforce the doctrine that men were doomed to an eternal struggle to obtain a limited amount of the goods necessary for subsistence.

Patten used Darwin in arguing against Malthus. The law of population assumed that men had a "definite set of attributes which were unalterable and unmodified by changes in surrounding circumstances." Darwin's theory, on the other hand, could be interpreted to mean that the succession of different environments through which a species passed during its history affected the attributes of the members of the species. If men, responding to environmental change, developed new concepts and techniques, they might learn to obtain a greater return from their environment. The amount of food, for instance, could be increased by the application of techniques developed by agronomists and industrial engineers during the nineteenth century.

Men's tastes were the major obstacle to guaranteeing subsistence to a growing population. If men could be taught to desire the kinds of goods their environment could produce, the pressure of population against the food supply would be reduced. Moreover, "up to a given figure," which Patten did not specify, an increasing population led to more efficient division of labor and permitted men to concentrate on specialized activities which resulted in new knowledge of techniques for getting the greatest return from the environment.[33]

Since men's tastes and habits could be changed in such a way as to eliminate scarcity, Patten was forced to take exception to Mill's doctrine that consumption has no influence on production—that a demand for commodities is not a demand for labor. If, Patten argued, men demanded goods not readily obtainable from the natural and human resources of their society, they would divert productive energies from the full utilization of the environment and create social distress. Patten criticized the upper classes for their excessive consumption of luxuries—what Thorstein Veblen would later call conspicuous consumption—and chided the lower classes for demanding a diet of wheat and potatoes, which prevented the cultivation of other vegetables and of fruits and led to the depletion of the soil. Full utilization of the environment required some redistribution of the wealth controlled by the upper classes and the educating of all classes to consume smaller quantities of a greater variety of goods.[34]

Patten did not yet have a specific program for redistributing wealth and changing the tastes of consumers. But he was critical of contemporary schemes for social reform. Doctrinaire liberals, who advocated the removal of all hindrances to free competition, neglected the fact that the qualities necessary to overcome competitors in the market place did not produce a greater variety of goods and more kinds of satisfaction in the consumption of wealth. Henry George's scheme for the nationalization of land and Karl Marx's proposal to appropriate "all the means of production" for the proletariat would redistribute wealth without changing men's desires. Patten saw no advantage in the lower classes' inheriting the earth if they were not taught to get the most out of their inheritance.[35]

In contrast to Marx, with his emphasis on changing modes of production, Patten viewed social welfare in terms of the "mode of consumption," of men's utilization of the material, aesthetic, and spiritual goods available in their environment. He was less concerned with overhauling political and economic systems than with introducing restraint and variety in consumption, so that men would realize that their environment was potentially productive of abundance. Social reform must induce men to "subordinate the physical and exclusive pleasures of life" —satisfactions that could not be shared with the community— and to utilize their environment in the "most productive manner." Protective tariffs, for example, would serve to enforce both restraint and variety. Free trade, responsive to the inappropriate demands of consumers, caused land and factories to be used for the production of a limited variety of staple goods, which exhausted natural resources and perpetuated inefficient habits of consumption.[36]

Although Patten looked forward to an age of abundance in which men would happily utilize the fruits of their environment, he had not forgotten the Calvinist injunction that affluence and ease would lead men to the City of Destruction. Moreover, social Darwinism seemed to reinforce the Protestant ethic. Patten recoiled from his own theories. A "high civilization" had been developed "only in countries where the obstacles were so great that only the more intelligent could survive." Since every improvement in techniques of production and habits of consumption meant that the "obstacles [would] decrease as the country advance[d] in civilization," it was possible that further progress would be "retarded" because less intelligent people would survive and even prosper. The weak and the strong would both survive, to the detriment of civilization.[37]

What Patten had observed of German social reform seemed to promise a way out of this dilemma. He proposed to strengthen the weak, not to eliminate them. Men must use their intelligence to "improve on" what had been "given them by nature." It was wrong to "fold our hands and allow a decline of intelligence" as scarcity gave way to abundance. Men did not "leave swamps undrained because water naturally" collected in them; they did not allow "mad dogs to run loose" because hydrophobia

was the "result of natural causes." Although Patten was eager
to drain the social swamp, he refused, unlike Yale University's
William Graham Sumner, the archenemy of German-trained
economists, to let weak men be annihilated in a struggle for survival. The lower classes would remain poor and ignorant if
they were not encouraged to "increase their intelligence" by
means of state-supported education, and if there were no enforcement of contract laws in favor of workers, no limitation
of consumer credit to prevent "slavery," and no restraint, in the
interest of "public welfare," on the "speculative spirit" of capitalists. Progress, Patten concluded, was hindered mainly by
ignorance and prejudice, which could be eradicated by a higher
standard of living, by education, and by increased economic
opportunity.[38]

In the *Premises,* his first search for a viable economics of
abundance, Patten struggled to create a frame of reference
which would encompass the two environments and value systems he had known, those of Illinois and Germany. He straddled
the ambiguities separating agrarian and religious values, which
emphasized the ethos of restraint, from urban and scientific attitudes, which embodied the preconditions for sustained abundance. On the one hand, he attempted to salvage those aspects
of the Protestant ethic which comported with the demands of
economic growth; on the other, he sought to restrain men from
abusing abundance by teaching them the lessons of the new sciences of nutrition and agronomy and of the new industrial technology.

Patten was not ready to announce the creation of a completely
new frame of reference. For the moment, he temporized, calling
on men to develop the qualities which would enable them to
survive in an "isolated state," in which they depended on their
own exertions; at the same time, he emphasized the interdependence enforced by the technological progress of modern civilization. These twin allegiances, to isolation and to interdependence,
had, at a lower level of complexity, enabled William Patten to
become the first citizen of De Kalb County. His son's desire for

men to "enjoy the pleasures of an isolated state along with the efficiency of civilization" would have less measurable results.[39] Before exploring the development of Patten's thought, however, it is necessary to examine the environment in which, against which, and for the sake of which he carried on his work.

CHAPTER II ✎

Professionalism and Social Change, 1885–1910

Patten was deeply involved in the complex problems and kaleidoscopic changes of an America which was becoming rapidly industrialized. In 1888, when he took up a professorship at the University of Pennsylvania, the United States was experiencing unprecedented economic growth and, with it, new forms of social and individual dislocation. Despite prosperity, tensions between rich and poor were growing. Although most Americans embraced the doctrines of *laissez faire*, increasingly powerful groups demanded collective action to regulate utilities and trusts. In a country with a growing sense of national pride and power, millions of immigrants and farmers, as well as a handful of intellectuals and professional men, felt estranged from the dominant mood of American life. Churches grew in wealth and numbers, but so did groups which regarded the existence of God as a hypothesis to be examined when time permitted. The precepts of traditional morality were broadcast from altars and lecterns, in the press and in popular literature, while some men found justification for their actions in an amoral mechanistic universe, others made success the leading virtue, and many discovered that graft oiled the wheels of American political machinery. To many thoughtful men of Patten's generation, the open society seemed its own greatest enemy.

Yet many people, Patten among them, believed that the open society could be reformed from within. If businessmen could gain strength by combining, so could reformers. If expertise and specialization were keys to material success, they were also means for changing men's social and personal goals. Doctors of philosophy, journalists, and teachers had never met a payroll; similarly, many businessmen had been denied a confrontation with ideas. Few American businessmen would tolerate outmoded machinery or methods of merchandizing in their enterprises. They might be taught that, as a result of recent developments in economic science, the dogma of *laissez faire*, the association of political economy with theology, the uncritical acceptance of the Malthusian law of population, the assumption of an unchanging set of social and economic institutions, and a preoccupation with the law of diminishing returns were also outmoded.

In an open society, reformers who prefer persuasion to force are usually not effective unless they have more goals in common with than in conflict with the men they hope to change. The group of about a hundred Americans who had studied social science in Germany in the 1870's and 1880's and who, over the next forty years, attained the leadership of American higher education were not alienated radicals. Most of them had origins, religious beliefs, a respect for material success, and an entrepreneurial zeal which were similar to those of the men who sat as trustees of their universities. Patten later recalled that he and his friends were "earnest, mature men" with definite plans. Each had "drawn the line on which he was to move." Like their German teachers, the Americans were determined to promote what they considered necessary evolutionary change within the established order. Their German training had reinforced their respect for gradualism, not turned them into ideologues.[1]

They were also young men impatient with the rate of American adjustment to an industrial society. Patten later recalled that the German-trained scholars protested "against the current

political and social ideas." They were frustrated by "wordy conflicts between free trade and protection advocates" and by "end-
less harangues on paper currency." In their first decade as university teachers, their impatience frequently came to the surface.
In July, 1885, for instance, Patten told Richard Ely, then teaching at The Johns Hopkins University, that the "arrogant demands of employers" were "mainly responsible for the growth
of socialism in our country." Ely and Henry Carter Adams, of
the University of Michigan, who were among the most conservative of the German-trained scholars, were accused of advocating socialism by national magazines, politicians, and even
university officials. By the mid-1880's, it was clear that the re-
form-minded scholars would have to improve their public image
if they were to be effective.[2]

The young economists, in Patten's words, "knew we had a
struggle before us and wanted no doubt as to our unity and
who our enemies were." It was easier to identify enemies—
businessmen who refused to look beyond *laissez faire* or intellectuals like William Graham Sumner who defended the harsh-
ness of an unregulated economic system—than to create unity.
The German-trained scholars disagreed among themselves about
methodology and public policy. Patten and John Bates Clark
of Columbia University defended deductive reasoning; Ely and
Adams preferred induction. Edwin R. A. Seligman of Columbia
and Clark were less favorable to state intervention in the economy than were Patten and Ely. Yet all these men came together
in 1885 and agreed to promote economic research and social reform through the American Economic Association.[3]

The Association unified economists as professional men, not as
social reformers. It met needs similar to those felt in the second
half of the nineteenth century by doctors, lawyers, and scholars
in every nation in which industrialization had accelerated the
pace of social and spatial mobility. In Germany, England, and
France, as well as in the United States, men whose livelihood
and social status depended on their possession of a particular
set of skills sought to control education in their discipline and

entry into their ranks. Professional identification enables a man to appear before the general public as a person of substance and responsibility. When a society vests control of entry into and advancement in a profession in the hands of its members, it publicly or tacitly acknowledges that this body of men is performing a socially useful task, worthy of financial support from laymen.[4]

Professional identification is also a brake on intellectual extravagance. In order to retain his status and the respect of his colleagues, a professional man must share most of their assumptions about, and methods of dealing with, their common body of knowledge. Diversity of opinion is tolerable within a profession if the divergent opinions stimulate new research or generate what a significant group of men at a particular time regard as reasonable alternative solutions to problems affecting the profession and the society which supports it. There are, however, limits to the expression of divergence. Professional organization generates a stake in the *status quo*. Economists, for example, can no more advocate a total overhaul of the existing order than they can call for a return to a lost past. A formally organized profession will usually work within the definition of the possible which is accepted by the society around it. For Patten and his friends, the American Economic Association was a source of both opportunities and restraints.

For most of the nineteenth century, the best economists in England and the United States had been amateurs—men who earned their livelihood in business, the law, the ministry, or journalism, not from research and teaching in economics. Only in Germany was economics recognized as a separate profession by mid-century. The German-trained Americans had to struggle against well-established patterns in their effort to attain professional status for economics. Three journalists, Edward L. Godkin, Henry Demarest Lloyd, and Henry George, exemplify the difference between professional and amateur social science in America during the last decades of the nineteenth century. These men had the freedom to oversimplify denied to professionals. Godkin, in the name of the Manchester school, railed against protectionism; professional economists, in contrast, accepted political reality and sought opportunities to construct tariff schedules which satisfied interest groups without doing serious damage to economic growth. Lloyd raised the specter of concentrated wealth threatening the welfare of the commonwealth; professional economists, whether or not they approved of the trend toward oligopoly, worked to measure the effect of competition on the economy. George was a man with a panacea, the single tax; professional economists, embarrassed by the flaws in his logic, accepted the fact that most Americans were committed to plurality in taxation and tried to prevent the imposition of any tax that might endanger the health of the economy.[5]

The restraint on vision imposed by professional commitments would eventually create serious problems for Patten as a social theorist. In 1883, however, when, with Ely and with Edmund J. James of the University of Pennsylvania, he began to discuss a constitution for an association of economists, these problems had not yet arisen. The three young scholars began their discussions with the recollection of an evening in Halle, almost five years earlier, when Johannes Conrad had urged them to create an American organization similar to the Verein für Sozialpolitik.[6]

The Verein, founded in 1872, united those German scholars and men of affairs who opposed extreme individualism in economic and social life—on the assumption that the scientific study of economics yielded conclusions which could be applied to social policy. In the opening address to the first meeting of the Verein, Gustav Schmoller, a leading spokesman of the younger historical school of economists, declared that scientifically derived policies would enable a "constantly increasing portion of our people" to "share in the great possessions of civilization, in culture, and material welfare." [7]

The Verein had a significant influence on German legislation. Its reports and recommendations were reflected in the 1878 modifications of the industrial code, in the tariff reform of 1879, and in the Kaiser's message of 1881, which promised compulsory insurance against accidents, infirmity, and old age. By the turn of the century, however, the Verein, like the organizations modeled on it in the United States and England, was torn by the tension between science and public affairs, by the problem of separating economic research from advocacy of social reform.[8]

In 1883, this tension was not yet apparent, and the three Americans were convinced that a professional association could serve both science and social reform. They were dissatisfied with existing American organizations—the Social Science Association, founded in 1866, and the Political Economy Club, organized in 1881. The former, they felt, was too broad in purpose to satisfy professional aspirations, the latter too exclusive in its membership and too much in the informal English tradition of polite after-dinner discussions.[9]

The early history of the American Economic Association has been obscured by the personal foibles of Richard Ely. A vain and suspicious man, Ely later claimed that in 1884 he had conceived a plan for an association of economists "who repudiated *laissez-faire.*" Although he admitted that Patten and James had written a program for a "Society for the Study of National Economy," he asserted that this plan was abortive because its political doctrines were too radical. A more accurate interpretation of the history of the Association would place the Patten-James draft of the program in perspective as a document which was never given an adequate chance to form the basis of an organization, because Ely ignored his commitments to his two friends. Ely, James, and Patten had discussed drafting the program for two years before James wrote it, "after careful consideration with Patten," in May, 1885. When copies of the program were sent to American economists early in June, 1885, Patten and James believed that Ely would help them organize the society.[10]

The society was to have three broad purposes. The first two were professional: to encourage careful investigation of economic problems and to publish monographs on economic sub-

jects. The third purpose, though it would have been obvious to
German-trained economists, was unfamiliar to most Americans:
"to combat the widespread view that our economic problems
will solve themselves and that our laws and institutions, which at
present favor individual instead of collective action, can promote
the best utilization of our material resources." According to
James and Patten, the state was a "positive factor in material
production" and had a claim to a "share of the product." They
indicted the leaders of American society for failing to "maintain
that standard of intelligence and industrial efficiency" below
which no nation should "allow its members to fall." [11]

Patten and James followed German models in setting forth a
program for labor, agriculture, and the allocation of natural resources. They recommended improved sanitary and industrial
conditions, higher wages, shorter hours, and the provision of
opportunities for "mental and moral growth." They called for
conservation laws to protect, preserve, and create forests, for
the establishment of agricultural experiment stations, for government subsidies to stimulate the production of desirable crops,
and for the dissemination of information about natural resources
and the best means of developing new industries. Unlike the
Verein für Sozialpolitik, however, they demanded the regulation of monopolies. James and Patten envisioned a "national
economy of smaller industries so distributed as best to utilize our
material resources." This was proposed policy, not dogma; they
were willing to change their views as social conditions changed.[12]

An earlier draft of the program reveals that, in the final version,
Patten and James consciously dissembled in order to broaden
the appeal of their society. The word "collective" was frequently
softened, and the phrase "collective action, the most efficient
means of individual development," was replaced with vaguer
language. In several passages, "capitalist" and "exploitation"
were changed to milder synonyms.[13]

A few days after Patten and James had sent their program
to economists, Ely told Seligman, "I am now about to organize
an Economic Association of which I send you the program."

Economists were probably confused when they received programs for two different organizations. The confusion lasted for about three months, by which time Ely had acquired so much support for his scheme that Patten and James relinquished their own program and promised to support Ely's proposed American Economic Association. But Ely's contention that the Patten-James proposal fell dead distorted the facts. Andrew D. White, President of Cornell University, had told Ely, "Should your association be founded, whether by itself or in connection with that suggested by Professor James, I should hope to connect myself with it." In the summer of 1885, Ely ignored Patten's reminder that he had promised to "revise" the program the three of them had discussed together. The call for the American Economic Association was issued in September, 1885, at the Saratoga Springs meeting of the American Historical Association. Ten economists attended the first meeting and subscribed to Ely's platform.[14]

Over the next two decades, the A.E.A., like the Verein and the British Economic Association, became more a professional than a political organization. In 1887, the A.E.A. abandoned Ely's "Statement of Principles," in an attempt to attract such conservative economists as Sumner and Arthur T. Hadley of Yale into the Association. Yet many economists denied that the A.E.A. had abandoned either ethics or a concern for public welfare. Patten and Ely believed they could afford to be magnanimous to their political enemies, since the German-trained economists dominated the teaching of their discipline in major universities, the spawning grounds of future economists. As Francis A. Walker, the first president of the A.E.A., declared in 1887, "The *a priori* economists will never again be numerous enough to dominate any catholic association in this country."[15]

Nevertheless, involvement in university affairs made economists more cautious in their pronouncements on public issues. In the last third of the century, the leading American colleges were transformed by energetic educators into universities on the German model. Such "captains of erudition" as Charles W.

Eliot of Harvard, Andrew D. White of Cornell, Daniel Coit
Gilman of Johns Hopkins, and Charles Kendall Adams of Wisconsin were determined to modernize the curriculum, encourage
research, and promote universities as dynamic forces in American life. The fulfillment of these goals required money, which
was obtained through the use of salesmanship and diplomacy in
dealing with leading businessmen and state legislators. Most of
the men who controlled the educational purse were dedicated to
the maintenance of the *status quo* in economic and political
life. The freedom to do research in a university setting and to
impart professional standards to students was obtained at a
price—not antagonizing the powerful men whose generosity
made universities possible.

Although Patten appreciated the need for caution, he was disturbed by the timidity of some of his colleagues in the Economic
Association. Even Ely, who had survived a public hearing in
1895 on his political views, began to take refuge in at attitude of
scientific impartiality after the turn of the century. Patten believed that the German-trained economists had won a sufficient
"victory" over men who assumed the eternal validity of the
laissez-faire dogma to permit the making of public recommendations, as a scientific group, on such questions as overproduction,
monetary policy, and tenement-house reform. In 1908, however,
when Patten, then president of A.E.A., attended the White
House Conference on Conservation, the Association refused to
give public support to Theodore Roosevelt's program. Winthrop
Daniels, secretary of the A.E.A., wrote to Gifford Pinchot,
Roosevelt's principal adviser on conservation policy, that although the members of the executive committee, as individuals,
supported Roosevelt's aims, they felt "obliged not to seem to
commit the Association to any propaganda, however laudable." [16]

In his presidential address, Patten attacked the attitude that
had inspired Daniels' letter and reminded his colleagues that the
economist's place was "on the firing line of civilization." As
several hundred economists digested a dinner that had proceeded
from canapé Rudolf through seven courses to *petits fours*, he

told them that economists were "by education and tradition revolutionists." Their "vehicle should be the newspaper and magazine, not the scientific journal." Economists must be concerned with the "pressing needs" of the American people.[17]

In 1908, Patten was speaking from what he thought was a safe position on the faculty of the University of Pennsylvania. For twenty years he had survived conflicts with members of the arts faculty who were suspicious of the social scientists at the university's Wharton School and with the Philadelphia businessmen on the university's Board of Trustees. When Patten arrived in Philadelphia, in September, 1888, the Wharton School had forty students and a faculty of five. Twenty years later, it had grown to almost six hundred students and a faculty of forty.[18]

The Wharton School, the oldest collegiate school of business in the United States, was founded in 1881 by Joseph Wharton, a Philadelphia iron magnate. Wharton stipulated that protectionist doctrines be taught, but he defended the faculty against attacks by conservative Philadelphians. The first classes were held in 1882, with Robert Ellis Thompson, who, in 1875, had become the first professor of social science in the United States, as the only teacher of economics. The goals and curriculum of the School began to change in 1883, when Edmund James became senior professor. James wanted the School to be both a business college and a place for advanced study in social science. A shrewd administrator, James invited leading Philadelphia businessmen and bankers to teach their specialties at the School and persuaded the trustees to appoint German-trained scholars to the faculty. In 1887, James obtained a professorship for Patten. In the *curriculum vitae* he prepared for his friend, James skirted the truth by implying that Patten had been hard at work, since his return from Germany, studying "such branches of law as are of special interest to the economist." [19]

The Wharton School expanded rapidly in the seven years Patten and James were together on the faculty. By 1895, the School had a professor of journalism, Joseph F. Johnson, who later became Dean of the School of Commerce at New York

University, the historians Edward P. Cheyney, Dana C. Munro, and James Harvey Robinson, the statistician Roland P. Falkner, who was the first to apply index numbers to American government statistics, and a sociologist, Samuel M. Lindsay. The School expanded its curriculum from two to four years in 1894 and awarded five Ph.D. degrees between 1891 and 1895. Patten and James enhanced the prestige of the School by inaugurating the "University of Pennsylvania Publications in Political and Social Science" in 1888 and, more important, by founding the American Academy of Political and Social Science a year later. The *Annals* of the Academy was only the third periodical in America devoted to professional discussion of the social sciences with a style and contents based on German models.[20]

The quality of instruction improved after Patten and James forced Robert Thompson out of the School in 1891. Thompson was a disciple of Henry Carey, the Philadelphia economist whose *Principles of Social Science* appeared in 1851. He considered Carey the leading figure in economics, superior to any Englishman or German. Moreover, Thompson disliked Patten. In a newspaper article in 1888, he condemned Patten and Richard Ely as "socialists." In 1891, Patten and James persuaded the trustees to fire Thompson, who countered by protesting to Joseph Wharton that his attackers were working against the traditions of Philadelphia with evil doctrines derived in equal parts from Johannes Conrad and William Graham Sumner. Wharton, however, agreed with Cyrus Adler, a business associate, who called Patten a "distinguished representative of the younger scientists."[21]

In 1895, when James went to the University of Chicago, Patten became administrative head of the Wharton School, a position he held until 1905, when the School acquired a dean and Patten's title was changed to Chairman of the Economics Department. The Wharton faculty was uneasy after James's departure. With James no longer present to exercise his diplomatic skills, the trustees became increasingly concerned about the political opinions of faculty members. Several men wondered if the

School could "manage to get along without" James. By 1897, when Patten went to Europe for a year, it was clear that the Wharton School could survive without a single dominant figure. It had become a complex institution with a national and even international reputation.[22]

The history of the Wharton School reflects the history of social science in America in the late nineteenth century. By 1900, America was, for the first time, part of the mainstream of Western development in social science and no longer a backwater. Twenty years of activity by Patten and his fellow German-trained scholars made it impossible for social scientists in any country to ignore the contributions of Americans. Articles by Americans and reviews of their books appeared in the leading European journals. Such outstanding European scholars as Alfred Marshall, Vilfredo Pareto, Eugen Böhm-Bawerk, and John A. Hobson contributed to American periodicals. Patten and his colleagues were in frequent correspondence with leading European social scientists: Marshall, Hobson, Böhm-Bawerk, Pareto, Schmoller, Max Weber, and Achille Loria, to name just a few. Scholars exchanged transatlantic hospitality on frequent visits.[23]

The Congress of Arts and Sciences held at the Louisiana Purchase Exposition in St. Louis in 1904 symbolized America's rise to world-wide prestige in social science. The Congress celebrated, in effect, a quarter-century of German influence on American thought and, more important, demonstrated that American and European scholars could gather as equals. Twenty-seven German, eighteen French, sixteen British, and ten Austrian scholars joined about a hundred Americans at the Congress.[24]

America became a "world power" in the life of the mind at the same time that American economic strength forced European nations to grant her great-power status in diplomatic affairs. A small group of Americans had shifted the center of gravity of Western social science.

CHAPTER III 🖎

The Standard of Living,
1885–1891

For thousands of years men have sought to solve the problems of production—to develop techniques for utilizing natural and human resources which would allay their gnawing fear of impending scarcity. Throughout history, the standard of living of most men has fluctuated greatly. Lean and fat years have alternated with depressing regularity. Men's longing for a golden age of abundance is expressed in many of the greatest documents of civilization, including the Bible and Plato's *Republic*. This longing for a standard of living that would satisfy the minimal needs of all men remained a utopian dream until the second half of the nineteenth century. As industrialization increased the rate of economic growth of Europe and the United States in the nineteenth century, economists shifted their attention from the problems of production to those of the distribution and consumption of wealth. Although this changing emphasis in economic thought reflected the changing environment of Western man, most economists clung to the assumption that scarcity was the normal condition of life. For a generation, Simon Patten's ideas were significant exceptions to this pattern of thought, which acknowledged the industrial triumphs of the nineteenth century while retaining older assumptions about the conditions of existence.

By 1888, Patten was convinced that the problems of production had been solved. The perennial dream of abundance could be realized if men would turn away from creating wealth to examining the problems of distributing and consuming it. Despite the fact that men devoted more thought to increasing production than to raising the standard of living, the "social environment of man" was "slowly, yet surely" creating a higher "standard of life." The rise in the standard was, however, retarded because the surplus wealth resulting from improved techniques of production remained in the possession of the men who could "present the strongest combination." The wealthy, in short, were getting wealthier, to the detriment of the lower classes. Moreover, inappropriate consumption of the fruits of production—consumption which depleted natural resources—might perpetuate scarcity and make the twentieth century, like all those which preceded it, the graveyard of men's aspirations.[1]

Economists had been concerned with the problems of creating and maintaining a decent standard of living since the beginning of the century. Those who accepted Malthus' law of population concluded that, unless more men developed hitherto uncommon qualities, the standard of life of most people could not rise above a level of bare subsistence. Although Malthus' subsistence theory provided a comforting rationale for the existence of pockets of middle-class affluence in a world of poverty, the theory was never sacred to leading economists. David Ricardo, for instance, used the subsistence theory only when it suited his purpose. At other times Ricardo argued, "Since population adjusts but slowly to changes in the reward of labor, an accelerated rate of capital accumulation pulls market wages above the natural rate, permitting an improvement in the labourer's standard of living." By the 1830's, the more optimistic wages-fund doctrine supplanted the subsistence theory in professional discourse. According to this doctrine, the wage-rate, which depended upon the volume of past production, the current birth-rate of the working class, and the supply of capital for investment could increase over time. Although the wages-fund concept assumed the permanence of social stratification and an upper limit to a rise in the standard of living of the lower classes during any period of time, it recognized the results of industrialization as new realities rather than as passing exceptions to fixed economic patterns.[2]

Two of the three factors which set the wages-fund—the volume of goods and the supply of capital—were primarily determined by production. But the centrality of production in determining the average standard of life in a society committed to industrial expansion was challenged from two directions in the second half of the nineteenth century. In Germany, historical economists explored the subtle interaction between psychological and traditional factors which influenced men's economic decisions. At about the same time, William Stanley Jevons in England and Karl Menger in Austria developed the concept of marginal utility analysis, which suggested that, at any level of economic development, men's standard of living was shaped by careful psychological discrimination between the pleasures and pains that result from the choice of various goods.[3]

Patten, who had studied the Germans and Austrians as well as the classical theorists, was convinced that the prosperity of a nation, the highest standard of life possible for each citizen, was determined, "not by the aggregate produce of industry," but by regular production, stable prices, uniform distribution, and proper habits of consumption. Simply to increase production, without regard for problems of ethics and health—for problems of distribution and consumption—would cause, not cure, social misery. Although Patten admitted that, at times, "improvements in production" were accompanied by a "change for the better in the standard of life," he was convinced that the "causes raising the standard" were not the same as those which were "so rapidly bringing into use so many improvements in production." Too many economists confused the laws which governed machines with those which ought to govern men. Unlike machines, men had to be educated to consume the varieties of goods, particularly food, their environment could produce. They must be persuaded that certain choices of food and shelter would produce better health than the choices they usually made. Men would have to replace their compulsive emphasis on production, which they justified by a fear of scarcity, with new values attuned to an age of abundance. Only by a new assessment of the reality around them could men raise their standard of life "so high" that there would be no surplus revenue for any selfish "class or combination" to squander on luxurious living while the poor remained ill-fed, ill-clothed, and ill-housed.[4]

Debilitating self-indulgence, a luxury of the rich during the long age of scarcity, might afflict entire societies if, in the age of abundance, uniform distribution of wealth made men affluent without making them more enlightened consumers. The moral restraint of the Protestant ethic might prevent destructive self-indulgence, but it also made a virtue of asceticism, which could inhibit production and diminish the surplus. Men must be persuaded that inclinations toward gluttony and intemperance were inappropriate in an age of abundance, because these urges, developed in an age of scarcity, were no longer justified by the hardships of life. Genuine improvement in the standard of life required that men substitute useful for dangerous consumption, not that they merely reduce their total consumption.[5]

Ironically, the techniques for producing and marketing the greatest variety of goods at the lowest cost and for persuading men to expand their consumption—the techniques of industrial combination and advertising—could also be used to abuse consumers. If monopolies were allowed to maintain high prices, they would be forced to use advertising in order to persuade consumers that they needed goods they could not afford. Cynical men, playing on "feeling or prejudice," could enrich themselves while damaging the standard of living which foreshadowed an age of affluence.[6]

Patten thought the danger from monopolists and their advertising men could be counteracted in three ways: by consumers' exercise of power, by businessmen's following principles of enlightened self-interest, and by state regulation. Once consumers' desires for an improvement in their standard of living were awakened, they could combine to make purchases at wholesale prices and to force sellers to substitute desirable for undesirable products. But the consumers' potential power had to be protected. This protection would come from new concepts of enlightened self-interest and the power of the state. In a scarcity economy, "individual selfishness" was necessary for survival. In the emerging abundance economy, on the other hand, socialized generosity could lead to increased well-being for all. Businessmen could be taught to recognize that generosity brought economic benefits. The standard of living of an entire society could be raised by educating consumers to appreciate and use the products made available as a result of technological progress, by raising the wages of labor so that workers could buy these products, and by regulating trusts in order to limit wasteful competition for markets.[7]

Patten was unwilling to grant the state a major role in enforcing the conditions which would make an age of abundance possible. His respect for German social legislation was in conflict with his admiration for the results of self-help among Illinois farmers. Although he was impatient with the laissez-faire philosophy of "our grandfathers," he gave the government only a limited role in utilizing the economic surplus to best advantage. Tax revenues should be used only to furnish the "conditions needed for a wholesome, regular social progress." More specifically, he wanted the government to provide a "well-organized system of public instruction, public parks, cheap, yet elevating places of amusement, good public roads, . . . an efficient system of drainage, and sanitation in the cities." But Patten was advocating more than minor reforms. The experience citizens and public officials gained from efforts to remedy "present evils," he declared, would be "invaluable" when it was necessary for "society to be reorganized on another basis." [8]

The growth of an economic surplus made possible the creation of a society attuned to the implications of abundance. Although Patten believed that it was possible and necessary to raise the standard of living in most societies, he was not certain what an improved standard would mean for individual consumers. He needed tools with which to analyze the merits of the different elements of a standard of living, to judge the value of various desires, and, most important, to decide which impulses must be restrained or redirected in the name of progress and social harmony. These concerns led him to explore the economics of consumption.

The classical economists had focused on problems of production. For David Ricardo, the rate of economic growth depended "solely upon the volume and efficiency of productive labor engaged in industry and agriculture." A generation later, John Stuart Mill, though forced by the prosperity around him to discuss the ways in which wealth was consumed, ignored the feelings and attitudes of consumers when he discussed the problems of production. The leading economists of the first half of the nineteenth century left the impression that men existed for the sake of goods.[9]

In the second half of the century, however, most economists gave a contrasting impression. The work of Jevons and Menger in introducing the concept of utility into economic analysis and the empirical research of such Germans as Ernst Engel, head of the Royal Statistical Bureau of Prussia, made demand precede supply in economic logic. The marginal-utility economists believed the most important part of an individual's economic activity to be the "constant weighing up and choosing of which needs shall be met and which not." Jevons, reintroducing Jeremy Bentham's utilitarian calculus into economic discourse, argued that every choice made by a consumer involved the maximizing of pleasure and the minimizing of pain. Even for Jevons, however, the utility of a particular good was a function of its supply.[10]

Less than a decade after Jevons wrote, the assumption that the utility of a commodity could be easily calculated was challenged from several directions. In England, F. Y. Edgeworth asserted that the balance of pleasure and pain in an individual's choices was a function of all the commodities available to him, not just of one commodity, as Jevons had believed. Since the utility of each commodity was related to an individual's entire pattern of consumption, it seemed almost impossible to discuss the habits of consumers with any clarity or precision. During this time, the German economists were examining the influence of non-economic factors on economic behavior. To many men, however, it appeared impossible for economists to assess the influence of tradition, education, ethical concepts, and social status on an individual's concept of utility.[11]

An art critic, John Ruskin, whose sensibilities were revolted by the worship of production, made a telling attack on classical economics in the 1860's. Ruskin's most famous dictum, "There is no wealth but life," was an epigrammatic statement of his thesis that consumption was the "end, crown, and perfection of production." He called for social reorganization to enable men to fulfill their yearning for beauty in their lives. Although Ruskin's theories influenced many social reformers in England and the United States, the lack of precision in his economic logic made his ideas suspect to most professional economists.[12]

The United States had become a melting pot for these new economic ideas. In Europe, a fierce methodological controversy between the historical-empirical economists and the marginalists during the last two decades of the century prevented the combining of facts and theories in a fruitful synthesis. Patten and his colleagues—such men as Richard T. Ely, John Bates Clark, and Henry Carter Adams—had been in Germany at a time when historical and deductive concepts of economics circulated freely. In the United States, between 1880 and the turn of the century, economists grouped themselves according to their attitudes toward government action in the cause of reform. Methodology was a subject for consideration within groups of economists rather than for argument between groups. In his search for an economics of consumption that would enable him to clarify the requirements of the emerging age of abundance, Patten was free to utilize the logic of the Englishmen and Austrians, the data of the Germans, and the aesthetic fervor of Ruskin.[13]

The starting point for Patten's economics of consumption was the problem of cultural lag: the survival, in a period of potential abundance, of behavior appropriate to an age of scarcity. Although the contemporary world was "better fitted for supplying our wants" than was the world of "our ancestors," men had "inherited laws, habits, and prejudices" suited to the past. A theory of consumption must create the basis for a "new society and a state whose power will be superior to that of any combination of selfish individuals and whose duties will be commensurate with human wants." [14]

The interaction between men's desires and the goods available to them produced two "orders" or types of consumption, the "natural" and the "economic." In the natural order, choice of commodities was dictated solely by the relationship between desire and the availability of goods. This condition prevailed for those goods available to a society, either naturally or as a result of a small expenditure of effort, in such abundance that the labor required to produce them was an insignificant factor in the individual's calculation of the utility he would derive from their consumption. Throughout history, however, the economic order, in which men's desire for an article was tempered by a consideration of the cost in labor and capital of producing it, had been more important than the natural order. Under "economic" conditions, for example, a man would first choose an article whose consumption offered the highest ratio of pleasure to pain, then select other articles in descending order of their pleasure-pain ratios. In short, men selected particular goods on the basis of the "ratio of their cost to their utility." [15]

As the economic surplus of a society increased, choices made according to "economic order" created a problem of cultural lag. The growth of a surplus, of a quantity of goods sufficient to raise the entire society above a subsistence standard of living, indicated that the cost of producing most articles was decreasing. According to the marginal-utility theory, as the cost of goods decreased, the amount of pleasure available to their consumers increased. It followed that, unless men changed their habits, traditions, and prejudices, they would increase their consumption of the goods to which they were accustomed. There was a real possibility that an age of abundance would produce communities of intemperate gluttons.[16]

It was not, however, inevitable that abundance would create a society in which sensual gratification sapped men's desire for the pleasures of the spirit and the intellect. Under proper guidance, noneconomic pleasures—art, religion, and patriotism, for instance—could become increasingly important to men as the economy of abundance matured. The assumption that the "pleasures of men" could be "narrowed down to one single controlling desire" was derived from the constant threat of hardship during the long age of scarcity. Although Patten was still uncertain about the extent to which human nature was malleable, he defined the "highest" civilization as the one which gratified the greatest variety of desires.[17]

At this point in his career, Patten was more comfortable with economics than with psychology and social theory. He appreciated the need to explore the sources of desire and the complexity of the concept of civilization, but he turned back to arguments based on economics. He defined the optimum standard of living, for example, in terms of economic welfare alone—as a supply of goods "equal to the number of articles" which had "about the same ratio of cost to utility" as was apparent in the food supply available in environments where abundance rather than scarcity was the rule. In order to attain this standard, it would be necessary, as he had argued before, to educate men to make a better selection among available goods and to raise wages in order to enable the lower classes to share in the expanding surplus of production. Education and wages had a reciprocal relationship. Higher wages provided the means to improve consumption. Improved consumption helped to maintain the rate of wages by creating a new standard of living, below which men would not sink without a fierce struggle. The new standard of living created a "safety valve" which averted the destructive results of the scarcity-based ethic of free competition.[18]

Two problems that might arise during the impending transition to an age of abundance especially worried Patten: overconsumption and an uneven adjustment of men's values to the new conditions of production and consumption. These problems could not be solved through the application of economic logic alone. With great hesitation, Patten turned from economic to psychological analysis in order to determine what restraints would enable men to avoid the personal and social costs of an age of plenty.

Overconsumption, Patten's term for intemperate gluttony, could prevent men from using the economic surplus to raise the standard of social, aesthetic, and moral life. In an economy of scarcity, sensuality was restrained by the "economic order" of choice—in short, by fear of misery. With starvation a real possibility, men tempered their appetites in order to avoid destruction. But when improvements in technology guaranteed a continuous surplus, fear of annihilation was unreasonable.[19]

In order to postulate the possibility of a restraint on overconsumption, Patten assumed that the intensity of pleasure derived from sensual gratification decreased with every increase in the variety of the goods consumed. If men could choose among twenty articles of food instead of five, for example, they would satisfy their essential physical needs quite rapidly and derive pleasure from sampling a variety of foods rather than from overeating. Life in an abundance economy would lead to a progressive weakening of appetite. Patten's analysis offered a solution to the problem of alcoholism. In his opinion, the increasing consumption of liquor in the United States reflected an effort to compensate for the inequitable distribution of the economic surplus and a lack of education in the potential variety of consumers' choices available in an economy of abundance. The remedy for intemperance was, not prohibition, but a "satisfying diet within everyone's means." [20]

The theory of the progressive weakening of appetites posed a terrifying paradox. Although progress seemed to depend on the victory of men with weak appetites, throughout history "strong races"—men with "vigorous appetites"—had displaced their "weaker neighbors." In "more advanced nations," moreover, the leaders of progress were usually men with "keen appetites and powerful passions." Progress seemed to have occurred in "apparent opposition to the primary laws of consumption." [21]

The paradox was, however, a result of the unevenness of most men's adjustment to the new conditions of life. Habits formed in the age of scarcity, for example, made men so willing to work that they injured themselves and their children. Only those with strong appetites could survive in a society in which men worked compulsively. Immigrants to America, moreover, were mainly people with strong appetites, drawn by the promise of fulfilling their desires in the New World. Since Americans did not teach these people the benefits of restraints on consumption—the pleasures of variety rather than quantity—the immigrants impeded the transition from the values of scarcity to the ethos of abundance. Furthermore, low wages and poor working conditions gave the mass of men no opportunity to seek variety in the goods they consumed. In addition, American taxes caused a rise in the price of the sugar and spices which were necessary to make palatable many of the vegetables which could be produced cheaply in America. These conditions created a conflict between strong and weak appetites which prevented the possibility of abundance from becoming reality. There was an increasingly wide gap between progressive, enlightened, self-restrained men and underprivileged men who were unprogressive, unenlightened, and unrestrained. [22]

Although Patten seemed to imply that life in an age of abundance would be one of restrained ease, he could not forget the lesson of an Illinois boyhood that prosperity came to those with the greatest capacity to endure hardship and suffering. He had not resolved the tension, evident at the end of his first book, between his regard for the virtues of lonely agrarian struggle and his insight into the new urban basis of civilization. Since he was not yet certain which of the older virtues would be valuable in an age of abundance, he begged the question. Men with weak appetites were not necessarily the "best." They were merely "used as a type." [23]

Patten was overwhelmed by doubts about the best way to implement the restraints appropriate to new economic conditions. He contradicted some of his most carefully argued earlier points—declaring, for instance, that "improved production" would eventually "cure its own evils." Faith was less painful than logic, and Patten confessed to a belief that society would progress toward the age of abundance no matter how men behaved. Yet he retained his desire to "shorten the period of transition as much as possible" and abhorred the prospect that the "destructive tendencies of modern civilization" might force the "weak and unwary" into a life of "misery and vice." [24]

He put aside a consideration of the long-range implications of his ideas to propose a public policy for the period of transition from the age of scarcity to the era of abundance. Because the "growth of waste" had "almost kept pace with the increase of productive power," America lacked adequate schools, parks, houses, streets, books, and art galleries. The creation of these things required money, which Patten proposed to obtain by taxing the revenue "wasted by competition." Taxes should be imposed on the surplus profits used for advertising, salesmanship, and the duplication of retail outlets. [25]

Patten was not completely at odds with the political realities of his time. Although he opposed the Sherman Antitrust Act of 1890 because it glorified the ethic of free competition which had been developed to meet the needs of an age of scarcity, he approved of the protective tariffs embodied in legislation in the 1890's. Philadelphia, his adopted home, had been the center of American protectionist thought since the early nineteenth century. Friedrich List, the leading German exponent of the virtues of protection, had spent several years in Philadelphia. Henry Carey, a native Philadelphian, was regarded as the most sophisticated American exponent of protectionist ideas during the first half of the century. But Patten had advocated tariffs long before he came to Philadelphia.[26]

His defense of tariffs was based on radically different premises from those of his predecessors. List and Carey had argued that tariffs were necessary to enable undeveloped nations to grow away from primitive conditions. Patten began with the assumption that the American economy was more advanced, more "dynamic," than any other in the history of the world. Tariffs were a tool with which to create new values attuned to abundance. To List and Carey, tariffs would protect natural resources from exploitation and infant industries from crushing international competition. Patten was more concerned with the effect of tariffs on patterns of consumption. If there was a heavy tax on incoming staples, Americans would be forced to consume a greater variety of goods.[27]

Patten's defense of tariffs raised a problem that, during the next three-quarters of a century, would disturb economists concerned with the possibility of abundance. Was it possible to talk of a transition from scarcity to abundance without being a nationalist in a world where the most enlightened men increasingly took an international point of view? A high-tariff policy implied that a nation had decided to protect and nurture its prosperity without regard for the poverty of other countries. Even if tariffs would improve the standard of living in the nations of the West, they might inhibit the economic development of Asia and Africa. To many men, it seemed crass to talk of an age of abundance while most of the world's population barely managed to subsist.[28]

Patten advocated economic nationalism because he believed it would benefit the entire world. His commitment to the stern morality of his Protestant heritage prevented him from feeling indifferent, hostile, or superior to other men. No progressive nation could accept any "industrial deficiency of its people as final." If Americans were to develop a "higher economic system," they would have "little difficulty finding imitators all over the world." Imitation alone would not, however, produce the most rapid progress. The giving of economic aid, to raise the standard of living in undeveloped countries, was "a duty devolving upon the more advanced nations of the world." New methods of production and new standards of consumption, if brought to the "partially civilized races," would destroy the patterns of exploitation which kept the great mass of the world's population in economic and social bondage.[29]

Christian morality alone could not, however, sustain Patten's conviction that it was necessary and possible to raise men's standard of living. The Protestant ethic might teach men how much to consume and what items to avoid. It could not help them to make the positive decisions required in an age of high mass consumption—to choose between potatoes and green vegetables, gas and oil heat, for example. Under the influence of Johannes Conrad, Patten had begun to move from justifications of human behavior by references to faith and works to a justification based on the findings of social and natural science.

In the years to come, Patten would shift from a trust in God to faith in the new sciences of nutrition and experimental psychology. Yet he shrewdly recognized that a normative decision must precede this change. He refused to claim that a higher standard of living, as it related to the consumption of material goods, needed no justification—that the relief of physical pain was obviously good. Patten remained loyal to the conviction of his childhood that all human actions must have a moral justification. Social and natural science must somehow make men better.

Between 1888 and 1891, Patten sought a moral justification for improvements in the standard of living. He began by attacking the contention of Herbert Spencer, the English evolutionary philosopher, that the goal of human action was the creation of a society in which pleasure was "unalloyed with pain." To Patten, a world without pain would be a world without progress, since, according to the doctrines of evolution, society progressed by the elimination of obstacles which produced pain. Given the presence of obstacles, morality was a function of the "external conditions surrounding the food supply." Moral behavior was simply conduct which enabled men to exercise all their faculties in getting the most they could out of the least land, which created the highest standard of living possible in an environment. But Patten was uncomfortable with this position, since it implied that hedonism, whose aim was the reduction of the "gross sum" of the pain of life, was the model for "perfect action." If hedonism was the goal of progress, intemperate self-indulgence in abundant goods would become the norm of behavior—and destroy the age of abundance.[30]

Patten seemed to have combined the concept of a struggle between man and nature with utilitarian philosophy's dictum of the "greatest happiness for the greatest number." His apparent agreement with William Graham Sumner and Jeremy Bentham conflicted with his vision of a new civilization in which technological progress diminished the need for struggle and in which the complexity of life made "happiness" an empty word, requiring radically new content.[31]

Patten, like the America he lived in, was in transition from an economy of scarcity to an economy of abundance. As he recognized the persistence of poverty in the midst of potential abundance, and the new possibility of enabling the lower classes to share in the fruits of abundance without society's dealing harshly with men who, by abstinence, investment, and careful management, had led the Industrial Revolution, he groped toward a new definition of morality.[32]

In 1892, Patten rejected the "necessity of renunciation," on which traditional morality was based, and substituted moral rules based on the concept of surplus. Men must select moral codes according to the same principles they followed in selecting the new goods to consume in an abundance economy: because the codes had a "greater surplus than the old passions had." Moral behavior, formerly based on fear of punishment for evil deeds, must become a result of the "pleasure of right actions." As in the past, however, men must learn to defer pleasure in the present in order to obtain greater satisfaction in the future. The deferment would be based on joy, not on fear.[33]

The relationship between the economics of consumption and the new morality would solve the problem of making choices among groups of "goods." The standard of material living would be raised because men would learn, by the psychological process of association, that certain articles could be included in "complements," or groups of goods, which provided a greater surplus of satisfactions than the consumption of isolated articles. Men would prefer, for example, the improvement in health and vigor that resulted from eating three vegetables and a steak rather than potatoes and bread. The standard of moral living would rise as men came to "appreciate the larger groups in which the moral and economic blend." In an age of abundance, for instance, men would define a city as a "source of growing pleasures" in varied consumption, not merely as an organization for defense against enemies. The pleasures of urban life, viewed as a "complement," would eventually include a shared enjoyment of art, religion, and right conduct toward one's fellows.[34]

Patten's efforts to discuss the problems of the standard of living in a context of abundance may appear to have resulted in an unappetizing cluster of ambiguities. Yet he was raising questions few men with a professional commitment to logic had asked before. Patten had begun to transfer the problems of an age of plenty from the fantasies of utopians to a more immediate and sophisticated context. It took insight and courage for a professional economist to question the assumption of scarcity—of a lamentably limited supply of goods and resources—on which most of his colleagues based their work. It may have required even greater courage to pursue his questioning where it next led him: away from the central concerns of his profession to a consideration of the broader issues involved in defining and increasing human welfare.

CHAPTER IV

The Problems of Welfare, 1892–1896

Improving and protecting the welfare of individuals and groups have been the dominant goals of political and social action throughout history. Yet the word welfare cannot be precisely defined. Within the last century alone, it has been used to justify every political and economic system. The word has served, in a narrow sense, to describe the efficiency of an economic system; in a broad sense, as a rather empty name for the purpose of political and social institutions; in an intermediate sense, as a label for a state which seeks to provide economic and social security without demolishing class distinctions.

To Simon Patten, welfare meant the fulfillment of the possibilities of abundance in such a way that the human race would behave according to the ethical precepts of the Sermon on the Mount. Because men had learned to produce an increasing surplus of goods, they could extirpate the signs of scarcity—poverty, vice, selfishness, and fear—and turn their attention to concerns of the spirit and intellect. The age of abundance had been made possible by an intellectual and industrial revolution which glorified the "selfish actions of individuals." But the liberal emphasis on the "welfare of individuals" must yield to a focus on the "welfare of society." Only by the "concerted action of society" could men complete the transition from the age of scarcity to the era of abundance.[1]

Patten sought to influence the collective action which would prevent needless suffering in the process of evolution toward a world in which there would be enough to go around. Yet he was not sure how much suffering was needless and how much planning would do more harm than good. He refused to disregard the nagging fear that unrestrained abundance might turn potential paradise into actual hell.

For three years, from 1892 to 1895, Patten did not confront his doubts directly. Instead, he explored the problems of distributing and consuming the surplus wealth of America in ways most conducive to social welfare. For the first time, he articulated a formal definition of the surplus which made abundance possible: "the excess of satisfaction obtained by society in the consumption of economic goods above the cost of producing them." Men would have to choose between "enjoying the surplus" and "using it to keep society progressive." The maintenance of abundance, in a society in which population increased and wants expanded, required men to "give up" part of the surplus in order to "create prosperity." This renunciation could be effected either by imposing taxes to raise money for public expenditures or by allowing an unequal distribution of wealth in order to encourage private investment.[2]

Patten violated neither economic nor moral logic by his willingness to allow capitalists to retain their profits. Unlike Karl Marx, he refused to credit the creation of surplus value to the action of a single factor in production. For Marx, surplus value was the amount of a product created by labor above what was needed for subsistence, and expropriated by the owners of the means of production for their own use. Patten, on the other hand, agreed with the marginalists that value was created by the demands of consumers rather than by the amount of labor embodied in goods. To him, the surplus was what a society retained after the costs of production, including labor and a return on capital, were paid.[3]

The state was entitled to a share of the surplus because it offered protection and privilege to economic institutions. If the state did not impose taxes, the "most static elements in society," conservative investors and *rentiers*, would probably use the surplus for selfish ends. It was, however, shortsighted to use taxation to eradicate the inequalities in society: "Taxes must be levied to secure the funds needed to carry through reforms, which will bring a greater equality among the members of society." [4]

The mere existence of a surplus, of an excess of satisfactions, would not destroy "ideas and feelings antagonistic to the general welfare." There were three requisites for improving the general welfare: abundance, education, and restraint. Improved techniques of production, the precondition of abundance, would increase the number and variety of available goods. Education would enable people to benefit from new goods and to perceive the advantages of consuming new "complements." Confidence in the abundance of goods, combined with education, would enable people to restrain "primitive appetites and passions." [5]

The general welfare could not reach its maximum development until men utilized the fruits of abundance to create a psychologically classless society, in which the "feelings developed by the opposition of class interests" would disappear. Patten hoped that, as the potentialities of an age of abundance were perceived, men would be more willing to allow the state to "retain their surplus for educational purposes." The state would use its share of the surplus to broaden the "scheme of education" in order to encourage the "productive qualities and feelings in men" and in order to destroy outmoded loyalties to class feelings.[6]

Patten wanted to influence the content of the new education. For the first time in his career, he attempted to popularize his ideas. In articles and lectures directed at American teachers, he stripped the complications of professional economic argument from the concepts of abundance and restraint and used these concepts as a basis for advocating reforms in individuals and society.

The 1890's were a time of ferment in educational ideas. At Clark University, G. Stanley Hall conducted experiments in child and adolescent psychology. John Dewey studied the perceptions and reflexes of children and organized an experimental school at the University of Chicago. In Cambridge, William James lectured to teachers about new developments in psychology. The high-school curriculum was revised by a committee of educational leaders, including Charles W. Eliot of Harvard and William Torrey Harris, the leading American Hegelian and the United States Commissioner of Education. Simon Patten read the same books as these men and contributed to the same new periodicals devoted to education.

Like them, also, Patten was impressed by the new experimental psychology developed in Germany in the late nineteenth century. The mind-body dualism and the compartmentalization of the psyche into "faculties," which had dominated psychological thought since the Middle Ages, in the nineteenth century was challenged from two directions: associationism and the physiology of sensation. The English associationists, following David Hartley and John Stuart Mill, conceived the mind to be made up of groups of ideas that had become associated in various ways. Understanding, feeling, and will were the result of complex associations based on simple perceptions, not of completely separate faculties. In the 1870's, Wilhelm Wundt, a professor of philosophy at Leipzig, combined evolutionary theories, new findings in physiology, and associationist concepts into a new experimental psychology. Under the influence of Wundt, German and American psychologists studied the relationship between patterns of behavior and the organization of mind and body.

The new psychology had immediate relevance for education. The curriculum and teaching methods in most American schools were based on faculty psychology. Certain subjects, the classics for example, were justified mainly because it was believed that they exercised important faculties. The traditional classroom procedure, the recitation method, reflected a view of mental processes in which discipline and memory were more important than insight and activity.

The new psychology complemented Patten's economics. The subjective factors in the choices made by consumers—the habits, traditions, and prejudices which impeded the transition to an age of abundance—could be explained by the new psychological knowledge. Moreover, psychological research confirmed Patten's suspicion that men would not seek new pleasures in consumption merely because they were made available. In addition, the new psychology might provide techniques for persuading and conditioning men in their adjustment to new environmental conditions. The new doctrines, grounded on the theory of evolution and emphasizing the strength of the emotions and the dynamics of the development of personality, supported Patten's theories of "dynamic" economics and his efforts to suggest restraints that would prevent men from squandering the fruits of evolution.

Patten's adherence to the new psychology relieved him of the need to rely on the sanctions of the Protestant ethic as means of maintaining the restraints that would safeguard human welfare. It would no longer be necessary for men to hold in check their "primitive appetites and passions." Psychology could be used to educate men to prefer the pleasures of varied consumption and altruism—to develop habits suitable for an age of plenty. The ethics of Christ would become universal because of conditioning and joy, not because of faith and fear. Moreover, when men no longer felt the need to satisfy selfish and self-destructive impulses, they would not backslide.[7]

Patten contributed ideas about both curriculum and methods to the American debate about the proper type of education. Children and adults should be taught the habits which would create abundance and the restraints which would prevent the squandering of human and natural resources. A society could not achieve the "high standard of material comfort" on which "further progress" depended unless men learned to avoid wasting "half of the food supply" and came to appreciate the value of goods, particularly articles of food, to which they were not accustomed.[8]

Elementary and secondary schools should teach the implications of abundance rather than the necessity of restraint. Childhood and adolescence were the best times to develop habits appropriate for an age of abundance. Yet American schools were a "fossilized remnant of past ages," because they continued to teach the "nobility of hardships." Children must be shown that the benefits of abundance could not be socially exclusive: "As the standard of the community rises, the minimum standard demanded of every free citizen should rise also." They should also be given a sense of the importance of using social power to restrain dangers to society—ugly billboards, drunkenness, and persons with "defective mental powers," for example. The old curriculum emphasized "historic heroes," men who tried to attain a "golden age" by holding a "frail humanity above its natural level" with the force of example. The new heroes would be social scientists who sought to "elevate mankind through the growth of common qualities and the ejection of discordant elements" which lowered the "tone of society." [9]

Unlike elementary and secondary schools, which should emphasize the benefits of abundance, colleges should inculcate the restraints which would preserve the new society: self-control, efficiency, economy, generosity, and service. In the age of scarcity, restraint was learned at home and the possibilities of "culture" at school and college. In the age of abundance, however, most adolescents would be consuming a wide variety and increasing quantity of goods. Their desires would help to keep the economy of plenty growing. The colleges must assume a new role—preventing the impairment of the general welfare by an overconsumption of material goods. Young men and women could be trained to take satisfaction in intellectual pursuits and in the creation of values appropriate to the new age in people still operating in the context of scarcity. Moreover, the education of

youths and adults could be a weapon against the mass conformity
in consumption made possible by the development of techniques
for mass production and persuasion. Higher education should
teach people how to escape from "devitalizing routine" and
should loosen the "undemocratic bonds of group life." In sum,
educational institutions must perform "social work" to train
citizens to live in an age of abundance. Good citizenship is a
result of instincts, feelings, and ideals, not merely of a calculation of material interests.[10]

The inculcation of a sense of citizenship appropriate to an age
of abundance required a new conception of pedagogy. The new
psychology emphasized the existence of a "subjective" as well
as an external "environment" for each individual and group.
The inner world of feelings and perceptions and the outer world
of objects could not be separated. Pedagogy which emphasized
formal logic and the accumulation of facts ignored the complexity of human nature. Teachers must recognize that education was an emotional as well as a cognitive process. The goal
of education, a rearrangement of the subjective environment to
make possible an adjustment to a civilization based on abundance,
required that teachers develop a "logic of conviction." Students
must be stimulated to modify patterns of behavior and to make
appropriate selections of the desires to be satisfied or restrained.
If education could give direction to an orderly process of development which would replace haphazard, unguided evolution,
a great deal of "misery and suffering" could be avoided.[11]

Patten was not specific about the content of an education for
abundance or about the techniques of the new pedagogy. He
was an economic and social theorist, not a formulator of specific
programs. His role was to suggest that the development of a
frame of reference for an age of abundance had consequences
for areas of life besides economics. As a self-conscious professional economist, he was content to leave the details of educational programs and pedagogical techniques to professional
educators.

Patten's attitude toward the new science of nutrition is another example of his desire to go no further into other men's fields of expertise than his own goals required. Although he recognized that the consumption of certain foods was essential for the maintenance of health and had learned something about the chemistry of nutrition from Johannes Conrad, he did not attempt to outline a program for teaching men the findings of nutritionists. Patten's professional interest was in the attainment of prosperity and the development of values suited to the new conditions of life. Diversified production and consumption, particularly of foods, made abundance possible. The discovery, in the closing decades of the nineteenth century, that a diversified diet was necessary for human welfare reinforced his economic doctrines. He was pleased to learn from the writings of such men as W. O. Atwater of the United States Department of Agriculture that variety in consumption had physiological as well as economic benefits. Just as Johannes Conrad used his friend Ernst Haeckel's concept of "ecology" to validate his research in economic history, Patten accepted the science of nutrition as an independent corroboration of the validity of his insight into the impending transition to an age of abundance. Deciding on the specific details of an education in the problems of nutrition was a task for other men.[12]

As chairman of the economics department at the Wharton School, nevertheless, Patten participated for thirty years in decisions about educational policy. The Wharton curriculum reflected the views he expressed in his articles on education. His conviction that education must be relevant to students' immediate concerns was embodied in a proposal that freshmen be taught American rather than Roman history, political economy rather than mathematics. His dislike of coercion and his doubts about the value of religious sanctions made him support a movement to abolish compulsory chapel services for Wharton undergraduates. On the other hand, his belief that colleges should emphasize the "consumption" of spiritual and aesthetic goods led him to accept literature and languages in the curriculum. Yet he was more concerned with inculcating the techniques for managing abundance than with promoting liberal education. Patten envisioned the Wharton School as a "College of Practical Affairs" modeled on Massachusetts Institute of Technology and providing "thorough training in politics, economics, statistics, and history." [13]

Despite Patten's belief that education should be enjoyable, opening up new possibilities for human satisfaction, rather than coercive, the Wharton faculty, like most American faculties of the period, did not have much confidence in student freedom. There was little *Lernfreiheit* at the School, despite the predominance of German-trained scholars on the faculty. Students were allowed few elective courses and, until the second decade of the twentieth century, were required to stay in the same classroom all day while the faculty took turns lecturing to them. [14]

In his own teaching, Patten was faithful to his ideas. Inside and outside the classroom, he tried to put himself into rapport with the feelings of his students, to identify with their aspirations and to make his ideas meaningful to them. He lectured with few notes, seated in a chair, with his elbows on the desk, speaking directly to his audience in a mild conversational tone. Although he was not a demanding teacher, his gentleness and warmth stimulated his students to work hard. Patten rarely read examinations and papers, seldom gave a failing grade, and suggested rather than required that particular books be read. Yet most of his students did more work for Patten's courses than "for anybody else's." [15]

Although Patten never made a comprehensive statement about the "logic of conviction," he cultivated a spirit of excitement and exploration in his classroom. One technique he used was deliberate exaggeration for pedagogical effect. Half a century after studying with Patten, all his surviving students recalled his argument that canned tomatoes, a symbol of mass production and international trade, made war impossible. He invited students to disagree with his ideas and dramatized the difficulties of economic thought. On one occasion, for instance, after Patten had expounded a theory at great length, a student "cited a string of statistics which clearly contradicted the theory" and asked, "What do you say to that, Professor Patten?" After a long silence, Patten replied, "I would say those are bad statistics." [16]

Patten's greatest personal influence was exerted outside the classroom: talking to anybody who came to see him at breakfast in the University Club, visiting students and colleagues, and presiding over informal discussions among young instructors and graduate students. J. Russell Smith, a noted geographer, remembered Patten's ability to "separate your ideas from yourself." Frances Perkins, the first woman to serve in the Cabinet, recalled that Patten was the "first person who ever indicated" to her that she "had talents of any importance." She visited him at breakfast when she was trying to decide whether to marry: "He said, 'It really doesn't matter if you complete your work, go ahead and get married.' He had a healthy attitude toward life." [17]

He kept in contact with his students "with something of the keen sense of responsibility which a military commander may feel for those whom he has sent upon this or that particular campaign." Although he never sought any public position for himself, he encouraged many students to enter social work and government service. On Patten's recommendation, Edward T. Devine was appointed general secretary of the New York Charity Organization Society in 1896. William Draper Lewis, who studied under him both as an undergraduate and as a graduate student, became Dean of the University of Pennsylvania Law School and an adviser to Theodore Roosevelt. Samuel M. Lindsay organized and administered the Puerto Rican school system from 1898 to 1902. Leo S. Rowe became an assistant secretary in both the Treasury and State Departments and first director of the Pan-American Union. Walter E. Weyl achieved fame as a journalist and as founding editor of the *New Republic*. Frances Perkins had an outstanding career in social work before becoming Industrial Commissioner of the State of New York and United States Secretary of Labor from 1932 to 1945. Rexford G. Tugwell, after teaching at Columbia University, had a notable public career as an adviser to Franklin D. Roosevelt, Assistant Secretary of Agriculture, Director of the Resettlement Administration, and Governor of Puerto Rico.[18]

It was easier to evince concern for the welfare of young people in a society which provided increasing opportunities for men and women trained in the social sciences than to grapple with the theoretical complexities of promoting human welfare in a society which was in transition from scarcity to abundance. 1895 was a year of crisis in Patten's intellectual development.

On the surface, Patten seemed to be extremely optimistic about the prospects for an improvement in human welfare in the United States. He had revised the classical laws of rent, cost, wages, and diminishing returns to fit America's dynamic economy. Higher tariffs, improved education, the elimination of wasteful production and consumption, and the provision of a few social services seemed to be the only reforms necessary to insure a satisfactory transition to an age of abundance.

As he probed more deeply into the complexities of the emerging economy of abundance, however, he became less optimistic. A number of problems which had nagged at him since he had begun to write, more than a decade earlier, loomed larger. The American economy might become static, might reach a state of equilibrium, before its resources were fully utilized. Some men were too selfish, others too generous. In a society increasingly dominated by group feelings and interests, individual integrity was frequently threatened. Most important, men had conquered their external environment without modifying their values and their aspirations. Although most Americans did not "know what it is to be hungry," they had not fully recognized that full stomachs alone would not create a better civilization.[19]

Now forty-five years of age and at the height of his powers, Patten attempted what he hoped would be a synthesis of science and philosophy that would resolve his doubts and enable men to maximize human welfare as they confronted the future. He sought to solve "all social problems" by exploring the implications of a new relationship between men and their environment.

His challenge to the concepts of the traditional frame of reference was stated with unequivocal clarity: "Human societies have at length emerged from the condition where the avoidance of pain is the requisite for survival. Man is now placed in a pleasure world and his needs demand a pleasure and not a pain economy." In order to demonstrate the implications of this alteration in the human condition, Patten returned to the first principles of evolutionary thought and experimental psychology.[20]

Evolution, the process of adjustment to new environments, was motivated by "competitive stress," which produced what Darwin called the struggle for survival. This stress was the result of a reciprocal relationship between human intelligence and environments which constantly posed new challenges. The external environment was a collection of desirable and undesirable "objects," the study of which was called "economics." This collection of objects was the most important stimulus for changes in the "subjective" environment, which consisted of men's perceptions and feelings. Changes in both environments were, therefore, dependent, first of all, upon economic conditions: "The causes of evolution lie in economic conditions and their effects show themselves in organisms." [21]

Neither economics nor the theory of evolution, however, revealed the "mental mechanism" which enabled men and external conditions to interact and produce changes in the subjective environment. In the psychological doctrines he used to justify his ideas on education and his concern for the feelings of his own students, Patten sought the mental mechanism which would guarantee social welfare. Yet psychology was an aid to the logical exposition of economic ideas, not a scientific prerequisite of these ideas. He had developed his insight into impending abundance by observing the relationship between the environment and men as producers and consumers before he knew enough psychology to see a relationship between the environment and the nervous system.[22]

The basis of Patten's psychology, derived mainly from the writings of William James and James Mark Baldwin, was a sharp distinction between sensory and motor ideas. Sensory ideas were impulses carried to the brain from the organs of perception. Motor ideas, the impulses carried by the autonomic nervous system to the organs of the human body, created the "movements in the organism" which produced an "adjustment between it and the objects of which it has knowledge." Following James, Patten criticized associationist psychology for conceiving of the mind in terms of "groups" of ideas and emotions. In his view, mental processes consisted of "waves of consciousness." [23]

These waves, the result of many complex internal processes, received their initial stimulus from the external environment. An environment which provided a surplus of pleasures stimulated the development of motor ideas. A surplus of pains, on the other hand, stimulated sensory ideas. Although Patten qualified his assertion that pleasure controlled motor development while sensory powers "depended upon the need of avoiding the sources of pain," he often forgot his doubts.[24]

Since motor impulses were stimulated by a surplus of pleasure in the environment, and since the American economy was making possible a growing surplus of pleasure, it followed that motor impulses deserved more attention from social scientists. The problems of welfare could be solved by stimulating particular motor responses. Simpler problems, related to the methods of increasing production and the proper patterns of consumption, had already been solved or were approaching solution, mainly as a result of sensory impulses.[25]

Men had learned to derive a surplus of satisfactions from their environment without modifying their motor behavior. The beliefs, ideas, and passions which molded "social forces" had not changed to fit new economic conditions. Abundance made traditional values obsolete. Patten wanted to provide new values which would enable men's inner lives to reflect economic reality.[26]

He believed that men could create a society in which "mastery over nature" was complete, while lethargy, vice, and overconsumption were not permitted. Patten envisioned restraints on pleasures derived from abundance, a world in which fear, but not the pain of renunciation, was absent. In the age of scarcity, men were forced to create institutions based on the "fear of enemies or pain." In the emerging abundance economy, on the other hand, the "evils" were "subjective." The new evils were caused by "defective relations . . . between men or between man and nature." Internal evils, the results of problems of "adjustment," had replaced the external threats of the age of scarcity. Yet if the pleasure economy abolished restraints by eliminating all pain, the result would be greater misery than men had known in the age of scarcity. Historically, a pleasure economy was an "impossibility," since "nation after nation" had "gone down" when "utilities instead of pains" became the "supreme object of interest." [27]

The "impossibility" was a result of the neglect of motor development, of the mechanism for adapting to satisfactions. Since, prior to Patten's generation, productive techniques did not make possible long-term abundance for the entire human race, men had sought to avoid pain—to develop sensory powers—rather than to create new values. They had been content to anticipate the lean years by gratifying their sensory desires in the fat years. As productive techniques improved, however, sensory impulses would relax, and an increasing surplus of satisfactions would stimulate motor development. The "extension of knowledge," governed by motor impulses, would persuade men to restrain material consumption in order to "consume" the pleasures of the spirit and the intellect.[28]

Patten was impatient with the slowness of unaided evolutionary processes. He wanted to speed up the relaxation of sensory impulses to enable men to enjoy an age of abundance more quickly. The new uses to which he put the insights of psychology, however, prevented him from assigning this task of adjustment to professional educators. Belief and reason, the tools of pedagogy, could not have much effect if motor development was influenced solely by interaction between men and their external environment. Inappropriate beliefs could be "weeded out" only by environmental change. Reason was a tool for manipulating beliefs and facts, not an "independent source of authority" and conviction. Neither education nor social planning could "alter the order of development nor eliminate any of its steps." [29]

Yet Patten could not bear the thought that human suffering must persist, since he thought he knew how men could prevent "many evils and economize much time." In desperation, he introduced a new assumption. There was a "normal line of social progress": the eternal desire to develop techniques for promoting human welfare. This "normal line" existed outside history. Historical development, like a river cutting its way to the sea, followed the course of least resistance, rather than the shortest, or normal, route. In the past, the urge to promote welfare had been sacrificed to the negative need to "ward off pain." Since a changed environment enabled men to maximize welfare, they might be able to create the impulses, habits, and ideas they would have had if the normal line had not "been abandoned." [30]

It would first be necessary to plot what human development might have been on the normal line, in order to discover the extent to which men, in their desire to avoid pain, had deviated from considerations of general welfare. For this purpose, Patten postulated two fixed points in time: the beginning of civilization, when the world's population was small enough so that there were enough material goods to go around; and the establishment of the "Social Commonwealth," a hypothetical society imagined by Patten to serve as a "basis for speculating in regard to future progress" on the ahistorical assumption that the "line of progress" had been direct. [31]

The Social Commonwealth was a model which purported to indicate what men would value in an age of abundance if, throughout history, scarcity had not made them more anxious to avoid pain than to "conform to the conditions of social welfare." This model reflected Patten's vision of a life of restraint amidst abundance. The inhabitants of a social commonwealth would develop four kinds of ideals, thwarted in the long age of scarcity, which would enable them to reshape old institutions and create new ones. The first type of new ideal would be economic and would lead to improved methods of producing and distributing wealth. The second group of ideals would be "aesthetic" and would transform the consumption of wealth by stimulating changes leading to its "best utilization." Third, new moral ideals would limit the activities of individuals to those fields in which "future welfare" was "prominent." Finally, religious ideals would illuminate the "defects and limitations of our planetary existence" and suggest another world where the "possibilities of a perfect existence" could be realized.[32]

The Social Commonwealth would not be the "highest or even a final social state." Moreover, it would not "satisfy all the aspirations of men." Patten was building a model, not planning a utopia. Like his German contemporary, the sociologist Max Weber, Patten realized that abstraction for the purpose of illuminating the past or projecting the future produced oversimplification. Patten's model of the "normal line" and Weber's "ideal types" were constructs of men who had studied history. Both men were painfully aware of the methodological perils of even the most severely qualified generalizations. Patten never tried to convince anyone that either of the terminal points on the normal line of progress had any basis in "reality" as most men understand this word. He was anxious to point out that the Social Commonwealth could not be construed as a utopia in which men would achieve some sort of "perfection." [33]

Patten wanted men to use his projection of the "normal" trend toward a social commonwealth as the basis for planning social and economic changes in the historical present, the transition period between the ages of scarcity and abundance. He could not, however, disregard the doubts raised by his conscience— his fear that planning could prove futile or destructive. Despite his profound concern for human welfare, he reasoned himself into a position so fraught with tortured ambiguity and contradiction that he could not proceed further without a leap of faith. His commitment to rigorous logic, however, which prevented his having faith in either individualism or collectivism, in either "natural" evolution or planning, also prevented him from carrying his social thought very much further. The intellectual honesty which condemned Patten, over the next quarter-century, to fitful attempts to resolve the ambiguities and paradoxes of his thought was a tribute to the power of his reason, to the sense of calling instilled by his Calvinist heritage, and to the sense of professional responsibility derived from his German education. More poignantly, his honesty provided an example of the paralysis inflicted on even the most gifted of men by the ethos of their age.

In 1895 and 1896, Patten tried to mold his contradictory ideas and feelings into a coherent system. He attempted, for instance, to combine his recognition of a need for new institutions with ideas prompted by his fear of the results of their operation. Each person must join a cooperative "group of producers"; "socialism," however, was a fantasy developed in a pain economy to provide a "more speedy remedy from present evils than the growth of social institutions can offer." Although, in a social commonwealth, everyone would develop the same "habits, customs, rights, and duties" and "blend into one race," Asian hordes might "break down" habits and ideals upon which "future progress" depended. Democracy produced "strong feelings tending to help the dependent classes"; but it might "hinder further differentiation and tend to keep in society all the classes it now contains." Improvements in the distribution of wealth would enable men to consume a greater variety of goods. Even expanding consumption might, however, produce a new age of scarcity if men were not restrained from sharing the new "equality of temptation." [34]

Patten proposed a three-part solution to the problems raised by these contradictions and ambiguities: an emphasis on the pleasures of aesthetic consumption, the "psychic control" of destructive passions, and a reinterpretation of the theory of evolution to relieve the tension between sympathy and a fear of coddling those who were unfit to survive. He wanted to show the "fortunate" men, who controlled the "social surplus," how to use it most profitably as a "trust fund" to serve the welfare of society as a whole. This solution was based on the assumption of the normal line—Patten's belief that it was better to provide "general measures of relief" against distress and inappropriate adjustment to the new basis of civilization than to encourage citizens to rely on "their own efforts." [35]

The general welfare could not be improved without changes in habits of consumption. "Crude appetites and vices" could be restrained by educating people to appreciate the "harmony of consumption." If their "aesthetic standards" were raised, men would perceive the possibilities of improved consumption in the emerging abundance economy. Aesthetic pleasure, which Patten defined as "non-exclusive" satisfaction, would replace the indulgence of physical appetites which could destroy the Social Commonwealth. Unlike John Ruskin, who was driven to advocate improved social aesthetics by his perception of the ugliness of industrial Britain, he embraced industrial change and believed that aesthetic pleasure must be predicated on abundance. Patten looked forward to a new concept of aesthetics, derived from the technology that made abundance possible, not backward, like Ruskin, to a simpler life, of which Gothic art was the highest expression. [36]

A mere increase in the quantity and quality of goods available to consumers would not automatically result in improvements in the general welfare. Passions and appetites must be restrained by a "steady improvement in psychic control." The goal of this control was increased productive power, combined with restraints against "overnutrition." Patten acquired the concept of social control, the means by which a society, defined as a group of interacting individuals, orders such social phenomena as the interests of individuals and the welfare of the group, from his friend Edward A. Ross, then professor of economics and sociology at Stanford University. He combined Ross's ideas with the findings of the science of nutrition in order to analyze the problem of overnutrition—the debilitating effect of retaining old wants after new wants were developed. When internal, or psychic, and social controls against overeating and excessive procreation were developed, men would become "socialized"—able to realize the four ideals of the Social Commonwealth. The socialization of consumers would enable them to value aesthetic and altruistic activities. As the restraints against overnutrition were internalized, selfish overeaters would be "gradually weeded out," and the "surviving part of society" could begin to transfer its attention from the getting and spending of wealth to concerns of the spirit and intellect.[37]

According to Patten, in conventional Darwinian theory the struggle for existence concluded with the "survival of the well-fed." Organisms which obtained less food than others were eliminated, whatever their aesthetic and spiritual accomplishments. Darwin, however, wrote in the context of the age of scarcity, when there was not enough food for the entire population of an environment. In the emerging abundance economy, on the other hand, everyone would have the food necessary for survival, and fitness would be determined by the "social and not the bodily qualities of a man." It was necessary to add three new stages to the theory of natural selection to make it applicable to a society in transition to abundance. Patten accepted Darwin's theory that the rapid multiplication of a species was followed by a struggle for existence and the survival of the fittest. In Patten's view, however, the struggle to exist in an age of abundance led first to the survival of the well-fed, then to the degeneration of the overfed. At a later stage, new restraints modified desires. Those who developed these restraints were "selected" as the fittest individuals.[38]

Aesthetic consumption, social and psychic control, and a new definition of what constituted fitness to survive in an age of abundance might provide a framework within which men could act to maximize the general welfare. Patten did not, however, rest content with the justifications and guidelines for social change he had developed between 1892 and 1896. He continued to seek authority for his speculations and a course of action to implement the values and restraints appropriate to an age of abundance.

CHAPTER V 🖋

Authority and Action,

1897–1903

It is one thing to propose a revision in the cluster of assumptions with which men view the human condition, quite another to demonstrate the validity and utility of a revised frame of reference. For a thoughtful social scientist in the mid-1890's, faith in insight or in divine sanction was insufficient authority for social theory. Patten had tried a third alternative, the methods and data of science, in his effort to place economics in "touch with the *Zeitgeist* of our age."[1] Psychology and ecology had not, however, resolved the contradictions and doubts that had disturbed him over the previous decade. Since it was possible to confound Patten by claiming that the productive surplus in America was only a temporary phenomenon, or that it was no easy matter to select and eliminate those who were genuinely unfit and not merely deprived of opportunity, agreement with Patten was a matter of opinion, not of logic.

The concept of the normal line, which Patten had used to validate his desire to mitigate suffering was based on a tenuous assumption—that men are motivated by a desire to maximize the general welfare. Moreover, the model he had erected on the basis of this assumption had produced contradictions and ambiguities. Patten published nothing in 1897, perhaps because he realized that his three-part solution to the dilemmas raised by his theory was not very convincing. Broader consumption, social control, and a revision of Darwin begged the basic question: What guaranteed that the surplus on which an abundance economy was predicated would continue to increase and that men would develop new attitudes toward the consumption of wealth?

Patten's study of psychology had forced him to conclude that reason, inductive or deductive, was an unsatisfactory authority. Reason was conditioned by assumptions based on feelings which men could not easily control. There were only two alternatives left to him, history and pragmatism: to justify his insight into contemporary changes in human behavior by comparing them with previous modifications of behavior or to back away from theoretical validation and propose courses of action which men could test to discover whether their results produced a more satisfactory society. Patten explored both alternatives between 1897 and 1903.

Like those eighteenth-century *philosophes* who despaired of reason as the sanction for moral behavior, Patten turned to history for the evidence he needed to solve the problems his theories raised. In order to write history, he traveled to Europe. By returning to the certainties of his youth, to the methods of the German economists, and to the places where the study of history had attained its highest development—the universities of Germany and England—Patten sought to escape the ambiguities and dilemmas which had gripped him during a decade of deduction in America.[2]

Patten's first months in Europe were depressing. He had come to find new insight and was merely refining his old ideas. In August, 1897, he told Franklin H. Giddings, professor of sociology at Columbia University, that the ideas he was "now trying out" were "old friends," with which he was "familiar enough to make them no longer fresh." After six months of hard work, Patten's spirits improved. He told Giddings that his thoughts had "run wild as they did when [he] was a boy." There was a "mass of new relations" to which he had been "partially blind before." Although he admitted, "What I see before me and would like to do is beyond my powers," he returned to the United States in the autumn of 1898 with a new book, *The Development of English Thought*.[3]

Patten found authority for his concept of a transition from an economy of scarcity to an economy of abundance in a theory of the economic and intellectual history of Western society. The same pattern of social development occurred in every environment. Whenever economic conditions changed, the motives, instincts, and habits of a race were modified, and new "modes of thought" were formed. All the "characteristics of civilization" were "reconstructed." Patten divided the history of thought into epochs, each characterized by a new mode of production and a modified physical environment. The pattern of events repeated in each epoch encompassed the four ideals he had developed in his model of the Social Commonwealth. As a new mode of production modified the physical environment, men developed new economic, aesthetic, moral, and religious ideas.[4]

Patten's economic interpretation of history was quite different from the theory of historical materialism advocated by Marxists in the 1890's. Friedrich Engels, the foremost interpreter of Karl Marx's ideas, deduced historical "laws" from the "operation of a nature conceived as an independent reality external to man." Patten, on the other hand, was closer to Marx's own view that "nature and man are complex realities whose interaction is studied in society." To Patten, economic change precipitated changes in aesthetics, morals, and religion which enabled men to visualize and bring about further changes in their modes and relationships of production. Patten was influenced by both Marx and the English historian Henry Thomas Buckle, whose *History of Civilization in England* appeared in 1857. Like Buckle, Patten was convinced that the most significant changes in men's perception of the human condition were the results of "tendencies" perceived "by the mind," not of events discerned "by the senses." Ignoring the crude empiricism of Engels and most Marxists, Patten reached for the more complicated ideas of process and the working of mind in history which had been explored by Buckle, the young Marx, and the Hegelian teachers of the German scholars from whom Patten had first learned economics.[5]

Patten's theory of history explained why men living in an age of potential abundance reacted to their environment as if they were still living in an era of scarcity. In each epoch, the values and attitudes essential for "race welfare" were internalized. They became motor responses—so automatic that they were passed on to the next generation by a process akin to heredity. Yet members of older generations were present at the beginning of each new epoch. The values necessary for welfare in each epoch were "formed anew from new conditions"; they did not "grow out of the similar ideas of the preceding epoch." Motor responses appropriate to the past produced cultural lag, since in each new epoch the "concepts and ideas of the preceding epoch" were "displaced or modified only with great difficulty." In time, however, "new aggregates" of thought were formed which "displaced" or "blended" with the ideas of the earlier epoch.[6]

Patten used the history of English economic thought to demonstrate the influence of environmental change on ideas and values. A radical change in economic relationships presented an economist with a mass of new data. He was forced to become a philosopher in order to generate concepts with which to comprehend these data. Because he was not familiar with philosophical conventions, new ones were "forced upon him by his own progress in an un-explored field." Conversely, a man who began as a philosopher found his assumptions and categories at odds with the data provided by his environment. He was compelled to trace a "downward curve" from abstraction to the "world of facts." As an economist became a philosopher, so a philosopher was transformed into an economist.[7]

English thought provided numerous examples of this pattern.

In the seventeenth century, the first period of the modern economy, Thomas Hobbes stated the problems of modern social organization but found no solution to them. John Locke, who began with data, moved toward philosophy. In the eighteenth century, as the Industrial Revolution gathered force, David Hume was transformed from an economist into a philosopher, Adam Smith and Thomas Malthus from philosophers into economists. In the next century, John Stuart Mill moved from economics to philosophy and Charles Darwin from philosophy to biology. Continental thought carried forward what Englishmen on an "upward curve" toward abstraction left unfinished. Locke raised problems which G. W. Leibnitz and J. J. Rousseau tried to solve, Hume awakened Immanuel Kant, and Mill stimulated Continental logicians and socialists. This relationship between English and Continental thought was a result of the fact that new economic conditions had their initial impact in England. When these conditions appeared on the Continent, economists, moralists, aestheticians, and philosophers carried forward the pioneering ideas of the English.[8]

The transformations in thought were the result of changing patterns of motor responses, not of reason. A "new group of sensory ideas" was transformed into new motor responses, or values, by a process which Patten called "conviction"—a conversion similar to the acceptance of religious faith. Patten's theory of conviction was similar to Max Weber's concept of charisma. Like Weber, Patten had been trained in historical economics and had grown up in a deeply religious environment. Several years before Weber announced his concept, Patten described conviction as the process by which impulses were imparted to groups. This process had the same emotional component, the "magnetism" exercised by a powerful personality, as Weber's charisma.[9] The leaders of thought whose curves Patten had described were, however, more often men who had experienced conversion to new values and had the ability to express them in words than charismatic figures who could attract followers.

To exemplify conversion to values appropriate to new conditions, Patten, like Weber, showed how new religious movements could integrate values that had seemed inconsistent in a different environment. Puritanism, for example, though it emphasized spiritual salvation, converted men to an acceptance of ideas appropriate to the development of capitalism—the concept of calling, wealth as an emblem of election, and the desirability of frugality.[10]

The conversion of intellectually gifted men to values which enabled them to formulate ideas appropriate to new conditions did not guarantee that whole societies would develop these values. Throughout history, there had been two obstacles to the communication of new ideas: the intellectuality which enabled gifted men to leap ahead of their contemporaries and the existence of different types of personalities in all societies. Economists and philosophers knew too much to be effective reformers. They failed to convert people to their doctrines because their insight into the complexity of reality led to paradox and contradiction rather than to communicable conviction. Promoting social reform was a job for simpler-minded men like Thomas Carlyle and John Ruskin. Men with "courage and decision" had "great advantages" over sophisticated thinkers, who were "trammelled" by tradition, by respect for social restraints, and by knowledge of contradictory facts.[11]

More important, each society consisted of men whose psychological characteristics forced them to respond to new conditions in different ways. There were four basic types of personality: clingers, sensualists, stalwarts, and mugwumps. Clingers were imitative, submissive people. Sensualists, their opposites, were unrestrained risk-takers, lovers of power, and seekers of continuous sensual gratification. Stalwarts, who appeared only in economically advanced societies, subordinated policy to principle, valued economic activity, and had strong restraints against self-indulgence. Mugwumps, whose name Patten borrowed from American politics, were men with strong powers of reasoning who were not prone to act on their ideas.[12]

These types of personality were products of the long age of scarcity. In the emerging abundance economy, clingers and sensualists were being eliminated, while stalwarts and mugwumps were growing in numbers and power. Stalwartism was the result of the highest development of the characteristics necessary for survival in an age of scarcity. It would "endure" as long as "frugalism" was "advantageous." But stalwarts refused to increase the variety of goods they consumed or to base their morality on pleasure rather than on fear. Mugwumps, on the other hand, could see the implications of changing economic conditions, even if they were too weak to force other men to change their habits of consumption. As the economy of abundance matured, all four types of personality would be replaced by new types which would reflect the new conditions of existence. Patten refused to predict what kinds of personality would dominate the future: "When better conditions open up new possibilities, bolder visualization enlarges the utopia until it is farther off than ever before." [13]

Despite his effort to find authority in history for the emergence of an age of abundance, Patten was still afraid that social reform would impede adjustment to the new economic conditions. Painfully aware of his own inconsistency, he argued that science, Christian morality, and the elimination of the unfit all provided proper justifications for reform. Neither science nor history prevented him from concluding that there was no essential difference between the Protestant ethic and the teachings of evolutionary theory. The "old contrast of the elect and the damned" had merely been transformed into an "opposition of the standardful and the standardless." Those who could not consume properly and those who consumed too much must be eliminated, though in a charitable manner—by depriving them of the right to reproduce. Conversion to new values, or positive reform, seemed more likely to protect clingers and sensualists than did negative reform, the withholding of sympathy in the name of science and progress. With considerable sadness, Patten decided that adjustment to the pleasure economy would not be complete for at least another century.[14]

History had failed to provide the authority Patten so desperately wanted. He probably realized that, although he bore some physical resemblance to Abraham Lincoln—long arms and legs, heavy, high jaw, melancholy eyes—he lacked the eloquence needed to create the personal charisma which might persuade men of the validity of his insight.[15] At the end of his lengthy volume of history, Patten edged toward the only justification of his doctrines still available to him: pragmatism. His efforts to find authority for purposive social action in the logic of economics, psychology, and history had failed.

A decade before he read William James's *Essays on Pragmatism*, Patten was willing to justify his ideas by the results of their application. "Habitual activity" would be the only "direct test" to which a judgment could be put. Yet Patten, like James, knew that pragmatic tests must be based on a set of values. Ideas and programs could be tested only in a context of commitment. By a process analogous to that of James in "The Will to Believe," Patten posited a theological justification for purposive action. In every epoch and every culture, men developed a belief in the "possibility of permanent life." The plan by which God worked in the world was discovered by examining concurrently the "laws" of life, reason, and economics. Because of the superb "plan upon which God works in nature," men had the power to attain their goals. The elements necessary for the "full attainment of every ideal" were present in the "life and character of men." In Patten's heavenly city on earth, for example, a "law of increasing altruism," which had beneficial pragmatic results, would emerge in an age of abundance. In their effort to realize the divine plan in an age of plenty, men would discover that they could maintain their own "vigor" only by devoting more time to the "welfare of other people." Like Auguste Comte fifty years earlier, Patten believed that altruism could be induced by social pressure if men were first committed to appropriate values.[16]

Patten built a program for action on these values. In 1899, a year after his historical theories were published, he began work on a new book, tentatively called *Progress toward Freedom*, in which he sought to find and eliminate the "causes of the slow progress toward social ideas." As the book advanced through successive drafts, its title and scope became more pragmatic. By the time it was published in 1902, as *The Theory of Prosperity*, Patten seemed to have abandoned his interest in the ultimate causes and effects of progress. He was concerned, instead, with the causes of and cures for the poverty that still existed in the midst of abundance in the United States. Disregarding the problems of finding authority for his theories, he explored the desires and restraints necessary for adjustment to an altered human condition.[17]

From the Middle Ages to the nineteenth century, most enlightened men, whatever their political sympathies, accepted the biblical injunction about the poor being always with us. Given the limits of production and the pressure of population, the argument ran, poverty was an inevitable condition of life. A man's worldly condition was, by and large, a function of his moral character. Private voluntary charity was the proper source of relief for the legitimate needs of the "deserving"—that is, the morally respectable—poor and contributed to the virtue of the donor.

This attitude toward poverty came under heavy attack in industrialized nations during Patten's generation. As the productive power of the West increased, scholars and reformers in Germany, England, and the United States subjected the traditional theory to empirical investigation. They concluded that drunkenness, sloth, and mendacity—the vices of the "undeserving" poor—were usually the results rather than the causes of poverty. A few men, the English scholars Charles Booth, John A. Hobson, and Seebohm Rowntree, for instance, had suggested that the existence of poverty placed limits on economic growth. At the time Patten applied his insight into the age of abundance to the problems of economic suffering, a new theory of poverty, which had nothing to do with morality, was emerging. The new theory, axiomatic to many men in the mid-twentieth century, was untenable to men who assumed that scarcity was the normal condition of life. According to the new concept, poverty is an economic phenomenon that can and must be abolished. Moreover, the state is the only social institution with sufficient resources to deal with the complex economic and social forces that create poverty.[18]

Although Patten never mentioned the works of Booth and Rowntree, it is probable that, given his interest in developing courses in social work at the University of Pennsylvania, he was familiar with their studies of poverty in London and York. In *The Theory of Prosperity*, he made a distinction between poverty and "misery" that was similar to Rowntree's differentiation between primary and secondary poverty. To Rowntree and Patten, people who suffered from primary poverty lacked sufficient income to purchase the requisites for physical efficiency. Secondary poverty, or misery, was the result of inappropriate consumption—in Patten's terms, of "nonadjustment" to the possibilities of a fuller life in the emerging age of abundance. Unlike Rowntree, who never accepted the assumption of potential abundance, Patten was confident that primary poverty could easily be abolished by improvements in productive techniques and a modest redistribution of wealth. Misery, which could grow, even in an age of abundance, until life was not "worth living," was a more tenacious problem.[19]

Patten's book was in two parts. In the first, he clarified his concept of surplus and examined the role of market forces in an emerging economy of abundance. Satisfied that a surplus of goods, combined with contemporary market forces, would abolish primary poverty, he went on, in the second part, to propose remedies for the "discontent" that resulted from misery.

Patten repeated his thesis that the source of "general welfare" was the "social surplus." But he added a new concept, "surplus energy," derived perhaps from the work of the German chemist Wilhelm Ostwald. In a dynamic society, each "round of production and consumption" left a "slight surplus," which was transformed into energy. The expenditure of energy so improved the environment that more energy could be "stored up for the subsequent use of men." Surplus energy enabled men to have a higher goal than mere survival and led to a process of evolution more efficient than that which resulted in the elimination of the unfit. Elimination had no "goal or end" except the removal of the "pain" caused by the unfit. If, however, elimination was controlled by a better distribution of the surplus and by sterilization of those who could not utilize it, a "clearly defined [personality] type" would appear, energy would be increased, and a "normal standard" by which individuals could be judged might be established.[20]

In a complex modern nation, the surplus was the result of interdependence and cooperation. By collective effort, rather than by struggling against one another, producers increased the surplus of goods and consumers the excess of satisfactions. Although Patten admitted that some competition was "necessary to make sure that the ordinary motives for production" were in operation, he believed that "effective competition" was not a "competition of men for places or of producers for cheapness but of position with position" within the market. As an economy moved toward abundance, the "most efficient positions" were always occupied, whether or not production was monopolized. Unregulated monopoly might lead to exploitation; but unfettered competition would set men against one another—make individual success rather than the general welfare the social goal. Monopoly, if regulated in the public interest, increased men's ability to plan their lives and to predict events and their results.[21]

Similarly, consumers were protected by their potential monopoly power—their ability to substitute one good for another or to restrain their consumption of particular goods—not by "rivalry among producers." Rising prices, for example, were a result of the behavior of consumers, not of the selfishness of "powerful trusts." Since men's wants were multiplying rapidly in the emerging economy of abundance, there was constant pressure on manufacturers to produce a greater variety of goods. This pressure enabled producers to increase their profits by producing new articles for which there was "urgent" demand, rather than by lowering prices, as they did in the competitive economy of scarcity. Prices would fall only if men restrained their consumption.[22]

Patten's theory of monopoly had important implications for American society. Every individual was, by definition, a consumer as well as a producer. "Class" solidarity, in the usual sense of the term, was outmoded. "Two isolated groups of laborers with different powers of substitution"—the result of differences in their rate of wages and level of education—could have less in common with each other than they had with their "employers and other associates within their own group." Moreover, since wants were constantly changing as the environment changed, there was no reason to accept the permanence of existing economic institutions. Because of consumers' power in an economy of abundance to substitute one good for another, monopolies would "struggle" with each other, and all existing monopolies would "give way to new ones." In addition, it made no difference who owned capital, as long as everyone was guaranteed an increasing share in the increasing "flow of income." In the long run, increased wages and the education of consumers would redistribute enough wealth and create a balance of desire and restraint sufficient to give consumers, through the power of substitution, dominant control of the economy. If society yielded to the forces of "monopoly" operating among both producers and consumers, poverty would be abolished.[23]

Society would not automatically embrace the new reality as Patten defined it. It was necessary to develop a system of values that guaranteed the permanence of new economic conditions, a theory of social change that justified these values, and a legislative program that would enforce adherence to the values and permit the theory to operate.

The values appropriate to abundance, which Patten had discussed over the previous decade, could not be inculcated unless men were protected against exploitation. Economic freedom was secure only where men could substitute one activity for another. Free land, which Achille Loria in Italy and Frederick Jackson Turner in America considered the most important protection against exploitation, was not highly regarded by Patten as a protective device. He believed that the benefits derived from free land could be "obtained in other ways"—principally by providing higher incomes and education to prevent situations in which the "exploited consent to the exploitation." In the long age of scarcity, exploitation had been necessary to produce enough to guarantee bare subsistence. Men had consented to being exploited, because traditional moral codes restrained the "free play of egoistic forces." Neither exploitation nor traditional moral codes, both based on the acceptance of pain, were appropriate to the new conditions of existence.[24]

These new conditions were producing a "cohesive" society in which misery—the poverty of ignorance—could be extirpated. This was the society described by Patten's model of a social commonwealth. As a result of his historical research, however, he no longer predicated attainment of the good society on the projection of a "normal," ahistorical line of development. Before becoming cohesive, a society was "adhesive"—in the last stages of a scarcity economy. During the transition from an adhesive to a cohesive society, men formed themselves into groups which surmounted obstacles, secured protection, and increased their stock of economic goods.[25]

Patten's theory of a transition from adhesion to cohesion had two related elements, abundance and restraint. Since American society was in the process of transition, the theory would be susceptible to pragmatic tests. He presented the values of abundance in a theory of full consumption. An increase in consumption was in the best interests of the dominant classes. Inefficient consumption, the result of low wages and inadequate education, would lead to economic crisis, since there would be no buyers for the increasing quantity of goods. Capitalists would learn that they gained more by increasing productivity than they lost by the "extra wages needed" to stimulate production.[26]

As Patten had said many times before, unregulated produc-

tion and consumption could create a society dedicated to gluttony and vice. On the basis of his refined view of economic
processes, he sought a "new group of restraints" that would
"keep men in touch with their economic conditions without
depressing their individuality." These new restraints would be
provided by the operation of the law of increasing altruism he
had announced three years earlier and of a corollary, the law
of "vicarious consumption," which asserted that men took pleasure in the "welfare of others." Altruism would reduce and
simplify individual wants and stimulate men to convert surplus
energy into programs to provide for all the exigencies individuals
could not control.[27]

The enforcement of these restraints would not create a utopia.
Progress would always lag behind men's ideals; "perfection"
was "never possible." Although "all men" could not be "made
wealthy," they could be "made comfortable by some of the
social surplus going to them" and could be protected by "public
control" of conditions which threatened to "lower the vitality
of the working population." [28]

A pragmatic approach to implementing the values appropriate
to an age of abundance did not, however, resolve Patten's
dilemmas. He wondered if the selfishness of American businessmen would prevent a capitalist economy from overcoming the
"difficulties that beset it." Although he believed that social
Darwinian concepts were valid only for a scarcity economy,
he suspected that some "natural elimination" was necessary to
"enforce social customs and traditions." Most important, he was
uncertain about the theological context in which he had placed
his pragmatism. Perhaps religious values could not prevent all
the deleterious effects of passion and conflict.[29]

A year later, in 1903, Patten tried to find in recent biological
thought values for his pragmatism. He sought the mechanism
by means of which the energy created by surplus production
and consumption stimulated "permanent changes in organisms"
and enabled the "effects of economic betterments to perpetuate
themselves." If this mechanism could be found, Patten would

no longer fear the destruction of the economy of abundance by inappropriate habits of behavior.[30]

In his search for scientific authority, Patten manipulated August Weismann's theory of cell growth and heredity and the findings of Patrick Geddes and J. Arthur Thomson on the evolution of primary and secondary sex characteristics. He presented a tortured and illogical argument to demonstrate that, although acquired characteristics—appropriate habits of consumption, for instance—could not be inherited, they might liberate surplus energy which would cause organic modification and allow the new characteristics to be perpetuated. Patten wanted to convince himself, as well as the few loyal readers who followed his confusing argument to its end, that an economic surplus would, in the future, provide the stimulus to evolution. Prosperity would create an "increase in energy" which would transform men more effectively than a struggle for scarce means of subsistence.[31]

Patten did not need the harsh comments of outraged reviewers of his *Heredity and Social Progress* in economic and scientific journals to know that his attempt to find scientific authority for his social theory had produced pseudoscientific gibberish. At the end of the book, he admitted that he had not justified his belief in continuous progress based on the production of an economic surplus. The age of abundance was "farther away" than he "had supposed." [32]

Some time after the book was published, Patten wrote on the flyleaf of his own copy, "Even in defeat there is hope." [33] Defeated in his efforts to find authority for his convictions and to resolve his theoretical dilemmas, Patten devoted the next fifteen years to agitation for various social reforms. At the age of fifty, he had reached the limit of his ability as a theorist. Perhaps he would fare better as an active pragmatist.

CHAPTER VI 📖

An Active Pragmatist, 1904–1914

The development of Patten's conviction that poverty could be abolished if men would accept values and restraints appropriate to an age of abundance coincided with the growth of professional philanthropy in America. The new and uncertain profession of social work experienced a remarkable growth in the 1890's. Charity organization societies, introduced from England in the 1880's to systematize the distribution of private relief funds, gained control of philanthropic activities in most large cities. Settlement houses, established in the 1890's and headed by such passionate and articulate persons as Jane Addams and Lillian Wald, were growing in number, size, and prestige. Professional training for social workers began at the turn of the century. Periodicals like *Charities* and *The Commons* had a growing number of readers who needed to be directed rather than convinced. A number of Patten's students—Edward T. Devine, Samuel M. Lindsay, Frances Perkins, William H. Allen, and Benjamin C. Marsh—held important positions in increasingly powerful organizations.

Patten's central theme, that the goal of social action was adjustment to the economy of abundance, has become so basic to modern social work that details about his influence are no longer known. Even the fact that he seems to have coined the term "social work"—or at least to have been mainly responsible for its adoption in preference to other terms—has been forgotten. In the official histories of American social work, Patten is scarcely recognizable in descriptions which refer to him as an "insurgent against social arrangements" or a man who saved the "entire field of social services" from "identification with the conservative classes of society." [1]

It is difficult to find another individual whose intellectual contribution to the development of American social work was more profound than Patten's. He lacked Jane Addams' fine sympathy for the poor and oppressed, Lillian Wald's delicate sense of the responsibilities of the administrators of benevolent causes, and Edward T. Devine's ability to transform ideas and sympathy into dynamic institutions. More than any of these people, however, he understood and contributed to the body of complex economic and social thought which lies behind agitation for evolutionary social reform in the twentieth century.

Patten's influence on social work was exerted through teaching, through conferences with students and friends in the profession, through books and articles. Many of the ideas he directed toward social workers reached a larger audience through nationwide newspaper coverage of his pronouncements on current affairs.

As early as 1893, Patten tried to interest his students in social work. The next year, Samuel M. Lindsay, later professor of social welfare at Columbia University, was awarded a Wharton School fellowship to study philanthropic activities at the Krupp factories in Germany. In 1896, Patten obtained the post of general secretary of the New York Charity Organization Society for Edward T. Devine. For the next quarter-century, Devine was the nation's leading philanthropic executive—administrative head of several organizations, founder of the New York School of Social Work, editor of *Charities,* and the first professor of social legislation at Columbia. In 1938, Devine recalled that, during the first two decades of the century, he had regular conferences with Patten about policies and programs. Patten had "far more to do with developments in social work" for which Devine was given the "main credit" than anyone had ever realized.[2]

Devine's books, which became basic texts for social workers, were based on Patten's ideas. In *Misery and Its Causes*, for example, he expounded Patten's thesis that secondary poverty had economic, not moral, causes, declared that the task of social work was to eliminate "surplus misery," and called for a "standard of living high enough to insure full nourishment, reasonable recreation, shelter, and other elementary necessities." [3]

William H. Allen, later director of the New York Bureau of Municipal Research, and Frances Perkins were profoundly influenced by Patten. Recalling a visit from Patten just after Allen had been appointed director of a "large relief society," Allen commented, "The next ninety-nine former teachers would have said, 'What do you plan to do with your job, Allen?' But Patten said . . . 'What are *we* going to do now?' " Miss Perkins recalled Patten's emphasis on "raising the standard of living as a way to help the poor." Patten, who obtained a job in a New York social welfare agency for her in 1910, helped her "come to terms" with herself.[4]

The writings Patten directed primarily to social workers dealt with the philosophy of social action rather than with specific ameliorative techniques. He discussed the major issues of dispute in the area of social welfare: the relative value of professional and voluntary workers, the respective merits of philanthropic and political action, the influence of social work on progress, and the attitudes of social workers toward such political and social problems as the cost of living, economic crises, social insurance, immigration restriction, and prohibition. Beneath all his proposals and opinions lay the economic and social theory he had developed since the 1880's.

"The economic revolution is here," Patten told the leading social workers of New York in 1905, in the first of ten lectures at the New York School of Social Work, but the "intellectual revolution that will rouse men to its stupendous meaning has not done its work." Patten again announced his central theme in unequivocal terms. The lectures, published as *The New Basis of Civilization*, became his most popular book, with eight editions in the next sixteen years.[5]

Patten stated his concept of cultural lag more succinctly than ever before. Despite a "surplus stored by cooperative effort," Americans retained "ancient social emotions" which prevented them from adapting to abundance. In the contemporary United States, there was a contrast between the "surfeited and the exploited," between those who consumed too much and those who had too little. This contrast could be obliterated only by social action to restrain the surfeited and provide opportunities for the exploited.[6]

In this argumentative form, Patten's theory of cultural lag was quite different from the lag theory to be made famous by William F. Ogburn of the University of Chicago two decades later. The concept of a lag between environmental change and men's perception of the implications of the change was not original with either Patten or Ogburn. It was an obvious deduction from the theoretical framework of the branch of sociology which emphasized imitation, invention, attitudes, and roles. Academic sociologists considered two varieties of lag: cultural, the maladjustment of social organization to changes in technology; and biological, the lack of adjustment between human nature and culture. The doctrine of cultural lag assumed the possibility of evolutionary change toward a society with fewer tensions and conflicts. The theory of biological lag, on the other hand, was a conservative doctrine. Men like the French scholar Gustave Le Bon and the Americans Franklin H. Giddings and Ogburn often regarded culture as a thin veneer over a fundamental human savagery which showed few signs of change. Although Patten had explored the possibility of biological lag in his earlier work, he disregarded it in *The New Basis of Civili-*

zation. As a moralist of abundance, anxious to get his message to a large audience, he put aside annoying possibilities.

The lag between the surfeited and the exploited raised a special problem for America, because the poor were becoming less visible to their affluent countrymen. Civilization increasingly spared men the "sight of anguish." The "imaginations" of affluent men must be "sharpened to see in the check book an agent as spiritual and poetic as the grime and bloodstain of ministering hands." Patten emphasized the importance of money—private and public—in raising the standard of life of the poor. In an age of abundance, men must recognize the ideological value of cash. Money, properly spent, would release "pent forces" far better than the moral platitudes of "Service Altruism." Patten preferred "Economic Altruism"—the willingness to "bestow gifts without conditions and to be taxed for public and far-reaching ends"—to the well-intentioned "paternal kindness that opens picture galleries to the public." [7]

Money in the hands of social workers could be used to abolish poverty. Whereas Lenin called for trained revolutionary cadres to implement Marx's theory of inevitable revolution, Patten wanted social workers to implement the age of abundance. But he was a shrewd and cautious man. Although he had little faith in alms-giving, he knew that social workers, the cadres of progress, needed the sympathy and financial support of the middle and upper classes. Accordingly, he refrained from advocating comprehensive social and economic planning to raise the standard of living.[8]

Instead of making a frontal attack on middle-class patterns of philanthropy, Patten assailed the affluent Americans' concept of culture. He revised the middle-class definition of culture as a higher authority, a set of standards invoked in moments of indecision. Culture was really the "perfecting of intercourse with one's group." Despite his moderation, Patten had attacked the values of scarcity where they were most vulnerable. The virtues of rugged individualism could be defended by others in ritualized debate. It was more difficult for his opponents to challenge the argument, which may have struck responsive chords in some very rugged individuals, that the middle class lacked culture because it lacked "group contacts." By focusing on isolation, Patten probed a central dilemma of liberal individualism.[9]

Their concept of culture as a set of frozen values enabled philanthropists to pride themselves on bestowing gifts and outmoded wisdom. Patten wanted them to create a new standard of living which would stimulate the development of new ideals of human behavior appropriate to an economy of abundance. America had "ample resources" to "abolish poverty by saving men instead of spending them." People who praised the "disciplinary values of hardship" and rewarded those who acquired them had not transcended the age of scarcity. Philanthropists should channel money to social workers who would teach the lower classes how variety in consumption could relieve the "inevitable monotony of work in the machine age" and who would agitate for higher wages and shorter working hours.[10]

Social workers could also inculcate in people restraints to protect the age of abundance from the effects of gluttony and vice. They might, for example, encourage men to take pleasure in the arts rather than in eating, drinking, and sexual indulgence. Patten's view of aesthetics was similar to that of Jane Addams and other leading social workers. Unlike Miss Addams' views, however, Patten's were part of a complex intellectual structure—the theory of consumption he had been developing for twenty years. Like the settlement workers, Patten preferred active participation in the arts to passive appreciation of prescribed values. Men should exhaust their "surplus energy" in constructive play. Although he valued popular culture and immigrant traditions, Patten, like many settlement workers, was occasionally condescending in his references to such culture and traditions. Many immigrant traditions were as "valuable as our own." Yet he rose above condescension and went beyond most of his contemporaries when he included national-holiday celebrations, camp meetings, circuses, and amusement parks in "culture." Social workers must take advantage of existing institutions—fraternal, political, economic, and cultural—which, by creating "bonds of control," enabled men to develop restraints against the evils of abundance.[11]

Patten's tone was pragmatic, but he could not, nevertheless, avoid being confronted with the dilemmas that had plagued him during the previous decade. On one page he warned that poverty would be "scarcely mitigated by prosperity," that it might be "many thousand" years before men were completely adjusted to abundance, and that, lacking convincing authority for his views, he was unsure of the long-range effects of his proposals. Moreover, he was ambivalent about the goals of social work. He believed that social workers must "go beyond the test of personality and family . . . and set up the standard of each locality as the norm by which the defects . . . of the poor are to be measured." On the next page, however, Patten offered to measure the success of social workers by the "number of independent, self-supporting families" they created.[12]

Pragmatism won out over despair. Social workers should be concerned with means, not ends. The ends of progress could not be defined. They would be attained, paradoxically, only when men lost "sight of them in the struggle for material improvements." It would be sufficient for social workers to concentrate on "moving people from the margin instead of aiding them at the margin"—to realize that the preconditions for the disappearance of poverty were the "extension of opportunity, the growth of efficiency, the spread of knowledge, and the increase of health." [13]

Patten's program for social work was directed at achieving many of the reforms advocated by the social-justice movement in America and the "new liberalism" in England. Like such American contemporaries as Jane Addams, Florence Kelley, Robert La Follette, and Louis D. Brandeis, Patten wanted public guarantees of better standards of income, working conditions, health, and housing. Unlike Patten, however, these reformers emphasized the elimination of abuses rather than the formulation of a positive program to improve the future. The English reformers Sidney and Beatrice Webb, William Beveridge, and David Lloyd George, however, were not content with the eradication of existing abuses. The years between 1905 and 1912, when *The New Basis of Civilization* was most influential in America, were years of ferment in English reform. The Webbs's minority report on the Poor Law and agitation for a "national minimum," Beveridge's program for unemployment compensation, and Lloyd George's health-insurance legislation anticipated analogous American reforms by more than a generation. Patten's persuasive argument that social workers should "fix the responsibility of the state in caring for the health and welfare of its citizens" caused many to work in the vanguard of American agitation for social legislation.

Not all social workers accepted Patten's definition of their role. His leading supporters were Devine, Perkins, and Lillian Wald, head worker of Henry Street Settlement in New York. Mary Richmond, director of the Philadelphia Charity Organization Society, was deeply disturbed by Patten's preference for public over voluntary action. In her book *The Good Neighbor*, she attacked Patten's proposal that social workers agitate for elimination of the causes of poverty. There was no relation between "money power" and "effective charity." No legislation could substitute for the "neighborly service of the Samaritan." [14]

Mary Richmond and her many supporters among social workers emphasized the moral causes of poverty. Unemployment, for example, was "*prima-facie* evidence of inefficiency or unwillingness to work." Since poverty was the result of the inadequacy of individuals, social workers must "learn to deal with each problem individually." The aim of social work was to "promote sound families who would produce personalities able to help themselves." [15]

In 1908, Patten rebutted the attacks of Miss Richmond and her most articulate supporter, Miss Zilpha Smith of the Boston Charity Organization Society. New social conditions required new values. The old values of charity—pity, sympathy, service, and character-development—were worthy of respect, but industrial civilization had created a "Great Public" which must adopt new values. Among the new values were organization, efficiency, generosity, and faith in humanity. For the first time in history, it was possible to offer the poor a "better environment" instead of "advice." Amateurs and volunteers—Miss Richmond's "friendly visitors"—lacked the knowledge to deal with contemporary social problems.[16]

The controversy between Patten and Miss Richmond placed Edward Devine in a difficult position. As director of several important organizations in the field of social work, he was forced to deal with Miss Richmond and those who admired her. He called Patten's position "profound and brilliant" but admitted that Miss Richmond represented the "orthodox charity organization view." Six months later, yielding to pressure from his colleagues, he praised the "utility and beauty of personal service" and declared that friendly visitors were "worthy of selection and training." By 1909, however, Patten's point of view had enough adherents to allow Devine to support him unequivocally. The poor, Devine wrote, needed "not more neighborliness but better citizenship," which would result from improvements in their environment.[17]

Even from the safety of his professorship, however, Patten, like Devine, was concerned with the strategy of influence. Although his arguments looked forward to a welfare state rather than to social work's struggling to make do with voluntary contributions, Patten did not, in his dispute with Mary Richmond, discuss state action. Since, before and after the dispute, he emphasized government action, it is probable that he consciously dissembled in order to avoid a debate on means before there was agreement on principles. He wanted social workers to realize that raising the standard of living of the poor, however this was done, would eliminate more misery than offering alms to the "deserving" poor. He feared that proposals for state action, though such action was inherent in the logic of his argument, might deflect the debate from a consideration of the painful subject of principles to a technical dispute over methods. As a pragmatic crusader, Patten was willing to sacrifice logic for power.

By 1908, operating mainly through *Charities* magazine, which was controlled by Devine, Patten had established himself as a consultant on contemporary social and political issues to the young profession.[18] For the next five years, he tried to mold social workers' opinions on such public problems as temperance, business cycles, immigration, and the cost of living.

Patten was less interested in the relationship between poverty and drunkenness than in the effect of alcoholism on the varied consumption necessary for adjustment to an affluent society. Many social workers favored prohibition, but, unlike Patten, for reasons of morality and health rather than of economics.[19] In the aftermath of the Mary Richmond debate, Devine asked Patten to reunite the progressive and traditionalist wings of the profession by defending prohibition—a major concern of the voluntarists—on the basis of the new principle of an improved standard of living. The immediate stimulus for Patten's comments on prohibition was an article by Hugo Münsterberg, professor of psychology at Harvard, in *McClure's Magazine*. According to Münsterberg, alcohol was necessary to overcome the "emptiness and monotony of an unstimulated life." If the use of alcohol was prohibited, men would seek stimulation in religious zealotism, tyranny, cruelty, sexual overindulgence, gambling, and recklessness. Alcohol, in short, restrained men from worse evils.[20]

Patten expanded his earlier view that alcohol had "no place in an age of surplus with its fuller life." Some control, some repression, of pain was necessary. "Drug control" of pain, through the use of alcohol or some other substance, would be unnecessary if men developed new means of social control. As men adjusted to the age of abundance, they would develop restraints which would prevent both alcoholism and anxiety. The increasing variety of consumer goods in the American economy would automatically reduce the use of alcohol. It was unnecessary to legislate prohibition and anger those "good citizens who must lose their non-economic habits gradually." [21]

In retrospect, it appears that Patten was looking ahead to the middle decades of the twentieth century, when the urge to restrain anxiety would affect the affluent as well as the poor. He understood the emotional strain on individuals in a society which subjected men to frequent tests of ability, which isolated them from their communities and from spiritual certitudes, and which demanded commitment to "tumultuous strenuosity" in carrying on the frustrating task of "reversing nature's processes." Since alcoholism was a result of anxiety more than of poverty and inadequate diets, "resignation" to the "irresistible changes" caused by evolution and adjustment might be more healthful than the vigorous pursuit of happiness. [22]

This insight into the dark side of living in an age of abundance was probably the result of a crisis in Patten's life. While he was preparing his rejoinder to Münsterberg, his wife of five years left him for a younger man. Charlotte Kimball Patten, twenty years younger than her husband, was an attractive woman from a wealthy family who came to Philadelphia in 1900 to study social work. Soon after her marriage to Patten in 1903, his friends began to detect strains in their relationship. Mrs. Patten tried to establish a *salon*, with her husband at the center. Patten, a reticent man, retreated into the background and became "her satellite." Stories circulated that the Pattens had a noncohabitation pact. In 1907, she began an affair with a young instructor in Patten's department, and in November, 1908, she initiated divorce proceedings. While the divorce was pending, Mrs. Patten aired her grievances in public—telling a newpaper reporter that her husband "wore shabby clothes and came to meet [her] at the station once wearing two days' growth of beard." [23]

The divorce was a blow to Patten's optimism and self-esteem. It gave personal meaning to his emphasis on restraint of the desires of the flesh. A continued commitment to restraint, even in the new context of resignation, had become important for the preservation of Patten's dignity, as well as for America's adjustment to an age of abundance.

In the wake of the divorce, the press poked fun at Patten's social theory. The *American Examiner*, for instance, published a full-page story with cartoons, headlined "How the Carefully Worked Out Matrimonial Theories of the Grave University Pedagogue Proved Too Much for his Society-Loving Mate." Patten had developed these theories between 1904 and 1908 in articles for monthly magazines and lectures to social workers. The major functions of women were motherhood and the consumption of wealth. Men, more concerned than women with sexuality, projected their desires onto their wives. The small group of sexual or "mistress type" women would be eliminated as society adjusted to the implications of abundance. In the emerging new civilization, families would be held together by common interests affecting consumption rather than by the need for mutual protection or affection.[24]

Patten slowly regained his sense of personal worth and reaffirmed his commitment to vigorous action in the cause of progress. In the spring of 1909, he returned to the problem of business cycles, which he had begun to explain to social workers in the wake of the Panic of 1907. Before the divorce, he was trying to integrate the "over-saving" theory of depressions, first announced in modern form by the English economist John A. Hobson in 1890, with his own theory of a transition from scarcity to abundance. Depressions represented a resurgence of the "motives of a scarcity economy." In the age of scarcity, a "moral brass band" encouraged abstinence and thrift. But the moral band was now out of tune. In a modern economy, personal savings were not a significant source of investment capital. Businessmen obtained new capital mainly from new profits resulting from the "growth of efficiency." Thrift, by curtailing consumption, reduced demand and threatened the rising "social standards" which made prosperity possible. Depressions, then, were the result of reduced consumption. Since consumption was reduced because of inappropriate adjustment to the new conditions of abundance, the acquisition of new values would be a more effective cure for fluctuations in the business cycle than would manipulation of the economy. Patten never did more than sketch out these ideas. After the divorce, he seemed to lack the confidence and the energy to refine his economic logic. In 1909 he was content to say that, when a depression occurred, economists were obligated to devise a "more perfect system." [25]

The next year, Patten regained his zeal for the active search for values appropriate to new economic conditions. Angered by the report of the commission appointed by the federal government to study the effects of unrestricted immigration, he called on social workers to protect the right of free entry into America. He accused the Immigration Commission of beginning with conclusions, of "asking what facts will prove these conclusions," and of then finding the "needed evidence." An unbiased view of the evidence indicated that no "large class of immigrants" differed in any "fundamental respect" from previous newcomers. Moreover, immigration, by providing new consumers, stimulated production and employment and, by thus promoting a higher standard of living in both Europe and America, caused wages to rise. Patten looked forward to the free movement of labor and capital between Europe and America. Any "ideal America" must "involve an ideal Europe." [26]

He clarified his meaning of "ideal" with a new call to social workers to engage in action subject to pragmatic tests. William James's *Essays on Pragmatism*, which he read for the first time in 1910, gave him a new vocabulary with which to present and sharpen the ideas he had been defending for a decade. Patten rejected James's "personal or empirical pragmatism," in favor of "social pragmatism." Where James emphasized "present desires and interests" and "psychic tests of truth," Patten looked toward the "future results of acts" and applied "objective tests of truth." There were, he asserted, nine tests of the social results of ideas: they must stimulate prosperity, peace, cooperation, efficiency, vigor, longevity, service, public spirit, and missionary zeal. Social pragmatism would establish standards of truth that would "make men work." [27]

Patten's pragmatism assumed the existence of four "ideals." There were three basic ideals: a political ideal, equality; an ideal of happiness, health; and an economic ideal, prosperity. To these, Patten added a fourth, individual action, embodied in the aggressive social worker, a type of Nietzschean Superman imbued with Patten's theories. Nietzsche and his followers were correct in their contention that the destruction of "slave morality" was the "essence of biologic progress." The social-worker supermen would use aggression to "secure social ends." Rebounding from the attack he had made on the strenuous life three years earlier, Patten asserted that strenuosity should be "favored" as the means to implement social reform. The new supermen would, however, emphasize social rather than individual values. Like the men William James sought in his contemporary essay "The Moral Equivalent of War," they would eliminate "poverty and disease" and throw their "whole energy into the uplift of humanity." [28]

Patten found authority for his pragmatic ideals in the same sources, religion and science, he had drawn upon for the past two decades. In 1911, he proposed to ground the values of both abundance and restraint on a "social" theology. He called for a "new birth," which would require no midwife if men were "made normal." The key to normality was a "large social surplus," used to provide a "standard of living capable of maintaining health and welfare." The new birth required a theology of joy, sacrifice, and service to replace the traditional theology of sorrow, penance, and misery. A new theology suitable to an age of "peace and plenty" would be more appropriate than attitudes developed under the "pressure of deficit." Mankind had the power to remove the "material obstacles to social progress" and create a "new City of God," which would be "well planned, healthy, and prosperous"—a "center for spiritual aspiration." [29]

Religion would be the ultimate restraint against the evils of the age of abundance—overconsumption, selfishness, and greed.

It would provide "psychic emancipation" to complement the "physical emancipation from want." The economy of abundance would degenerate into primitive chaos unless men developed a new "discipline more rigid than that of fear." Material progress could not "compensate" for spiritual "stagnation." [30]

Patten could not accept justification by faith when he might use the logic of science, social and natural, to sanction his opinions. In 1911 and 1912, he sought economic and sociological justifications for the restraints appropriate to abundance and explored the new scientific fad of eugenics and the implications of new psychological ideas. Economic progress had increased the surplus wealth of the United States. Social pressures and political developments during Patten's lifetime had distributed this wealth so widely that almost every citizen had the means to become a discerning consumer. Perhaps economics, through the new tool of budgeting—the projection of "social estimates" by groups and families—could enable men to consume in a manner appropriate to the new conditions of life.[31]

As a society entered the age of abundance, wants increased "more rapidly than the means of satisfying them." This increase condemned family budgets to a condition of chronic deficit, as a rising standard of living intensified consumers' demands. The cost of improvements in health, nutrition, housing, education, recreation, and social services put increasing pressure on family and government budgets. This pressure to spend could be balanced by increased income and restrained desires. If families wished to balance their budgets, they would be forced to accept the values and restraints appropriate to abundance. They would agitate for higher wages, for increased industrial efficiency, for better education to improve their power of substitution, and for the development of a generous and selfless spirit. The achievement of these goals would require less indulgence in luxury, a reduced use of intoxicating liquor, a greater investment in life insurance, and birth control.[32]

Patten oscillated between a desire for the relative asceticism required to balance budgets and a feeling that deficit spending—

installment buying, for instance—was necessary until all men acquired what later economists would call the "basic consumer-goods package" available in an affluent society. But he was un-equivocal about the need for sexual restraint. Reproduction "dwarfed" men's better natures. Marriages based on sexual de-sire led to a "steady decline in physical vigor." Patten could not, however, deny the power of the sexual instinct. "Sex freedom" was "too deep a force to yield without a struggle." Men were "renewed" by "climaxes of satisfaction." In the age of abun-dance, men would restrain sexuality and achieve climaxes in more rewarding activities—particularly athletics and the arts. Un-restrained satisfaction of desire was destructive; concentration on production to the neglect of consumption was worse. The mo-rality appropriate to abundance must be based, not on the sup-pression of desires, but on their sublimation into the "most ef-fective climax for all." [33]

For a time, Patten flirted with eugenics—the program of con-trolled heredity developed by the English biologists Francis Galton and Karl Pearson—as a possible restraint against sexual indulgence. He was never a consistent eugenicist. At the same time that he called for "eugenic marriages" to replace "emo-tional" attachments, he stated that the world needed "better feed-ing more than better breeding." Heredity was the "one power" that could transform man into a "superman." But it was "more reasonable to assume" that "virtues" were conditioned by society rather than by heredity. Although Patten approved the eugeni-cists' eagerness to base marital relationships on a calculation of the desirable traits that the partners would bestow on their prog-eny, he worried about the basis for selecting the characteristics of the "best" men and women.[34]

By 1912, Patten realized that his exhortations to social workers and his theory of a transition to abundance contradicted the doctrines of eugenics. The eugenicists believed that progress was a result of controlled heredity rather than of "taking the surplus of the prosperous and adding to the welfare of those injured by poverty." Most of the evils which eugenicists ascribed to heredity could be accounted for by the effects of scarcity or of a surplus which men had not yet turned to best advantage. Character traits were so complex that the study of the relationships between groups of traits must "precede attempts to modify races by the elimination of single traits." Eugenics was a pseudo science, advocating "methods that might work among tigers and wolves" but which human beings had "outgrown." [35]

If eugenics could not provide either a sanction for restraints or an explanation for the lag between environmental change and men's adjustment to it, perhaps the findings of the new research in abnormal psychology and psychiatry could. Patten probably encountered the work of Sigmund Freud at about this time. He seemed to be aware of the research on the physiological aspects of mental illness which had been conducted in Germany, France, and the United States since the 1890's. The findings suggested that many of the defects which eugenicists blamed on heredity were the result of "mental disorders" caused by an improper diet or by "poisons" formed within the body. Like Freud, however, Patten believed that repression—of sexual desires and fears—was the major cause of mental illness.[36]

Since repression had a social origin—in external restraints which men internalized—it could be dealt with by social reform. If, in an economy of abundance, men were forced, from earliest childhood, to restrain their desires as the Protestant ethic decreed, they would be unable to recognize appropriate desires when they came of age. Repression should begin in maturity, as a "relative pressure, not an absolute prohibition." Childhood must be a time of freedom to explore desires and appreciate the joys of varied consumption. Childhood could be extended by increasing the required number of school years and prohibiting child labor. These reforms would "bring compensation in a longer working period and in new forms of social activity from which would come a better art, a higher morality, and a purer religion." [37]

By the summer of 1912, Patten was spiritually exhausted from his efforts to revise his theories and make them meaningful to social workers and the general public. He was unable to respond to the torrid presidential campaign, in which Theodore Roosevelt and Woodrow Wilson advocated some of the reforms he had called for. Although his most faithful disciples—Walter E. Weyl, Samuel Lindsay, William Draper Lewis, and Edward T. Devine—worked actively for Roosevelt, Patten refused to be drawn into political controversy. He told social workers to "stick to their own tasks," and warned them that new laws were less important than new ideas and feelings. He even despaired of democracy, declaring that the old "banners of political democracy" should be put away "in a museum." In November, he cast his vote for William Howard Taft, because, he told friends, he felt compelled to remain loyal to the party of Lincoln.[38]

After the election, Patten declared that "progress does not come by dozens of little coercions, but by doses of freedom." When people were emotionally stimulated to appreciate the values appropriate to abundance, they would exercise their freedom by choosing restraints. Social workers, the cadres of progress, must eschew logical debate and political agitation and must stimulate people by "words, contrasts, art, and song." The social worker must become a "social poet," who emphasized "voluntary effort," which must "precede coercion." For a time, he appeared to accept the methods of Mary Richmond.[39]

By the end of 1913, Patten had regained his optimism and dedication to pragmatic social reform. He advocated the reorganization of social work, sketched a comprehensive program of welfare legislation, and, as if to quiet fears that he had been seduced by voluntarism, attacked mothers' pensions—Mary Richmond's scheme to offer a dole to worthy but poor women with dependent children.

Patten's plan for the reorganization of social work reflected his increased sensitivity to unnecessary suffering. More strongly than ever before, he urged social workers to attack the causes rather than the results of misery. Isolated and uncoordinated activity by a multitude of welfare agencies would merely "alleviate suffering which might have been prevented." Only state action could deal with "great environmental changes." Voluntary action was important, but it should be mainly supportive. The most pressing task was the legislation of "urgent reforms" that would "alter the environment" and enable men to adjust to abundance. The goal of social work was not "present adjustment" but the utilization of human and mechanical energy for "future ends." [40]

Patten's goals were embodied in a program for social legislation. New laws must provide for industrial stability, regularity of employment, a minimum wage, the segregation of the physically defective, the elimination of disease germs, the prohibition of child labor, efficient schools, and a greater number of productive years in each worker's life. This was, however, a minimal program; the new laws would "conserve more than they uplift." Adjustment to abundance required public action on behalf of prosperity, conservation, health, culture, and efficiency.[41]

Although Patten was vague about the specific provisions he desired in new social legislation, he left no ambiguities in his attack on mothers' pensions and traditional philanthropy. Denouncing the concept of "rehabilitation," he declared that "instead of striving to restore the fallen we should let no one sink to a level where rehabilitation is necessary." He saw no point in giving pensions to mothers, since the real problem was "long life for fathers." Similarly, workers who earned high wages were better for society than "all the minimum-wage laws" that could be devised. Making Americans efficient consumers was more sensible than seeking the "exclusion of the downtrodden workers of other races." Soup kitchens and "moral sun-parlors" were perverse substitutes for the removal of the forces which drew families "down to the depths of poverty and moral degradation."[42]

Never again did Patten attempt to work out in such detail the implications of the pleasure economy for public policy. He lacked the knowledge, the experience, and perhaps the energy to make more specific recommendations. Moreover, the tense balance he had advocated between voluntary action and coercive legislation, between reason and emotion, and, most important, between abundance and restraint, could not be disturbed without wholesale adjustments in the complex theories behind his policy recommendations.

At the age of sixty-two, Patten was reluctant to make another attempt to bring order into the confused mass of insight, assertion, and logic on which his programs for social reform were based. Moreover, the outbreak of war in Europe in the summer of 1914 and the national debate about America's role in the conflict challenged Patten as an admirer of German civilization and a prophet of abundance. The war did not, however, take him by surprise. He had long ago admitted that there were "obstacles" to progress which no civilization had been "able to overcome." [43]

CHAPTER VII 🖾

War and Social Reform,

1914–1918

The First World War shattered Patten's hope that men would gradually and peacefully adjust to the age of abundance. Prosperity seemed to provoke national ambition and a desire for conquest rather than lead to altruism and restrained emotion. Patten had never, however, shared the pacifism of many social workers and a few academics of his generation—Jane Addams of Hull House and David Starr Jordan, President of Stanford University, for example. Like such contemporary progressives as Theodore Roosevelt and Senator Albert J. Beveridge, Patten had a strong sense of American nationality and a belief in the civilizing mission of the United States. His social and economic ideas, grounded on German concepts of organicism and of the unique historical development of each society, had a nationalist emphasis. The United States was the first nation in which a transition from scarcity to abundance was possible. It was the national mission to set an example for Europe and to bring, perhaps by the use of force, the benefits of industrialization to the "uncivilized" races. Moreover, like many German historical economists and like such English reformers as Sidney and Beatrice Webb, Joseph Chamberlain, and Benjamin Kidd, Patten sometimes implied that imperialism would provide the impetus and wealth needed for social reforms at home.

In 1898, Patten had regarded imperialism as a temporary solution for problems that would eventually be solved by changes in men's habits and values. The Spanish-American War was a "happy opportunity," because the development of the American economy—the full utilization of the "best lands and industrial advantage"—threatened to reduce the social mobility of workingmen. Migration to America's new territories would relieve the "congestion of industry" and thus diminish the "frequency of strikes." Men would someday realize, however, that the fruits of abundance could be available to everyone if the values of an age of scarcity were rejected—particularly the greed and selfishness resulting from the assumption that the economy could not produce enough to give everyone a comfortable standard of living. When the values which conditioned the ways men distributed and consumed wealth were changed and men learned restraints appropriate to the new age, national territorial expansion would become unnecessary.[1]

Although territorial expansion was based on the values of scarcity, the members of an affluent society had an economic and political burden. Patten's conscience was disturbed by the prospect of an abundant America in a world of scarcity. There must be a "forceful application" of industrial and political "rights" to "inferior races." If Cubans, for example, were given a "free and safe government" and taught modern methods of agriculture, they "could supply the world with sugar." In 1914, Patten argued that the United States should intervene in Mexico to maintain order, protect the security of capital and the sacredness of contracts, prevent economic exploitation, educate the masses, and provide a living wage. "Moral responsibility" followed commerce.[2]

Unlike many American imperialists of his generation, however, Patten did not believe that the American form of government could be exported. Americans should be proud of their "civilization," not of their constitution. They should export the "conditions of a higher civilization," not the Bill of Rights. This doctrine did not mean that Americans must respect the wishes of Mexicans. The Mexican state should be broken up into "natural units" and controlled by the United States, regardless of Mexican "sentiment." It would be necessary to have a different policy for each undeveloped area of the world. Central America was an "integral part of our industrial system." But South America should be allowed to progress by "internal development." [3]

In the decade before 1914, Patten made it clear that he favored an imperialism of persuasion and example rather than of force. In 1903, he argued that modern war was a senseless struggle whose outcome was decided by industrial superiority rather than by personal or social virtues. The better, not the weaker, men were destroyed in contemporary warfare. Eight years later, he claimed that the growth of commerce, a rising standard of living, the increased circulation of magazines and newspapers, and the "spread" of art and literature restrained the "warlike feelings" that had wrought such havoc in the past. Since intense emotion must be "local and vivid," the mass media would not be effective instruments for warlike propaganda. Patten's psychological doctrines led him to what, in retrospect, appears to be shallow optimism. [4]

Patten's Calvinist heritage and his commitment to science prevented his becoming an unrestrained optimist. He was sensitive to the presence in the world of both sin and behavior inappropriate to contemporary economic conditions. War would cease to threaten human welfare only when men worked to create a world-wide economy of abundance. Patten could not share the optimism of men like Norman Angell, the English journalist who argued in *The Great Illusion*, published in 1910, that economic progress made war impossible. Like Joseph Schumpeter, Patten believed that atavistic feelings—yearnings for violence—prevented complete acceptance of the logic of modern technology. The forces that promoted war were only temporarily "held in check by the interests and sentiments of modern industry." [5]

In the summer of 1914, the interests and sentiments of industry did not restrain the martial feelings of the people of Europe. For the next three years, Patten, in lectures, interviews, and articles, argued against America's becoming involved in the destruction of European welfare and prosperity. Americans must work to make the world safe for abundance. They must realize that participation in the war, on the side of either the Allies or the Central Powers, would hinder the amalgamation of German and Anglo-American ideas into a productive synthesis and would damage America's emerging pleasure economy.

Patten's first impulse had been to defend German civilization against the Anglophilia of many influential Americans. In November, 1914, he declared that Germany had developed the ideas which enabled men to recognize the implications of the transition from scarcity to abundance. Germany stood for centralization instead of regionalism, for a superracial culture instead of racism, and for a United States of Europe instead of nationalism. German thought, controlled by the "professor not the Kaiser," was superior to the selfish and backward ideas of the Allies. No nation had ever gone to war with so much "idealism" or "enthusiasm." Russia, not Germany, was the real aggressor. Germany had merely taken the opportunity to increase the rate of European progress. Patten's praise of German ideas and methods was similar to the views expressed by Charles McCarthy in *The Wisconsin Idea*, published in 1913. Unlike McCarthy, however, who ignored German militarism, Patten, for the moment, applauded it. Progress was, of necessity, a "ruthless crushing," which required the elimination of the "weak to the advantage of the strong." Yet Patten could not forget his arguments for peaceful progress and his sympathy for the oppressed and exploited. Discussing the wise leadership of German professors, he added a *non sequitur*: "If they have gone wrong this time. . . ." [6]

By 1915, Patten was less concerned with defending Germany than with demonstrating the influence a combination of German imagination and Anglo-American restraint could have on the emergence of a new civilization based on economic surplus. The warring nations were acting out the conflict between Anglo-

American ideals of personal freedom—the restraint of power—
and German concepts of social welfare—the use of power. The
drama must end, not in the bankruptcy of one side, or even in
compromise, but in the "amalgamation" of the best features of
both cultures.[7]

Germany was the first nation to realize that societies evolved
"from the status of freedom to that of welfare." Efficiency,
which Patten defined as the increasingly economical use of
"mechanism," was the key to improved welfare. The imminence
of a world-wide economy of abundance forced men to choose
welfare as their ideal, not the "Goddess of Liberty." Although
German efficiency provided the tools for creating an economy
of abundance, Anglo-American traditions offered the restraints
which would prevent the welfare state from becoming a totali-
tarian society. Mechanism and freedom were "complementary
goods," not "opposing ideals." The war could be the "melting
pot" in which the "dross of yesterday" was "separated from the
ringing truth of tomorrow." [8]

In *Culture and War*, written in the summer of 1915, Patten
tried to synthesize German and Anglo-American thought. He
sought a middle course between the values of liberal individualism and those evident in the boast of the German chemist and
social philosopher Wilhelm Ostwald: "While other nations still
live under the regime of individualism, we have already achieved
that of organization." According to Patten, German thought had
three central principles, *Dienst, Ordnung,* and *Kraft,* which he
translated as "service, conformity, and growth." In German
terms, there was only one "valid judgment" of an act of state:
"Did it produce adjustment and hence increase the vitality and
concentration needed for growth?" Unlike Englishmen, who regarded self-interest and personal salvation as the highest ideals,
Germans emphasized service. Growth and service became effective, however, only by "conforming to natural law." To Germans, this law was not a set of unalterable concepts but a "ceaseless flow drawing all life together, yielding joy through the increase of its speed." [9]

Yet Patten was "bitterly disappointed" with many of the results of German philosophy. Most important, he disliked the "philosophy of conflict with its battle cries of war and degeneration." Those men—Germans, Americans, or English—who advocated either conflict or a "moral equivalent" of war ignored the most important social development of the twentieth century, the possibility of an age of abundance.[10]

The "way out from war" was "not moral restraint, but economic liberation." Forgetting for a moment his praise of Anglo-American restraint, Patten declared that the world needed, "not a restraining morality, but activity, not sacrifice but joy, not toil but harvest." The war was merely a temporary setback in the process of transition from a scarcity to a pleasure economy. Poverty, he reminded his readers, was a result of "bad external conditions," not of heredity or moral inadequacy. The remedies for poverty were increased income, improvements in public health, and a "purer family life."[11]

Some moral restraint was, however, necessary in the new civilization. The "pressure of income" would not necessarily "insure character." Income was "merely a condition to the appearance of character," the "soil in which the spiritual may grow." Nevertheless, generosity was more important than restraint. Income, sympathy, and planning would ease the "hardships of the unfortunate." Foreshadowing Franklin D. Roosevelt's "one third of a nation" speech, Patten declared that "perhaps forty percent of the population" was "sufficiently nourished and protected to participate in the social advance of the nation."[12]

America needed a "new society, not a new heredity." But the new American society could be created only by combining the German concept of welfare with the American ideal of political freedom. Twentieth-century progress required expertise as well as benevolence. Moreover, progress required the moral restraint of a religious idea. This ideal must develop from the American tradition of humane theology rather than from the "tribal gods" of the Germans.[13]

Although America needed a new society, the nation could

maintain its current level of adjustment to abundance only by remaining out of the war. Patten analyzed the ways in which the war threatened America's emerging pleasure economy. In November, 1914, he had asserted that the Allies could win the war only by enlisting American capital and resources. Three months later, he called war a destructive transformation from "productive consumption to unproductive expenditures." The contest would "end in bankruptcy of one or both parties rather than in general defeat." Bankruptcy could be prevented by immediate victory—which was "improbable." Even though Germany would "become bankrupt before England," her "enthusiasm" was greater than England's and transcended "monetary values." Without American aid to the Allies, Germany would be the victor in a struggle which would bankrupt all participating nations. If America remained neutral, the war could last for only about three years.[14]

The war would, moreover, create a severe economic crisis. Speculative investments in war industries would merely postpone a crash that could destroy the "economic gains of a century." It would take "another half century" to repair the damage to the emerging economy of abundance. Only accelerated technological progress, such as had occurred after the Napoleonic Wars and the American Civil War, could quickly replace the losses and create greater future prosperity. But technological advance might not be rapid enough to compensate for the unprecedented amount of capital used up in twentieth-century warfare.[15]

The impending economic crisis obscured the "most important" question of the generation: "How much of the national wealth can be taken from producers and given to the state?" Because of the war, Americans faced, for the first time, an "actual decrease in the quantity of capital." Patten contradicted his theory that investment capital was derived from undivided profits. Returning to John Stuart Mill's theory of capital, he asserted that, with the middle class "spending all it earns" and the upper class "taxed to death," only the "savings of the workers" could increase capital. Moreover, the war, by provoking fears of "future want," caused men to "cut down their present consumption in favor of future consumption." The most important question of the generation could not be discussed cogently until peace reduced fears and made risks "static" again. Yet there were some grounds for hope. The technology of warfare was not sufficiently advanced to destroy the "permanent resources of the world." Losses would eventually be "liquidated" and values "recreated." [16]

By the autumn of 1915, Patten believed that a "slump" in American morality might follow the setback to the emerging economy of abundance. The growing support for an American economic boycott of Germany offended Patten's "moral sense." Abundance should reinforce Christ's message that the way to halt aggression was by appeasement based on love. Even a warrior's morality was superior to that of the proposal to hit the Germans when their backs were turned. More important, a boycott would injure both Germany and America. Diminished trade could "kill" as surely as could war.[17]

In 1916, Patten amplified his prophecies of disaster. England would be bankrupt in a year unless she received cash credits from the United States. The English and American governments faced a "day of reckoning," when they would learn that men could not spend more than they earned. The Federal Reserve Board was merely a "national trinket" to postpone this day of reckoning. The best way to prevent an economic crisis was to end devastation and "Hun brutality." For the first time, Patten was affected by the increasing exasperation with Germany evident in the United States.[18]

Patten feared that American expenditures for preparedness would destroy the surplus wealth on which the new basis of civilization must be built. Because of inadequate taxes on capital gains from wartime speculation, the results of the "material advantage of the nineteenth century" would go, not to every citizen, but "into the hands of the bond-owner and his heirs." The destruction of abundance was made more probable by the fact that neither the Allies nor the Central Powers would win a "decisive victory" and be able to "demand huge indemnities from their opponents." Since indemnities could not pay for the war, Patten proposed a "triple tax" on income, inheritance, and land. This tax would fall entirely on surplus income, which he defined as income above what was necessary to maintain the standard of living Patten considered "normal." Although this triple tax would provide public funds "without trenching on the standards of the marginal workers," the heaviest burden would fall on the middle class, who would have to forego many comforts so that the country could "meet the increased national expenditure." [19]

In the summer of 1916, Patten sensed a "panic of fear" threatening America's emerging abundance economy. He worried about the ease with which a "vivid description of how New York may be captured" could "upset the nerves of the nation without a single foe being in sight." The preparedness campaign and the new concept of "Americanism" endangered minority rights and frightened people who were just beginning to recognize the possibilities of life in a pleasure economy. America had "progressed," however, by according "rights" to minorities, not by enforcing the "mandates" of the majority. Yet some form of national defense was necessary—less to "ward off danger" than to "suppress our inherited timidity." [20]

A defense program based on abundance must emphasize social as well as military values. Americans should develop a "lofty ideal of subordination of the person to the state," but without the "taint of military domination." National unity must be promoted, but not at the cost of "our culture, our liberty, and our institutions." The nation could best defend itself against external threats by providing increased income for the average citizen, by encouraging cooperative living, and by educating men to bring their "emotional nature" into "harmony with culture, science, and brotherly love." Until the whole world was attuned to the implications of abundance and to the restraints appropriate to new conditions, a naval alliance with England for "joint control of the ocean" would be necessary. This alliance would keep peace in a world divided into three economic zones: Anglo-American, Continental European, and Asian.[21]

This program, which Patten called "National Pacifism," had little in common with the pacifism of Jane Addams and other leaders of the American peace movement. Pacifists like Miss Addams "ignored human nature." The "great evil in the world" was not war but the "docility," the passivity in the face of environmental change, imposed by "martial discipline." By opposing docility rather than war itself, Patten was in a position to support the American war effort while struggling against the domestic evils due to war.[22]

As America's entrance into the war became imminent, Patten sailed closer to the national wind. In February, 1917, he urged the United States to fight for "definite principles" rather than "blindly join in the brutal effort to crush a strong nation." A month later, commenting that the United States was now the only nation with the "necessary elements for the successful carrying out of war," he comforted himself with the hope that "it would just be a war of words," since the battlefield was so far away.[23]

By April, 1917, Patten had decided to support the war effort and work to preserve the economy of abundance in the wartime and postwar world. But his defense of German values over the previous three years had offended the prominent Philadelphians on the University of Pennsylvania Board of Trustees. These men, already disturbed by Patten's advocacy of social reform, deprived him of his rostrum when America entered the war.

Like many other men of his generation who had been trained in Germany, Patten objected to the image of the brutal Hun in Allied propaganda. Most of his friends, however, yielded earlier than he did to patriotic feeling and the Anglophilia of those prominent Americans who controlled university funds. Richard T. Ely held a membership card in the Wisconsin Loyalty League. John Bates Clark accused his pacifist and neutralist friends of trying to "hold America in a helpless state." Franklin H. Giddings acknowledged the German contribution to "solving the problem of social organization" but considered the Prussian a "mongrel," a "wretched cur," a "savage," and a "brute." Edmund J. James, President of the University of Illinois and Patten's closest friend, was a strong supporter of Germany in 1914 but became a leader in the preparedness campaign and went to Washington in 1917 to offer his services to the war effort.[24]

The Scott Nearing case, a bitter conflict between the Wharton School faculty and the university trustees over the reappointment of a radical assistant professor in 1915, set the stage for Patten's dismissal. Nearing came to Wharton as a graduate student in 1903 and became a champion of principles based on implications of Patten's logic—implications which Patten himself hesitated to draw. For a decade, Patten was able to persuade Nearing about the wisdom of restraint. In 1911, for instance, when Nearing's speeches on social reform aroused criticism of the Wharton School, Patten persuaded him to "do no public talking for one year." In 1915, however, Nearing refused to restrain himself. When Billy Sunday conducted a revival in Philadelphia in February, Patten sat among his sponsors on the platform. Nearing, in a public letter, asked Sunday to notice that the city was "filled with unemployment and poverty," that "multitudes" were "literally starving." He described Sunday's sponsors as the "chief priests, scribes, and Pharisees of Philadelphia," and invited him to use his "oratorical brilliancy . . . against low wages, overwork, unemployment, monopoly, and special privilege." [25]

After the trustees dismissed Nearing for creating "strife and turmoil" which were "neither necessary nor desirable accompaniments of the objects for which young men are sent to college by their parents," Patten directed the campaign to defend him. "No resignations," Patten insisted to his colleagues the day Nearing was fired; "we all stay and make a positive fight." The defense of Nearing had two prongs; muckraking the Philadelphia vested interests represented by the trustees and trying to enlist the support of the recently formed American Association of University Professors against a violation of academic freedom. Nearing, Patten told a committee of the Association, had not forced his views on his students. His speeches outside the university were talks to "high-grade audiences" any "conservative teacher would gladly elect." It was necessary to separate what a man taught to adolescents from the "general right of teachers to impart to the public the contents of their science." The A.A.U.P. decided, however, that the mystique of science could not be used to justify unpopular views. They accused Nearing of being "singularly destitute of courtesy, tact, and ordinary common sense in the manner and occasion of his utterances." [26]

Patten did not have very much faith in the argument he had used on Nearing's behalf. Two years later, he did not try to defend as "science" his own reservations about America's participation in the war. The ostensible reason for Patten's "retirement" from the Wharton faculty was the fact that he had reached the mandatory age of sixty-five. But John Bach McMaster, the noted historian, who was also sixty-five in 1917 and who was not as effective a teacher as Patten, was asked to remain at the university. The Philadelphia *Public Ledger* suggested another reason for Patten's retirement: The trustees had been "gunning" for Patten because he was the "fount and origin of the doctrines against vested interests" which were "rife" among the Wharton faculty. It was impossible to "deal with the Nearings," the *Ledger* concluded, "until you have reckoned with the teacher of the Nearings." [27]

The trustees ignored the fact that, from the end of 1916 on, Patten was willing to accept American intervention in the war. They capitalized on a tactical error Patten had committed in his zeal for free expression of ideas. On March 30, 1917, at a rally in Philadelphia, Patten introduced David Starr Jordan, a leading pacifist, who declared that Germany had "never intentionally injured us." Early in the following week, the trustees notified Patten that his connection with the university would end in July, 1917. The Wharton faculty protested that Patten was an "inspiring teacher" and a writer of "national and international reputation," whose achievements "shed lustre on the University." But the protest was submerged in the excitement over American entry into the war, which occurred on the day it was published.[28]

Patten continued to comment on public affairs. Two weeks after he was notified of his retirement, he asserted that the passions which had led the United States into war were a result of the "educated classes'" failure to realize the implications of abundance. It would not be necessary to change human nature in order to restrain these passions. American "tradition and antiquated class opinion" must be "revised." Despite his disillusionment with education, Patten still believed in the power of ideas and in world leadership by example. If one nation, accepting the logic of abundance, were to create a "super standard," it could show the others the "possibility of peaceful progress." [29]

In late 1917 and the early months of 1918, Patten emphasized the need to preserve the results of a generation of economic surplus while the country was financing the war and its aftermath. The same forces that produced abundance could enable the nation to conduct the war efficiently and could prevent suffering in the postwar period. "Recovery after the war" was not the "logical consequence of war" but a result of "agents that would have been more effective if no war had occurred." These agents, the resources and techniques which provided a new basis for civilization, must be preserved during and after the war.[30]

One important way to preserve the agents of abundance would be to improve the system of taxation. Patten expanded his "triple tax" proposal of 1916. He called for "conscription of profit and resource to match the conscription of men." This conscription would be effected by a tax on "differential advantage" in ability and capital. In an economy capable of producing a surplus, income was the "measure of advantage and not of effort, of situation and education and not of heredity." By taxing only differential advantage, the nation would not exhaust its surplus of resources and capital. It would also be necessary to restrain consumption. The war experience could be turned to advantage if coercion and education were used to destroy patterns of consumption which undermined character in an abundance economy. Patten demanded prohibition of alcohol, "checks to conspicuous consumption," and education to improve habits of nutrition, cleanliness, and recreation.[31]

Victory in the war would be a result of productive capacity rather than of behavior in the trenches. Similarly, the "key to prosperity" after the war would not be expanded credit and increased consumption but efficiency and the use of planning in the production and distribution of wealth. The effort to expand production to meet the needs of war had demonstrated that efficiency and exploitation were incompatible. War production had revealed that the "hours of work must be shortened and labor conditions improved to get the maximum efficiency from laborers." [32]

The United States had sufficient resources and productive capacity to create an economy of abundance. The "struggle of the coming years" would be a "struggle of conflicting motives," not a "struggle with nature." If the motives of abundance prevailed over the motives of scarcity, production and consumption would "complement each other." A society attuned to the possibility of abundance for all would have an increased regard for health, length of life, and leisure. The new society "must be a working organization, active and efficient." It could not "afford to be one hundred percent efficient in work and only twenty percent efficient in its amusement, recreation, and leisure." True democracy was a "many sided life," not an "alley leading to a single goal." [33]

Yet the United States faced new problems in the creation and distribution of the social surplus. The closing of the frontier had eliminated an easy method for increasing agricultural production. The decline of immigration had destroyed the easiest means of increasing consumer demand. "Increased knowledge and greater skill," not intensified "price competition," would compensate for these changes and create a larger surplus. Similarly, the remedy for a declining industrial growth rate and the tendency for wages to become stable was an improvement in the "conditions which surround the worker." This improvement would create a higher standard of living and, consequently, greater consumer demand.[34]

The conditions of war and Patten's fear that there would no longer be abundance forced him to modify three central concepts of his economic theory: his views on thrift, on substitution, and on inflation. His opposition to credit financing of the war led him to contradict his earlier view of thrift, derived from John A. Hobson's concept of oversaving. Patten had criticized the exercise of thrift as unnecessary moral behavior inherited from the age of scarcity. Now, however, he argued that an "inducement to save" would be more beneficial to skilled workers than higher wages. Invested savings would increase production and "modify" workers' characters to make them more efficient. Rejecting another basic concept of his earlier theories of economics, Patten contended that the power of consumers to substitute one good for another might not check the rising cost of living. Prices were fixed by men who refused to produce and consume—by the satisfied and the overrestrained—not by people adjusted to the abundance economy. Moreover, Patten was no longer confident that rising prices were an indication of adjustment to the new civilization. Production and prosperity would grow most steadily if prices were kept at a "normal" level—a little above the level of the average in years of relative scarcity.[35]

More important, the war forced Patten to reject his belief that the activities of individuals and small groups of men could have a significant effect on the emergence of an economy of abundance. Government action, not the independent behavior of consumers and producers, was necessary to insure prosperity. The remedy for the fluctuation of prices would be "price regulation to prevent the upward movement in prices and rigid restraints on consumption to prevent a misuse of lowering prices." Both abundance and restraint should be implemented by coercive public action.[36]

Adjustment to the potential abundance of the modern world demanded new attitudes toward agriculture, labor, business, and foreign affairs. Price fixing was necessary for both agricultural and industrial goods. Moreover, cooperative farming was as beneficial as "large scale production in industry." Patten's program for labor included an immediate 50-per-cent increase in wages, an eight-hour day and forty-hour week, worker control of labor unions, equal pay for men and women, social insurance, the regulation of working conditions, and a comprehensive educational system. His program for industry foreshadowed the National Recovery Administration of the New Deal: "Joint mass production shall be encouraged under such regulations as conserve public interest. To this end a national board of industrial control shall be formed with powers similar to the Interstate Commerce Commission." If Americans modified their political and economic institutions immediately, the next generation would "bless the war instead of regarding it as a curse." In foreign affairs, Patten suggested an alliance with England for "humanitarian ends." He suspected that an "international league of peace" would lack sufficient political and economic power to enforce its decisions. Only England and the United States together could exercise a protectorate over the undeveloped nations of the world.[37]

At the heart of Patten's recommendations was his conviction that the abundance economy could be realized. He envisioned a world in which "none are ignorant, few die before the age of sixty, where poverty is unknown, and disease ceases to terrify." It was appalling that "old antagonisms and senseless stupidity" kept men from a "goal which mutual good will could readily attain." [38]

Patten no longer believed that "good will" could be generated by either a religious code or acceptance of the logic of science. By the end of the war, he was disillusioned with both the exercise of benevolence and the use of evolutionary methods as means to his end. The age of abundance, which required new values and new restraints, could only be created by coercion.[39] In the last five years of his life, he explored the psychological, social, and economic implications of a revolution in the name of abundance.

CHAPTER VIII ⚑

Materialism, Collectivism, and Abundance, 1917–1922

Between 1917 and 1922, Patten tried to repair the damage inflicted by the war on his hope for a world attuned to abundance. Neither the Protestant ethic nor the lessons of social science had restrained the passions rooted in the long age of scarcity. Most men, or at least most public men, ignored the implications of technological progress. They preferred struggle to cooperation, selfishness to generosity, force to persuasion. Patten realized that he must find more powerful authority for his belief that all men, if they developed appropriate restraints, could participate in abundance.

For twenty years Patten had been content with a pragmatic sanction for his theories. Like William James, he had been a pluralist, accepting the possibility of supernatural interference in human affairs while trying to explain as many phenomena as possible according to mechanistic principles. Like James, Patten preferred to test the validity of ideas by their results rather than by their logical and empirical relationship to a set of assumptions about the universe. Yet pragmatism and the political context in which it operated—the liberal belief that the peaceful competition of ideas would enable men to select the most effective modes of action—had failed dismally in the second decade of the century. Patten decided that, before they could create an age of abundance, men must have clear and consistent assumptions about the operation of the universe.

Patten had rejected an uncompromising theological world view as a young man. Another set of consistent assumptions, the doctrines of materialism, had been available to him since his years as a student in Germany. In the 1850's and 1860's, a group of German intellectuals constructed scientific and social philosophy on the premise that fundamental life processes could be explained by mechanistic analysis. Such scholars as Jacob Moleschott, Ludwig Büchner, and Rudolf Virchow bitterly attacked the conventional scientific and political doctrines of their time. They combined an animus against the hypothesis of a human spirit separate from the body with a passion for social justice. Proposals to redistribute wealth so that everyone could obtain an equitable share of the most beneficial nutriment blended materialism—expressed in the epigram "Man is what he eats"—with the new science of nutrition.[1]

Patten had encountered scientific materialism as a student at Halle. His teacher, Johannes Conrad, was a friend and colleague of the materialists. Like many of them, Conrad was a student of agricultural chemistry. One of his closest friends was Ernst Haeckel, who inspired the formal organization of German materialists and who was a dogmatic believer in the power of science to solve all problems. Although there is no direct evidence that Patten was inspired by the scientific materialists, it is difficult to believe that he could have avoided thinking about the issues they raised.[2]

The leading scientific monist of Patten's generation, Jacques Loeb, seems to have had no influence on Patten's work until 1917, when Patten used some of his ideas to establish a material basis for converting people to the values of abundance. Yet it is likely that Patten was familiar with Loeb's ideas as early as 1892. Loeb came to America from Germany in 1891 and taught for several years at Bryn Mawr College before moving on to

Chicago, Berkeley, and the Rockefeller Institute. Patten had several close friends on the Bryn Mawr faculty. Since the small college for women was so near Philadelphia, it is likely that Patten's friends introduced him to the German physiologist who shared his interest in the science of nutrition and in social reform.[3]

There are several possible explanations for Patten's refusal to declare himself a materialist until 1917. Perhaps he could not jettison the Presbyterian and Methodist influences of his youth. Another possible explanation is that his commitment to professionalism in social science inhibited him from grappling with universal riddles in public. Moreover, materialism in social science was associated with Marxism. Patten scorned Marxist economics and knew that any taint of socialism would destroy his potential influence on leading Americans. In 1903, however, he had published *Heredity and Social Progress*, in which he sought biological explanations for social change. But in the book Patten was ambiguous about scientific materialism and angered professional scientists by his obscurantist approach to biological doctrines.

In 1917, Patten began to write as a convinced scientific monist. For the next three years, he sought in the ideas of Sigmund Freud, whose work he had encountered five years earlier, as well as in those of Loeb, authority for the restraints appropriate to abundance. In May, 1917, contradicting his earlier opinion that sexual desire was a destructive force, Patten accepted Freud's contention that "all fundamental surplus emotions center about the sex act" and the corollary that "cultural forces" were "organized in ways that repress sex." To Patten, the conflict pointed out by Freud between unconscious desires and internalized restraints was appropriate only in an age of scarcity. As men adjusted to the emerging economy of abundance, this conflict would cease. Nerves and glands would somehow generate strong desires for nonsexual gratification. These desires could be satisfied by the material and aesthetic goods available in the pleasure economy. Patten's presentation of these ideas was not clear. Perhaps he did not fully comprehend the complex dynamics of Freudian psychology. On the other hand, he may have been groping toward a restatement of the Freudian reality principle. Because the external environment in which men operated was being transformed, consumption was becoming more important than production, expression more useful than repression. If reality provided more pleasure than pain, Freudian doctrines would have to be modified.[4]

Six months later, Patten combined Freud's emphasis on sexual desire with the German medical materialists' emphasis on nutritional science to support his theory, first stated in 1885, that evolution had an economic basis. Every "sex discharge" was the result of an impetus from the blood or a gland. This impetus was a "nutric discharge" created in the body as a result of particular patterns of nutrition. Since habits of nutrition were determined by the mode of consumption in each environment, evolutionary "improvements" were a result of "economic changes reducing the cost of food, saving waste, and increasing personal efficiency." These economic changes "transformed" the stomach, blood, glands, and sensory nerves "into more effective means of promoting evolution." [5]

Scientific materialism provided Patten with an explanation for the mechanism of social transformation. From 1885 to 1898, he had based the concept of a transition from scarcity to abundance on the existence of surplus wealth. Technological advance made surplus wealth possible. Patten did not inquire, in his public statements, into what motivated technological advance. Between 1898 and 1917, he asserted that surplus energy was the source of the increased production of wealth that made abundance possible. But he was vague about the source of surplus energy. In 1918, he postulated a scientific basis for the surplus and for the values and restraints appropriate to new social conditions.

Social change was a result of the fulfillment of wishes. A wish was a "pulse of surplus energy" generated by the bloodstream, the "seat of surplus mechanisms." The process of wish fulfillment formed a circuit, which began with a "tropism." To Jacques Loeb, who had endeavored to "found a science of animal tropisms" since the 1880's, a tropism was an automatic and predictable response to an external stimulus. Patten, exercising a social scientist's license, defined it as a vaguely perceived wish. In his theory, a tropism became a "strain," which was transformed into will. The action of the will satisfied the initial wish; the results of action created new wishes. These new wishes stimulated new circuits—each in a context of more material goods and more fulfilled wishes than men had had in earlier circuits. The physiological pressure to make wishes come true was more powerful than the struggle for survival. In other words, "natural compulsion" was a more effective mechanism of evolution than natural selection. Just as Loeb believed that environmental conditions "may warp or inhibit the inherited instincts," Patten claimed that progress occurred when men freed the "elemental pulses from the distortion" imposed by "ages of adjustment" to scarcity.[6]

His acceptance of scientific materialism placed Patten in a paradoxical position. He seemed to despair of the possibility of manipulating the environment before individual psyches were changed. At the same time, it appeared impossible to stimulate new internal "circuits" until the environment was changed. Patten resolved this paradox by arguing that mental illness, the pain created by the retention in an age of abundance of attitudes appropriate to an era of scarcity, prevented the start of new circuits which would produce adjustment to the new conditions of life. He was impressed by the possibilities of psychoanalysis, the "true starting point for the study of mental disorders." Yet "mental analysis" alone could not cure emotional illness. It would be necessary to combine psychoanalysis with changes in social institutions. According to Patten, mental illness was a result of "shock and fear" stimulated by "external happenings." Race hatred, for example, was an illness caused by "external" traumatic experiences. Social reform—the carrying-out of the programs Patten had outlined over the previous two decades—

would remove the causes of shock and fear and would provide the context for successful psychoanalysis.[7]

Patten's commitment to materialism and psychoanalysis enabled him to regain some of the optimism which had been destroyed by the war. He had a new assumption and a new vocabulary with which to express his long-held conviction that changes in a potentially benevolent external world could have a direct and rapid influence on mental life. In 1920, he challenged social workers and economists to reject discredited ideas and to look boldly into the future.

In the tone of an old prophet disturbed by the cautious and wicked ways of the young, Patten accused social workers of being unprepared to meet the challenges of the postwar period. Social workers were using outmoded principles: "crude views of distribution, sloppy politics, thread-worn biology, and milk-bottle sociology." While social workers comforted themselves with platitudes, more than half of the American people were too deficient, physically or mentally, to enjoy the benefits of the age of abundance.[8]

Specifically, individual casework was a "vain struggle against impossibilities" in a society acquiring the characteristics of a "monotonous plain without variety or color or form, due to the uniform pressure of group emotion." The poor, the helpless, the mentally ill were "beyond the influence of social work as now constituted." Only groups larger than the family exerted sufficient "influence on personality" to bring out "inherent possibilities"—and the poor were excluded from these groups by the "rigor of their conditions."[9]

The final solution for poverty lay in "institutional measures" which would accomplish what "personal casework" could not. Extreme poverty should be dealt with by the government, assisted by "charities of the old type." The immediate task for social workers, however, was to extend the economic standards of middle-class life to 60 per cent of the population, instead of a mere 30 per cent. Values and restraints appropriate to conditions of abundance could be inculcated only in people who first adopted middle-class standards. Patten emphasized the importance of psychological factors in the transition from the attitudes of a period of scarcity to those of an age of abundance. He had a prophetic presentiment that psychiatry might help to make individuals more effective in an affluent society.[10]

The economy of abundance could never materialize, however, if economists and statesmen did not realize that "liberal idealism" had proved "wholly unworkable" in the aftermath of the war. If statesmen had not thought in terms of liberal individualism, the economic losses of the war could have been recouped "in a year." Liberalism, derived from the values of scarcity, created the likelihood that a "century [might] pass before the efforts of contemporary statesmen" could be "corrected." Sometime sooner, the liberals and their heirs might be overwhelmed by the "insurgence of the disillusioned masses." [11]

The best interests of individuals and groups could be served only by conscious social planning and collective action. Patten believed that John Maynard Keynes's *The Economic Consequences of the Peace* was the "only worthy discussion" of the condition of postwar Europe. But Keynes's program for rehabilitation was inadequate. Unlike Keynes, Patten was confident that techniques could be developed to increase the economic surplus of Europe and the United States. The "question of the future" was "Who is going to obtain this surplus, and what are to be the means of distribution?" Although he agreed with Keynes that the "present suffering of Europe" was "not due to the war but the peace which followed," he wanted to plan, not merely predict, the economic events of the immediate future.[12]

Statesmen and their economic advisers must eschew the "liberal idealism" which caused them to confuse the "relief of urgent physical distress" with the "rehabilitation of destroyed European industry." Rehabilitation required new concepts, which Patten presented in a program for economic planning. His program was frankly collectivist, based on such premises as "Political rights shall be no defense of the individual against the mass, but a concession of the mass to the individual" and "The claims of property, persons, and classes shall be conditioned by the needs of the whole people." Scientific materialism appeared to have led Patten, as it had led Jacques Loeb, toward socialism.[13]

Patten's conversion to materialism and collectivism was, however, incomplete. The liberal and pluralist strains in his thought re-emerged in the half-tract, half-novel *Mud Hollow*, written during the last year of his life. Patten regarded the novel as an attempt to eradicate the "obsessions" which prevented "truth" from becoming "mass opinion." Since the world had not responded to the logical arguments of the far-seeing men of his generation, he would appeal to "emotion." *Mud Hollow* was, however, more than propaganda. It was thinly disguised autobiography and a personal testament, prompted perhaps by a desire to express his feelings, unrestrained by his lifelong reticence and by the Christian assumption that a man is revealed by his works. Moreover, Patten was angered by the popularity of Sinclair Lewis' *Main Street*, which challenged his affection for small-town America by its evocation of pessimism and despair. Mud Hollow, the town from which the novel took its name, unlike Lewis' Gopher Prairie, was not "living on but half of what it produce[d] and the worst half at that." It was a "normal village," which had "prosperity without culture," abundance without values appropriate to new conditions.[14]

Paul, the hero of the novel, like the young Simon Patten, had talents which a farming community did not recognize. "But for the reputation of his family," Paul would have been considered "stupid." Like Patten, Paul's "visions lay in the future, not in the past." Paul's only concession to the past, his idealization of his hard-working mother, may have been based on similar feelings in Patten. Although Paul eventually embraced new ideals, his wishes, like Patten's, "failed where wishes always do, just at the point of fulfillment." In a sense, writing the novel was a form of wish fulfillment for Patten. Paul transcended his physical and emotional limitations more successfully than Patten had. Moreover, Paul and Ruth, the heroine, unlike Patten and

Charlotte Kimball, found the key to marital happiness and lived happily ever after.[15]

Ruth's father, Professor Stuart, also resembled Patten. His ideas about women and social welfare were similar to Patten's. In the professor, as in Paul, some of the author's dreams were realized. Patten must have enjoyed the thought of a "hundred boys" rushing to "seize the Professor's hand." He may have longed for a prose style "reminiscent of Webster, Macaulay, and Cicero." [16]

The professor had brought up his daughter to be an emancipated woman. Like a Wordsworth maiden, Ruth did "what nature dictated." She projected the "throbs of a primitive environment" into a "modern situation." Yet, like Zenobia in Hawthorne's *Blithedale Romance*, she "hoped to influence men by a resemblance to them." Moreover, like D. H. Lawrence's Lady Chatterley, Ruth was a "plumed bird, alive to the present" and eager for sexual fulfillment.[17]

In the course of the novel, Patten explored the implications of Paul's meeting a "primitive woman" in a "cosy nook by the river." At times, Patten laid on sexual imagery with excessive thickness—and perhaps voyeuristic delight. Describing a boat ride, for example, he noted the "wavelike motion on the still stream": "with each stroke of his arm the prow dove, then rose, slowed and dove again. The boat had Paul's pulse . . . and her own fell into rhythm with it." Yet Paul was restrained by "convention, tradition, and custom." He had been influenced by those "hopeless boobs," the respectable and repressed leaders of the American middle class.[18]

Patten was not convinced that Paul should give Ruth what she passionately wanted. On the one hand, he called on men to conform to nature, to have the "courage to accept its revelations"; on the other, he urged men to "rise above sex and reach the land where all is soul." Because sexuality was not sufficiently restrained, men were "dragged back into sex relations." Fortunately, "each generation" strove to "rise above them." [19]

Paul, mysteriously transformed from a confused undergraduate into a lecturer on economics, needed an exhausting conversion experience to discover that his idealization of his mother had inhibited his capacity for restrained love for a woman as well as for mere sex. After Paul's conversion to a belief in love, he and Ruth formed a partnership with common tasks and goals. At the end of the novel, Paul and Ruth, carefully restraining their sexual desires, began the struggle to implement the age of abundance by conducting a campaign against an exploiter of the working class.[20]

The last half of *Mud Hollow* embodied an intensely personal assessment of Patten's life and thought. He regarded his career as evidence of man's ability to transcend his environment. The members of the Presbyterian church in which he was reared had "maintained their isolation" for centuries. Moreover, Sandwich, Illinois, was a "village where every one thought the same thoughts, ate the same pie, and used the same tools." Yet the "mere accident" of a German education and a professorship in Philadelphia had enabled him to become the prophet of a new basis for civilization.[21]

Before 1914, Patten had thought that the "world was nearing the end of a splendid epoch." The war and the affluence of postwar America had taught him that human nature was "vaguer, more emotional, with fewer of the rock attributes than was thought." The "rigid sameness" which prevailed in the "prosperous sections of the land" was deplorable. Men were "conformists or non-conformists," not "Democrats or Republicans, Protestants and Catholics, or even moral or immoral." He regretted that machines had more "emotional force than what is merely looked at or heard." The automobile, for example, was becoming "ourselves extended." But Patten had no nostalgia for a lost America. The past was worse than the present. It was senseless to return to the scarcity and hardship of pioneer life. The United States of the 1920's, with all its faults, was less "crude and degenerate" than in any previous time in its history.[22]

The collectivist spirit of his proposals during the preceding few years jarred with the liberal individualism he had internalized as a boy. He applauded prohibition and the progressive income tax because they gave "mass judgment a greater control over minorities." Yet he wanted to protect minority groups from the effects of "one hundred percent Americanism." Although private action could not check "community vice," and although social justice was "due a person regardless of his character," it was wrong for social workers to assume the "helplessness" of the working class. The lower classes could attain a higher standard of living through the pressure exerted on the economy by their increasing wants. The pressure for social adjustment to the age of abundance was a result of individual desires, which increased "more rapidly than the means of satisfying them." In the future, however, the *"person* will be as nothing; his *class* everything." Nevertheless, Patten continued to define adjustment as the "full development" of the "inherent possibilities" of individuals, not of groups.[23]

His belief that men must adopt values and restraints appropriate to the age of abundance was as evident in *Mud Hollow* as at any time in the previous thirty years. Men could not "thrive under exploitation." They needed, "not a new heredity, but the removal of complexes and the fun of spending what they earn." Yet if "sex desires" were not "curbed," the "rise of man" would be "retarded." After reading Freud, Patten could not question the "power of sex, merely its primacy." If sexual activity could be restrained, the greatest enemy of the economy of abundance would be defeated. The surplus energy saved by restraining sexuality could be used for altruistic purposes.[24]

Patten concluded this novel which was his personal testament with an avowal of faith and a prophecy. The metaphysical discomfort produced in this son of Protestant pioneers by a temporary allegiance to collectivism and materialism was resolved by compromise and emotive rhetoric. He rejected liberal individualism and materialism. A combination of pluralism and collectivism seemed best-suited to a future of restraint amid abundance. The modern world had "broken" with the past. The future belonged to cooperating groups, not to individuals. Patten was pleased to predict that "our children will live longer and have better times even if they scoff at our dearest traditions." Yet men might be protected from their passions, might take advantage of material wealth and at the same time learn to value aesthetic and altruistic action, by embracing a religious vision. Patten was confident that men might hope for a "new paradise" on earth, though not for "Eden." Despite Loeb and Freud, despite four years of human butchery, Patten's last public words expressed his hope that "paradises" would be "sought and gained" until "Eden reopens her gates." [25]

Mud Hollow was the last statement of a lonely and isolated man. For the last five years of his life, Patten lived in a cluttered apartment in Philadelphia, in a one-room cabin in East Alstead, New Hampshire, or at a hotel in Browns Mills, New Jersey. He was out of touch with his contemporaries. Only a few younger men, particularly Edward Devine, Scott Nearing, and Rexford Tugwell, were solicitous of his welfare. Most of his time was spent in reading, writing, and playing bridge. In May, 1922, Patten suffered a stroke at Browns Mills and lost the power of speech. On June 5, the doctors declared that his paralysis was progressive. A week later, the University of Pennsylvania Board of Trustees, refusing to allow old wounds to heal, rejected a petition from the Wharton faculty to grant Patten an honorary degree. Patten died on July 24, a man who had outlived his contemporary reputation.[26]

In 1725, Giambattista Vico, outlining the course of history, declared, "Men first feel necessity, then look for utility, next attend to comfort, still later amuse themselves with pleasure, thence grow dissolute in luxury, and finally go mad and waste their substance." Every society was "first crude, then severe, then benign, then delicate, finally dissolute." Patten, a social scientist in the tradition begun by Vico, had a similar vision of history. He hoped, however, that his own time, the period of transition from an age of scarcity to an age of abundance, would end in comfort and delicacy rather than in madness, waste, and dissolution. Like Vico, Patten perceived the new developments of his age and projected them boldly into the future. Just as Vico's rationalistic message was undercut, in the last chapter of *The New Science*, by an inconsistent obeisance to Christianity, Patten's belief in progress through the wise disposition of surplus wealth and energy was compromised by the continual pressure of the doctrines of social Darwinism and the Protestant ethic. Patten could not entirely reject these doctrines, although he knew that they had been generated in an age of scarcity, just as Vico, two centuries earlier, could not reject the mystical doctrines of the preceding heroic age.[27]

Vico is remembered, not for suffering from cultural lag, but for creating a foundation for the study of society in the nineteenth and twentieth centuries. Similarly, Simon Patten's reputation should rest, not on his limitations, but on his ability to transcend them and to lay the basis for social planning in an age of abundance. He deserves attention as the most astute and prophetic student in his generation of the economics of human values.

Patten outlined a new basis for civilization according to four broad categories: economic institutions, government activity, voluntary civic action, and family life. Although he was educated in the empirical methods of German historical economics, he tempered positivism with a consciousness of subjective phenomena. His desire to promote values and restraints appropriate to an age of abundance led him to study sociology, psychology, biology, metaphysics, history, and literature.

Patten's social theory was fraught with contradictions and ambiguities. He believed in the inevitability of progress but crusaded for immediate social reform to achieve progress more efficiently. A belief in the perfectibility of most men often jarred with his suspicion that some men had irremediable defects which could not be removed by manipulating their environment. Although he demanded collective action, he had a deep respect for liberal individualism. Despite an attraction to a mechanistic conception of life, he remained a member of the Presbyterian Church. He adhered to an essentially hedonistic psychology which was inconsistent with his insight into the complexity of human nature.

Patten was the first man to study systematically an important change in the life of the West—the transition from an economy of scarcity to an economy of abundance. He was the first to realize that, because men would no longer be forced to struggle for the basic necessities and comforts of life, they must develop new social, aesthetic, moral, and religious values and new restraints against destructive desires. Patten believed that the emotional discipline of the Protestant ethic, combined with the implications of biology, psychology, and social science, would provide standards of behavior based on pleasure rather than on suffering. His thought connected the world of John Stuart Mill with the age of John Maynard Keynes, the psychology of the eighteenth century with the insight and challenge of Freudian psychoanalysis, and the politics of Lincoln's America and Bismarck's Germany with the politics of the New Deal and later periods.

Some problems remain. Patten, a nonconformist only in ideas, a recognized leader in a growing profession, was not hailed as a prophet in his own time. Most of his friends and colleagues respected him as an economic theorist and a teacher but ignored his effort to change the frame of reference according to which they viewed the human condition. Yet, in the forty years since Patten's death, an increasing number of scholars and statesmen have accepted the assumption that men have, or will shortly attain, the power to produce enough material goods to guarantee everyone a constantly improving standard of living. Patten's writings played only a small role in the acceptance of the concept of abundance after his death. Nevertheless, the later intellectual history of the concept which received its first clear expression in his work may reveal some of the problems faced by men who challenge the assumptions which comfort most of their contemporaries.

CHAPTER IX ✍

The Communication
of Abundance, 1890–1920

Patten was one of the most widely read, highly regarded, and least understood economists of his time. In retrospect, his central themes—the transition from scarcity to abundance and the need for imposing restraints on behavior which have been justified by modern science—appear to dominate his numerous books and articles. Yet, despite considerable evidence that Patten's writings were read, and more often praised than condemned, by professional economists and sociologists in Europe and the United States, most of his fellow social scientists did not accept his challenge to their assumption that enough goods could not be produced to satisfy men's basic needs.

During Patten's lifetime, only a few men considered his central thesis. Most of these men were not professional economists. Lester F. Ward, for example, was a self-educated biologist and sociologist. Edward A. Ross, though trained as an economist, identified himself as a sociologist early in his career. Edward Devine left economics to become an administrator of social welfare institutions, and Walter E. Weyl turned to journalism after graduate study under Patten. The only economists who perceived the import of Patten's doctrines, Thorstein Veblen and

John A. Hobson, were conscious rebels against professional assumptions and practices—and Veblen showed awareness of Patten's thesis only to reject it.

Patten's fellow economists praised his originality without taking account of his central idea. Although John Bates Clark of Columbia University declared in 1892 that Patten was providing a "scientific basis of an optimistic faith that is in all of us," he never mentioned the concept of a transition, but engaged in lengthy conflict with Patten about the definitions of cost and price. Frank W. Taussig of Harvard, the leading expert on American tariffs, praised Patten's "undaunted disposition to challenge accepted conventions" but deplored his "judgment as to what things are practicable." Edwin R. A. Seligman of Columbia, an expert on taxation and economic history, though he believed that Patten "inspired more of the younger scholars in the United States than any other individual," never mentioned his central thesis.[1]

Patten's closest friends, Edmund J. James, Richard T. Ely, and Franklin H. Giddings, never attached much importance, in public writings or in correspondence, to his central theme. Their friendship with Patten transcended intellectual issues. It was based on shared experiences in Germany and the United States, on a common struggle against amateurism in social science, and on commitment to social reform. James considered Patten "one of the most distinguished economists of modern times," but rarely mentioned his friend's ideas. Ely assigned Patten's books to his classes yet misunderstood his methodology and read his work for its contributions to social reform rather than to social theory. Giddings, a sociologist, rejected Patten's thesis. The two men battled affectionately—and with decreasing comprehension of the premises of each other's arguments—for the next thirty years. Ideas were less important to the friendship among these men than the desire to "stand close together," to defend their group against dogmatic promoters of the *status quo* in economics, politics, and education.[2]

Why did most of Patten's contemporaries ignore his most

original and compelling ideas? Part of the explanation may lie in Patten's inability to write with the clarity or grace of, for example, John Maynard Keynes. Even his closest friends were appalled by his inability to state his theories clearly and concisely and to marshal his evidence with scholarly rigor. Few of his colleagues could spare time from their own research and teaching to unravel the theories Patten spun out in twenty-two books and a hundred and fifty articles. Moreover, despite several painful efforts, Patten was unable to bring his ideas together in a comprehensive synthesis. Each of his books and articles dealt with separate problems of the transition to abundance and the development of appropriate restraints. As Clark told Ely in 1902, Patten needed someone to help him work "into a systematic whole his various thoughts." [3]

The professionalism which led to Patten's acquiring readers and influence also limited his impact on his contemporaries. A profession's existence depends on its members' willingness to accept and discuss a common body of knowledge. Patten, a committed professional economist, devoted large segments of his work to the discussion of technical points of economic theory which could be viewed as having no relation to abundance. His colleagues could debate his views on such problems as marginal utility, tariffs, and the theory of prices without acknowledging that they were part of an overarching conception of a transition from an age of scarcity to an age of abundance. Moreover, Patten was interested in the traditionally disputed questions of economics for their own sake. He gave most of his colleagues in the American Economic Association little reason to suspect that his fundamental assumptions about the prospects for economic progress were different from their own. [4]

Paradoxically, although Patten's professional involvement often obscured his major theme, it made his work more significant to future social scientists. The professional ethic to which Patten subscribed demanded careful reasoning and a dedication to presenting ideas in their fullest complexity. Patten felt responsible for making the most detailed examination possible of the way in which societies moved from one economic stage to another.

Professionalism limited the scope of Patten's vision. Without a profound sense of his calling as an economist and of his responsibility to colleagues living, dead, and unborn, he might have yielded to his enthusiasm and become a free-lance prophet like John Ruskin, William Morris, or Edward Bellamy. These visionary social theorists, who stated their ideas simply and repeatedly, had a greater impact on popular opinion in their own time than Patten had. But Patten's professional conscience, by restraining his impulse to prophesy, forced him to present the most complete analysis ever made of the implications of affluence. Patten was painfully aware of the tension within him between the prophet and the professional. In 1898, he suspected that economists knew too much to be effective reformers. Simpler-minded men like Ruskin or Bellamy had "great advantages" over the economist, who was "trammeled" by tradition, respect for existing social forms, and knowledge of contradictory facts. Yet, throughout his career, Patten straddled the fence between polemic and precision.[5]

Patten's style and professionalism do not entirely account for his lack of impact on his contemporaries. More important is the reluctance of men to modify assumptions which are still serviceable. During Patten's lifetime, the most sophisticated economists in the world could still explain most of the phenomena they observed without adopting Patten's belief that within the foreseeable future enough goods could be produced to guarantee every appropriately restrained individual the requisites for survival and a constantly improving standard of living. The fact that the traditional assumption of scarcity could still be used as the basis for economic theory does not mean that economists suffered from cultural lag, from what John K. Galbraith calls devotion to the "conventional wisdom." Within the personal memory and historical knowledge of Patten's contemporaries, prosperity had been a short-run trend, alternating with periods of economic crisis. It would have been difficult for

Alfred Marshall, the leading British economist of the generation, to accept Patten's frame of reference at a time when England's rate of economic growth was declining and large numbers of Englishmen seemed to be mired in poverty. The burden of proof was on Patten—and a great many of Patten's new ideas were based on faith in his own imaginative projections.[6]

Yet in the traditional assumption of scarcity there was more comfort for economists than for sociologists like Lester Ward and Edward Ross. In economics, as practiced by professionals between 1890 and 1920, important methodological and theoretical concerns interfered with the reception of Patten's ideas: the debate over deductive and inductive approaches to economic phenomena, the problem of separating normative and positive economics, the allocation of professional resources to research to which Patten's ideas were not immediately relevant, uncertainty about the relationship between economics and psychology, and semantic confusion about the meaning of "scarcity."

Patten's approach to methodology probably made most of his professional contemporaries uneasy. His central thesis was historical, a statement about economic and social change over time. Yet he presented and developed this thesis through the deductive analysis of models, or abstractions from reality. Patten's belief that, in the intellectual melting pot of America, deductive and inductive approaches to economics could be combined was a naïve resolution of the methodological controversies of the 1880's and 1890's. The *Methodenstreit*, the debate between the German historical economists and the deductive economists of Vienna, produced a cleavage in the profession outside of the borders of these countries. By the 1890's, the most prestigious economic writing in England, Sweden, Austria, and the United States was both deductive and ahistorical. Economists who might have accepted Patten's historical arguments were suspicious of his deductive presentation. On the other hand, deductive economists rejected his historicism. Max Weber, a German contemporary faced with a similar problem, rejected the profession of economics and called himself a sociologist. Unlike Weber, however, Patten's work emphasized the traditional problems of economics—the production, distribution, and consumption of wealth. Even if economists rejected his ideas, they were the only group capable of fully understanding them.[7]

Patten's frequent pronouncements on public policy, particularly in the first two decades of the twentieth century, made many contemporary economists suspicious of his professionalism. Since the early nineteenth century, most economists had distinguished between the "science" and the "art" of political economy. The science of economics, the study of the production, distribution, and consumption of wealth, was repeatedly purged of any implication that economic theory was relevant to public policy. Economists were conditioned to claim "neutrality" on all disputed political and social issues. The art of economics, the formulation of recommendations based on the economist's concern for the world around him, was generally held to be separate from economic theory and analysis. Although there were "always critics or dissenters who rejected either the possibility or the desirability of economists' " remaining aloof from political dispute, most professional economists of Patten's generation accepted a commitment to scientific neutrality as a methodological principle. Alfred Marshall, for instance, emphasized the need for a "clear distinction" between questions which "lay within the compass of economic science and those concerning the desirability of different social aims which . . . lay outside." [8]

The problem of maintaining a clear distinction between positive and normative economics was particularly acute for Americans of Patten's generation. Their teachers, the historical economists who founded the Verein für Sozialpolitik, opposed the claims of scientific objectivity made by English classical economists. The Americans were caught between a desire to become involved in problems of ethics and a growing commitment to the positivism of English and Austrian economists. Richard Ely, for example, who rejected the possibility of complete objectivity, deplored Patten's interest in neoclassical positivism. But the second generation of American professional economists, men like Wesley C. Mitchell, H. J. Davenport, and Irving Fisher, were impatient with Patten's inability to draw a clear line between economic theory and proposals for social reform.[9]

The hypothesis of a transition from scarcity to abundance may have seemed an irrelevant idea to many sophisticated economists of Patten's generation. The traditions of the discipline and the subjects on which laymen demanded enlightenment from professionals dictated the allocation of most research time to questions which required more precise answers than Patten's thesis could provide. Between 1885 and 1920, the most important objectives of economists were to increase the precision of microeconomic static formulae, to refine economic statistics, and to study cyclical fluctuations in mature economies. Many questions about the behavior of producers and consumers in situations in which resources and markets did not change had not been answered by economists in the first three-quarters of the nineteenth century. The one element of German social science which influenced economists of every school was the desire to accumulate increasingly accurate and useful data. The goals of economists were reinforced by the interest of influential businessmen in studies of individual firms and of buyers and sellers in the market place and in statistics on which to base industrial planning. Most important, to many men the basic fact of Western economic life in this period was not abundance but the dislocation caused by periodic world-wide depressions of increasing seriousness.[10]

Patten's thesis was not logically irrelevant to these concerns. He could not influence his colleagues, however, unless he made the concept of abundance immediately and specifically relevant to the problems they were examining. Yet he dealt with the economics of the firm and business cycles only in passing, and in rather opaque language. A generation later, when John Maynard Keynes, in examining the causes and remedies for depressions, used assumptions similar to Patten's, economists were more receptive than they had ever been to Patten's work.[11]

Even when Patten dealt with microeconomic formulae or business cycles, his emphasis on the complexity of human behavior, on the need for psychological analysis, made his colleagues uneasy. For Patten, the concept of utility was qualitative as well as quantitative. His analysis of abundance and the need for restraints required him to evaluate the various satisfactions men experienced in their economic and social life. In the period between 1880 and 1910, however, most of the world's leading economists drew back in uncertainty from the increasing complexity of psychological research. In these years, the concept of utility was excluded from economic theory by such leading scholars as Irving Fisher in the United States, Alfred Marshall in England, Vilfredo Pareto in Switzerland, and Gustav Cassel in Sweden. These men were convinced that it was impossible to measure satisfactions accurately, particularly when it was necessary to relate the satisfaction obtained from one economic good to an individual's entire consumption. For Patten, consumers' tastes were the starting point for economic analysis; for an increasing number of his contemporaries, they were not susceptible to analysis.[12]

Many economists were, however, uncomfortable with the exclusion of qualitative utility. In this period, men like the Englishman A. C. Pigou developed the new subdiscipline of "welfare economics," which attempted to make "policy recommendations while dispensing with value-judgments or . . . reducing them to a minimum." But welfare economists, unlike Patten, were willing to accept ethical neutrality as a possible and desirable methodological principle.[13]

Since the eighteenth century, moreover, economists had assumed that the desire for satisfaction was the major motive for economic action. Economists needed a new motive, which they found in the concept of scarcity. Men engaged in economic activity in order to obtain goods which were in limited supply. Gustav Cassel, for instance, declared that "scarcity is the fundamental fact which makes economizing necessary." For him, economics was the "pure logic of choice between scarce means."

The word economy came to connote a "sense of compulsion, of having something to contend against, and in the case of industry this is taken to be the fact of scarcity." The meaning of scarcity was taken as "self-evident," and few economists offered any definition of it.[14]

The usual concept of scarcity was quite different from Patten's. To most economists of his generation, scarcity meant merely the existence of unsatisfied wants and an inequitable distribution of goods. To Patten, scarcity meant the inability of a society to produce enough goods and services to guarantee everyone a standard of living which would support a healthy, productive life. What his colleagues regarded as a word to label a vague assumption which they found useful in explaining the world around them, Patten used as a descriptive term relevant to history and social reform. Most economists used the word scarcity to represent an absolute which enabled them to avoid the problems of measuring satisfactions. Patten used it as a relative term whose meaning was based on an assessment of satisfactions. Patten and his colleagues were talking at cross-purposes.

Patten did not, however, talk at cross-purposes to the British economist John A. Hobson, a self-proclaimed "heretic" who had a significant influence on the British Labour Party, on Lenin, and on John Maynard Keynes. In his first book, written in 1889, Hobson, who had not yet read Patten's work, argued that the central problem in contemporary economies was not production but the "check that undue saving and the consequent accumulation of over-supply exerts on production." Hobson seemed to imply that only outmoded attitudes and institutions kept men from producing enough to go around. Yet Hobson also accepted the conventional definition of scarcity. A few years later, he wrote that value "is determined on the supply side by natural scarcity."[15]

As Hobson's ideas developed, he integrated concepts derived from John Ruskin and Patten. From Ruskin, he acquired a concern for the aesthetic and spiritual components of "wealth." Patten's work gave him theoretical tools with which to make

Ruskin's vision of a welfare state a plausible goal for British social reformers. In 1892, Hobson accepted Patten's thesis that increasing the variety of goods consumed would utilize enough resources to minimize the effect of the law of diminishing returns. From Patten's books and articles, Hobson learned that men could "escape the niggardliness of nature" by applying a Ruskinian "preference of quality to quantity of life" to the "production of 'consumers' as well as consumables." Like Patten, Hobson had come to believe that the limits to an expanding standard of living were in men, not in machines or resources.[16]

In 1900, Richard Ely remarked that a "synthesis of the work of Patten and Hobson" would be a "great thing." Hobson himself made this synthesis in 1902, in his most influential book, *Imperialism*. In 1892, Hobson had emphasized the importance of Patten's theory of taxation, which demonstrated "conclusively" that taxes should not be imposed on the "cost of production but always on the surplus value created by all the factors in production." Before this time, Hobson had not thought of taxing any surplus except the unearned increment of land, the surplus value made possible by labor. For Hobson, what Henry George and Karl Marx had begun, Patten completed. Imperialism, Hobson argued, was essentially an outlet for surplus capital. The drain of this surplus caused underconsumption and, more important, impeded social reform, because capital was not available for public uses. A tax on surplus wealth need not disturb the standard of living of the rich. But it could make possible the redistribution of enough wealth to increase consumers' demand and thus stimulate even higher levels of production.[17]

Patten's belief that, in an economy of abundance, public needs could be met by taxing the surplus and not the cost of production gave Hobson the theoretical basis for the central argument of *Imperialism*. Hobson's book, which was the basis of Lenin's *Imperialism: The Highest State of Capitalism*, has had considerable influence on political affairs in the twentieth century. It is partly as a result of Patten's theory of the emergence of an economy of abundance that modern Communists regard

American investments abroad as imperialistic but view their own analogous activities as altruistic service to humanity. In a communistic society, there is no private investment and hence no surplus to tax or to spend on what Hobson and Lenin defined as imperialism.[18]

Closer to home, Patten's central thesis was accepted and promoted by Walter E. Weyl, a University of Pennsylvania Ph.D. in economics who turned to journalism and became a founding editor of the *New Republic*. Weyl conceived his most influential book, *The New Democracy*, published in 1912, as a popularization of Patten's concept of a transition from scarcity to abundance. "My original idea," he told Patten, was to "simplify the first chapter of your *New Basis [of Civilization]* and to give it a statistical foundation." Weyl's book was a ringing call for social reform based on Patten's doctrines. Social action to "extirpate misery" and plan economic development was "simply a quicker turn of the wheel in the direction in which the wheel is already turning." [19]

Weyl's intellectual dilemmas were similar to Patten's. Like Patten, he wanted social reconstruction to be "gradual and quiet, though rapid." In short, he wanted to equalize opportunity and consumption without a major redistribution of wealth. "Gradual rapidity" required faith in a permanent condition of surplus. Weyl, like Patten, left the disturbing implication that if the surplus diminished or if the population curve went up sharply instead of leveling off, efforts at social reform would either have to diminish or to cease entirely. For Weyl as for Patten, the redistribution of wealth and the provision of social services must be sacrificed whenever the economy of abundance was threatened.[20] Hobson and Weyl cared more for social reform than for professional status or the cautious analysis which was beginning to mark "scientific economics."

The third rebel of the period who might have stood with Patten was Thorstein Veblen. The two men had much in common. Both were born on Midwestern farms in the 1850's, and, though Veblen never studied in Germany, he did graduate work at The

Johns Hopkins, Yale, and Cornell universities with men who had. Like Patten, Veblen was deeply influenced by the evolutionary hypothesis and impatient with the traditional boundaries of economics, particularly with the exclusion from consideration of nonrational aspects of human behavior.[21]

There is much in Veblen's work that might have made him hospitable to the concept of abundance. As a young man, he had been deeply influenced by Edward Bellamy's fantasy of abundance, *Looking Backward*. Moreover, Veblen discerned in his own time the "most rapid advance in average wealth and industrial efficiency that the world has ever seen." In addition, his belief that outmoded institutions prevented the realization of the advances of modern technology seems, on the surface, to complement Patten's demand for adjustment to the new basis of civilization.[22]

Yet Veblen took a paradoxical attitude toward Patten's work. Although he believed that Patten's approach to history was a "marked advance over the somewhat crude form" in which Marx and Engels "left their fundamental concept," he rejected the theory of a transition to an age of abundance. Veblen deplored Patten's methodology and psychology. On the one hand, he applauded the "modern scientific animus" which enabled Patten to "look more closely into the causal relations between the economic situation and the resulting culture"; on the other, he rejected Patten's projection of a "normal line of development" which led him to equate the words evolution, amelioration, and progress. To Veblen, Patten was a naïve hedonist and meliorist who did not assign sufficient importance to the dark side of human nature and ignored the disintegration of personality produced by "machine discipline." Veblen was an ascetic who glorified workmanship, or the values of production, and deplored wastemanship, the pursuit of consumption. He emphasized the need for more goods and the value of hard work and of the development of new industrial techniques—what Patten considered virtues of the age of scarcity—rather than the need to educate consumers. Nevertheless, Veblen, unlike most economists, had assumptions and interests which enabled him to acknowledge at least the importance of Patten's ideas.[23]

The frame of reference most hospitable to Patten's ideas was that of the first generation of American sociologists. These men, most of them trained as economists in Germany or the United States, found scientific economics too constricting a discipline. They wanted the freedom to explore social change and its implications in the broadest possible manner, untrammeled by the restriction of economics to the consideration of the classical questions of how material wealth is produced, distributed, and consumed. In the 1890's, American social science was being transformed from a chaotic mixture of approaches to and methods of research into a branch of knowledge divided into increasingly separate disciplines with different conceptual schemes, publications, and vested professional interests. Heated discussions about the scope of political economy, about the relation between economics and sociology, and about the validity of biological analogies destroyed the unity which had characterized the German-trained group of social scientists in the 1880's.[24]

Patten worked hard in the 1890's to maintain the unity of the social sciences. In a debate at the annual meeting of the American Economic Association in 1894, he stood alone for what had already become a lost cause: "We have arrived at a point in the development of the social sciences where we cannot let one another alone." But he foresaw a "cleft between the economic and sociological camps" which was "likely to grow." The cleavage was institutionalized in 1905, when the American Sociological Society was founded at a meeting of the A.E.A. Of the nine men who signed the notice for the first meeting of the Society, all except one, William Graham Sumner, were members of the A.E.A., and all except Sumner and Lester F. Ward had been trained as economists. Six of the thirty-six men who drafted the constitution of the Sociological Society had taken their doctorates under Patten.[25]

Until the 1920's, sociologists in England, Germany, and America were more eager than economists to use "science" to reform society. Following the pattern established by Auguste Comte, who named their discipline, sociologists felt obliged to make pronouncements on disputed public questions. They were a generation behind economists in the development of a public relativism—a desire to view their own society coldly, as one among many in the history of the world. From 1885 to 1920, sociology was a refuge for economists with an urge to preach. To Americans like Patten, Edward A. Ross, and Albion W. Small, sociology was a release from the constraint of talking about change when they yearned to explore the problems of progress.

Lester F. Ward, a self-educated biologist and sociologist with a deep commitment to reforming American society, was the first to perceive that Patten was probing a profound question which was an embarrassment to professional economists. Patten, Ward pointed out, offered an exciting answer to the "most pressing problem of practical philosophy": whether "life is worth living." The concept of a transition from scarcity to abundance was as significant as Charles Darwin's doctrine of natural selection. Patten's work provided the "key to the solution of many psychic puzzles" and justified "meliorism" in moral philosophy.[26]

Ward brought Patten's thesis to the attention of European and American sociologists and used it extensively in his own writings. In July, 1897, for example, he discussed the transition from an economy of scarcity to an economy of abundance at a meeting of the *Institut International de Sociologie* in Paris, at which such renowned sociologists as Gabriel Tarde, Emile Durkheim, and Jacques Novicow were present. Patten's insight, Ward told the Frenchmen in a paper of almost fifty pages, placed the problem of the "purpose of life" in a new context. In 1899, Ward defined "social betterment" in Patten's terms, as the "passing out of a pain economy into a pleasure economy or from an economy that yields only the satisfactions of physical needs to one that fills out the higher spiritual aspirations." Four years later, he generalized Patten's theory of economic change into a broad theory of progress. Rejecting his earlier view, based on the work of Herbert Spencer, that progress was the "objective fact of increasing complexity of organization," Ward declared that a "state in which function is everything and feeling nothing is a typical pain economy." Progress required the growth of feelings—subjective change—as well as the "objective" increase of complexity. "All social progress," Ward asserted, was a "movement from a pain economy toward a pleasure economy." [27]

Nevertheless, Ward had serious reservations about Patten's work. He attacked Patten as intellectually lazy, as perhaps dishonest and possibly "mad." Laziness was reflected in his ignorance of the "general volume of psychological knowledge of the time." Ward felt that Patten had been less than honest in not admitting that "he was driven to the study" of the transition to an age of abundance by dissatisfaction with the concept of the English social theorist Benjamin Kidd that religion is an "ultra-rational sanction" for social reform. Patten seemed "very much afraid that some one [might] imagine that he [was] indebted to others for suggestions." Ward admitted, however, that Kidd's "whole notion of social evolution" was "such as may take place in a pain economy." Finally, Ward attributed the "unevenness" of Patten's thought and his opaque style to a "form of genius" that was "strongly suggestive of paranoia." He concluded, nevertheless, "Dr. Patten may be mad, but he certainly has lucid intervals." [28]

Ward's reservations about Patten were in part personal, in part theoretical. Patten had angered him in 1892 by severely editing an article he had invited Ward to submit to the *Annals*. Ward may have felt that Patten challenged his position as America's leading philosopher of social change. More important, Patten was never comfortable with the assumptions underlying sociological methodology in his time.[29]

Although he told Ward that sociology had "come to stay and for this fact the science owes to no one more than" Ward, Patten publicly vilified the premises of the work of Ward and other sociologists. He denied that the social behavior of the human race was a result of imitation and suggestion. Sociology must rest on "economics as an underlying science." Social change was a result of the increasingly sophisticated calculation of utilities—a result of economic processes. Sociologists like Ward were bemused by analogies drawn from biology. In Ward's books, "analogy and deduction" replaced "true induction." Other sociologists, by using organic metaphors, implicitly denied men freedom and mobility. If men were to regard themselves as cells in a particular part of a social organism, they would lose the ability to transcend their local environments and to work toward blending the "different races of men into a common type." Those who practiced Auguste Comte's "ghost science" were cultivating a "barren and negative field." Only economics, for all its limitations, could provide an appropriately tough-minded underpinning for a general social science.[30]

In his relationship with Edward A. Ross, Patten carried his capricious battle against his strongest supporters to a destructive extreme. When they first met in 1892, Patten tried to enroll Ross as a disciple. In 1894, Patten and Ross quarreled over Ward's *Dynamic Sociology*, which, Ross later recalled, "switched me from economics to sociology." Patten infuriated Ross by rejecting his review of Ward's book for the *Annals* and by announcing a "considerable aversion to Spencer, Ward, and similar writers." Two years later, Patten chided Ross for "giving a little too much time to politics lately." Ross's opposition to unrestricted immigration and his flirtation with doctrines of racial superiority provoked Patten's wrath. After berating him for ignoring the "force of environment as a source of progress," Patten added pedagogy to insult: "You are capable of good work, Ross, and you ought to get down to it." [31]

Patten's petulance was directed against a man who had grasped his challenge to conventional assumptions about economic reality. In his most influential book, *Social Control*, Ross declared that the world was "passing from a 'pain economy' . . . to a 'pleasure economy.' " His exploration of the formation and function of the "collective mind," the source of social control, was based on Patten's thesis. According to Ross, "With the diffusion of higher tastes, society may safely soften its official rancor against life and serenely look forward to the time when ascetic ideas may be dismissed with thanks for their services." Moreover, Ross clearly perceived the problem of restraint, the essential complement to the doctrine of abundance. *Social Control* was an exploration of the genesis and application of restraints in a society moving toward abundance. Yet the two men could not work together to bring home to Ross' audience, a larger group than Patten's, the importance of Patten's thought. They were divided by too deep a personal and theoretical gulf. Nevertheless, in 1937, Ross recalled Patten as a "simple, honest man . . . about as formal and pretentious as Socrates," whose influence was "with me still" and "alive in the minds of thousands of men and women." [32]

It is ironic that the one leading sociologist with whom Patten was in personal accord, Franklin H. Giddings, had no use for the concept of abundance. Giddings served Patten as a confidant and editor but lamented his "strange combination of vision and myopia." They disagreed bitterly over the origin of social feelings, Giddings defending imitation—what he called "consciousness of kind"—and Patten holding fast to the calculation of utility. In methodology and politics the two men were poles apart. Giddings alternated between scientific relativism and blatant espousal of doctrines of Anglo-Saxon superiority and rugged individualism. Patten, impatient with relativism, was committed to a belief in environmentalism and cooperative action. How Patten could remain affectionate to Giddings while feuding with Ross and Ward must remain a psychological riddle.[33]

When Patten died in 1922, the outlook for acceptance of his central thesis seemed dim. His strongest supporters were either dead, like Ward and Weyl, or past their point of greatest influence, like Ross and Hobson. Ross' work was soon eclipsed by the more empirical sociology of the University of Chicago school and the more relativistic theories of men like Max Weber. Hobson's best work was behind him, and even he never completely accepted the theory of a transition from scarcity to abundance. Rexford G. Tugwell, Patten's last doctoral student, showed few signs of becoming an influential theorist.

In the forty years since Patten's death, however, ideas similar to those he pioneered have attracted more adherents than during his lifetime. Many men have noted that, despite a great depression, wars hot and cold, and an unexpected population explosion, the world's productive capacity has increased and the standard of living of most men has been gradually rising. Changes in the external environment have persuaded men in a way that Patten's arguments have not. As Patten discovered in 1898, intellectual history is not the story of the filiation of ideas but an account of men's responses to economic changes around them.[34]

The Triumph of Abundance, 1920–1965

Simon Patten was a forebear, not a source, of present-day thought about the problems of economic abundance. Although his ideas have been relegated to, at best, the status of footnotes, the problems he raised and the arguments he put forward have, in the past forty years, moved from the periphery to the center of economic and social controversy.

Rexford G. Tugwell is the only contemporary theorist on the subject of abundance to consider Patten's ideas the "greatest single influence on [his] thought." Throughout his career as a teacher, presidential adviser, and public administrator, Tugwell, who studied with Patten from 1912 to 1917, has accepted Patten's central thesis. "Not until recently," he declared in 1924, "has it been necessary to consider what ought to be done with an economic surplus." Like Patten, he envisioned a "struggle toward cooperation and coordination . . . to raise living levels and to meet the conditions of new ideals of life." In 1933, justifying national planning for the utilization of natural resources, Tugwell assumed, like Patten, that America had "every needful material for Utopia." He deplored the persistence of misery in a society which could produce enough goods to guarantee every individual the requisites for survival.[1]

Tugwell had more effect on public policy than on social thought. Yet even in his area of greatest influence, the New Deal agricultural program, he supported a plan which used the rhetoric of abundance to justify a policy of scarcity. Under Tugwell's guidance, Henry A. Wallace, Secretary of Agriculture in the first two administrations of Franklin D. Roosevelt, embraced Patten's theme. "The pioneers lived in a scarcity economy," Wallace wrote in 1934; "we have now come to a time of abundance." But because Americans "have not learned how to live with abundance, men go hungry and ragged." Agricultural policy must bring our "social machinery . . . up to date with modern science and modern methods of mass production." At the same time, however, Wallace and Tugwell endorsed the domestic allotment program for the rehabilitation of American agriculture. This plan, based on crop restriction, contradicted the ideas of Simon Patten. Tugwell and Wallace were, in effect, eliminating plenty in a period of want.[2]

This contradiction was perceived by former President Herbert Hoover, whose affection for the competitive principles of the age of scarcity jarred with his engineer's perception of the implications of technological change. Attacking the crop-restriction policy of the Agricultural Adjustment Administration, Hoover claimed that the "economy of plenty through the huge increase in productive power which science has given us" was threatened by "processes of nationalism and regimentation." He was certain that the "triumph of our degree of economic plenty over an economy of scarcity" meant that the "problem of assurance against undeserved poverty is soluble." The solution lay in not disturbing the social and economic arrangements which had made abundance possible. Yet Hoover, like Tugwell and Wallace, was unwilling to carry the logic of abundance as far as Patten had. He refused to admit the possibility that some of these arrangements were based on assumptions appropriate only to the preceding age of scarcity.[3]

Other engineers and scientists did not have Hoover's reluctance. From the time of Justus von Liebig and the medical materialists in the mid-nineteenth century to the present day, many practitioners of science, pure and applied, have been impatient with society's failure to realize the social and economic implications of advances in biology, medicine, chemistry, and physics. In the 1920's, Frederick Soddy, British Nobel laureate in chemistry, looked forward to "universal peace and prosperity" if the industrialized nations would replace an outmoded monetary structure, based on specie and faith, with units based on calculations of energy. During the next two decades, such men of science as J. Arthur Thomson, C. H. Waddington, and Julian Huxley argued that there were no technical obstacles to the creation of an age of plenty. The only obstacles were short-sighted men who did not perceive that the organization of society had not kept pace with the inventive momentum of science and engineering.[4]

In the 1930's, these ideas were publicized in the United States by the Technocrats, led by an engineer, Howard Scott, and were supported by a few popularizers of contemporary economic thought, notably Stuart Chase. Patten's theory of the emergence of an economy of abundance and Thorstein Veblen's emphasis on the central role of engineers in a modern economy blended in the ideas of these men. Scott and the more extreme Technocrats wanted to measure the costs of production in ergs rather than in cash. Chase called for an "industrial general staff" to administer the American economy. Even John Dewey, America's leading philosopher, who had ignored Patten's ideas before the 1930's, sympathized with some of the Technocrats' goals. According to Dewey, the "vision of an age of abundance" was obscured because men's minds were "pathetically held in the clutch of old habits and haunted by old memories."[5]

Simon Patten would have rejected the notion that science and technology provide most of the solutions to the painful problems involved in reorganizing society to enable everyone to partake of abundance. To professional economists, scientists' impatience with the stupidity of social arrangements seems naïve. For most scientists and engineers, discovery and invention, not social organization, are the crucial variables in modern society. All rational men who understand the progress of science and technology can agree on the organizational changes that should follow scientific and technological changes. Economists, on the other hand, are trained to regard the state of invention at any instant in time as a constant. Since organization is the dominant variable, economists are continually aware of the complexity of the human psyche and the messiness of social arrangements. For scientists, the formulation of social policy is generally an exercise in logic; for economists, it has more often been a painful exploration of partial solutions to insoluble problems.[6]

The economist whose solution to some of the problems of the 1930's triggered what many men consider a revolution in economic thought was sure of man's ability to produce enough to go around. John Maynard Keynes's most influential work, *The General Theory of Employment, Interest, and Money,* published in 1936, found an "explanation of the paradox of poverty in the midst of plenty" in the "insufficiency of effective demand," which could "bring the increase of employment to a standstill *before* a level of full employment has been reached." His analysis aimed at "depriving capital of its scarcity-value within one or two generations." [7]

Like Patten and unlike the scientists and engineers, Keynes emphasized the need for restraint in the present to preserve abundance for the future. After full employment was achieved, "it would remain for separate decision . . . by what means it is right and reasonable to call on the living generation to restrict their consumption so as to establish . . . a state of full investment for their descendants." Two years later, in a letter to the *Times* of London, Keynes forestalled any possibility of doubt about the assumption on which his theories were based: "The resources of the country lie in its physical capacity for current production and no shortage exists there. . . . We are still allowing a great volume of potential wealth to evaporate un-utilized." [8]

Keynes had for many years been fascinated by the prospect of an age of abundance. In 1919, attacking the economic arrangements of the Treaty of Versailles, he spoke wistfully of the lost dream that "perhaps a day might come when there would be enough to go round . . . and men, secure of the comforts and necessities of the body, could proceed to the nobler exercise of their faculties." Six years later, addressing a meeting of English Liberals, he emphasized the "economic transition amidst the early stages of which we are now living"—a transition from an "Era of Scarcity" to an "Era of Abundance." The era of abundance would be succeeded by an "Era of Stabilization," when men would "deliberately" control and direct "economic forces in the interests of social justice and social stability." In 1930, Keynes foresaw the end of the "struggle for subsistence" and worried about the implications of mankind's being "deprived of its traditional purpose." [9]

There is no evidence that Keynes read Patten. He assigned credit for the concept of a transition from scarcity to abundance to a man who had pondered Patten's ideas with great care, John R. Commons of the University of Wisconsin. Commons, a student of Richard T. Ely, was ambivalent about Patten's theme throughout his long career. In his first book, published in 1893, Commons quoted Patten frequently but was unwilling to take an unequivocal position on whether the assumption underlying economic analysis was scarcity or abundance. At one point he declared, "Nature, while lavish in her supply of our intense need for air, is niggardly in her supply of food, clothing, and shelter"; at another, that the "control of man over nature has more than compensated for . . . diminished natural resources." In his most important theoretical works, written after Patten's death, he was somewhat less equivocal. [10]

During the 1920's and 1930's, Commons could not decide whether to use the words scarcity and abundance as relative terms applicable to all times and societies or as terms referring to a transformation caused by the Industrial Revolution. In 1924, he defined scarcity, in the manner of most economic theorists, as the "relation of living things to limited resources." A few years later, he argued that although the "workingman's liberty of choice increases with abundance of jobs . . . it is the common law of property, not the abundance of nature's benevolence that regulates." Yet in the same work, which contained the passages later quoted by Keynes, Commons discussed the transition from scarcity to abundance as a specific event and defined the "fundamental contrast between the European and American systems" as the "contrast of poverty with abundance, of low standards of living with high standards of living." [11]

Commons may have believed that his ideas were markedly different from Patten's. He claimed, for example, that the alternative to scarcity was efficiency, not abundance. For Commons, efficiency usually meant an "engineering economy"—a phrase which recalls Thorstein Veblen's concentration on the need for more goods rather than Patten's emphasis on the relationship between increased production and a rising standard of living. Like Veblen, Commons sometimes resembled those scientists who believe that technology will automatically transform social arrangements and individual attitudes.[12]

Yet Commons was uncomfortable with this belief. His commitment to economics forced him to consider in detail men's attitudes toward technology and production. The consideration led him, as it had led Patten and would lead Keynes, to explore the problem of restraining desires and eliminating values inappropriate to the contemporary environment. The period of stabilization—analogous to Patten's "creative economy"—required "new restraints on individual liberty enforced . . . by governmental sanctions . . . but mainly . . . by economic sanctions through concerted action" by cooperating groups. Commons' examination of restraints forced him to expand his earlier definition of efficiency until it contained the implications of Patten's ideas on "adjustment" to abundance. Efficiency,

Commons declared at the end of *Institutional Economics*, "acquires the double meaning of increase of output and increase of income." [13]

Keynes was attracted by Commons' insight into the social and political implications of the transition from scarcity to abundance, not by his efforts to make the concept independent of social philosophy. He ignored Commons' emphasis on the different modes of "legal control and transfer" in periods of scarcity and abundance, quoting only his remarks on the implications for social arrangements of man's ability to produce enough to go around.[14]

Keynes hesitated to claim that acceptance of the doctrines presented in his *General Theory* required a new set of assumptions about economic life. Tracing his forebears in the history of economic thought, he aligned himself with those men, from Malthus to Hobson, who rejected the theory that supply and demand were self-adjusting. The concept of underconsumption, of goods without buyers, does not necessarily imply that enough can be produced to guarantee everyone a minimum standard of living. Full consumption does not have to be adequate consumption. Keynes would have been more accurate if he had claimed Malthus' whipping boy, William Godwin, as his intellectual ancestor.[15]

During the Second World War, moreover, Keynes revealed that his conversion to the point of view supported by Simon Patten was not complete. Responding to the work of William Beveridge and Friedrich Hayek, he accepted both the scarcity and abundance frames of reference. Keynes gave enthusiastic support to the Beveridge plan for overhauling British social insurance. He agreed with Sir William that the "abolition of want just before this war was easily within the economic resources of the community." Two years later, however, he was in "deeply moved agreement" with "virtually the whole" of Hayek's *The Road to Serfdom*. Hayek's book rested on the assumption of scarcity. In order to justify the social arrangements of laissez-faire liberalism, he heaped abuse on the "familiar clichés and baseless generalizations about 'potential plenty.' " According to Hayek, "Whoever talks about potential plenty is either dishonest or does not know what he is talking about." [16]

Unlike Keynes, who pulled back from the assumption of abundance, Colin Clark, an English economist on whose work Hayek based his attack on prophets of plenty, moved from a scarcity to an abundance frame of reference. The first edition of Clark's *The Conditions of Economic Progress*, published in 1940, made so convincing a case against the possibility of enough to go around that Hayek neglected to cite any other source. By 1947, Clark had reversed his opinion. In a new edition of his book, he deleted his attack on the "clichés" about "poverty in the midst of plenty" and asserted that the "existence of Increasing Returns . . . the state of affairs in which the net quantity of real product obtained per unit of effort expended increases as a consequence of an increased scale of production." [17]

Many of the points Clark made on the basis of his new frame of reference supported arguments put forward by Patten a half-century earlier. He attacked Malthusians for ignoring the possibility that "many of the refinements and economies of civilization only become possible under conditions of much higher population density." Moreover, like Patten, he defended the use of protective tariffs to "build up increasing returns industries" and government control of competition to secure the "most satisfactory output and prices." Like Patten, Clark asserted that the restraints necessary to prevent inappropriate consumption in an age of abundance should not be based on the "false spirituality" developed in the long age of scarcity. For the present, expanding consumption was more important than restraint: "Anything we can do to enable other people to satisfy their material wants is a . . . genuine act of charity." [18]

Clark's transformation was part of a more general acceptance of the abundance frame of reference in the 1940's and 1950's. In these decades, many economists, scientists, and social theorists wrote as if the affluence of the West and the potential plenty of the undeveloped nations were established facts. The rapid ex-

pansion of production in the United States and England during
the war and the recovery of the European economy after 1945
removed many men's doubts about the possibility of plenty. By
1950, rapid economic growth and the success of Keynes's proposals as guides to public policy had led many men to regard as
obvious truths what, a generation earlier, seemed the imaginings
of misguided optimism. In 1949, for example, D. H. Macgregor,
professor of economics at Oxford, brought the themes of scientists and economists together in a new synthesis. According
to Macgregor, the problems of abundance could be solved by
placing equal emphasis on the analysis of invention, discovery,
organization, and the attitudes of individuals. Although many
economists objected to the vagueness and subjectivity of the
concept of abundance, and although many socialists clung to
their belief that a decent standard of living for all must wait
upon a thoroughgoing redistribution of wealth, it seemed clear
by the early 1950's that most men professionally concerned
with social change were content to work within the existing
order to make more efficient the distribution of the goods with
which an age of abundance had begun to be established.[19]

During the past fifteen years, it has not been necessary to defend the possibility of a transformation from an age of scarcity
to an age of abundance. The most frequently debated issues
have been whether social theorists should talk of an affluent
society as an established fact or as a potential condition, and
what the existence, or the approach, of abundance implies for
social policy. In 1965, as the legislative and administrative machinery of the American government moved toward the establishment of a "Great Society" based on the capacity to produce
enough goods to guarantee everyone a constantly improving
standard of living, the questions which disturbed Simon Patten
at the turn of the century had not been answered. It is one thing
to agree that social policy shall be concerned with *optima* rather
than *minima*, quite another to define the characteristics of the
good life. It is easier to decide that men must restrain certain
desires than to find efficient ways of inculcating these restraints.

J. K. Galbraith's 1958 best seller, *The Affluent Society*, focused public attention on the concepts and rhetoric pioneered
by Simon Patten. For the first time in history, "Western man"
has "escaped" from the "cycle of poverty." The momentous
task of social theory and public policy is to build a "bridge" between the "world of scarcity and that of affluence." Although
men have solved the "problems of producing goods," they spend
more time worrying about production than about the "next
task," that of adapting public and private values to the new conditions of economic life. Like Patten, Galbraith is concerned
about the increasing invisibility of the poor, the problems of
overconsumption, and the neglect of education to improve
habits of consumption. Solutions to these problems are thwarted
by inappropriate values which create a situation in which private
affluence exists in contrast to "public squalor." Galbraith, like
Patten a son of rural Presbyterians, is uneasy about the desire for
material goods which prevents wealth from being used to create a "social balance" in which all men have equal access to the
fruits of abundance. Like Patten, he yearns for a reassertion of
the Protestant ethic, updated to suit modern conditions. If men
can restrain the greed and prevent the insecurity born of scarcity, new public virtues, attuned to abundance, will develop.[20]

Two years later, Walt W. Rostow, a prominent student of
economic development, took issue with Galbraith's optimism
about the American economy and argued that abundance in
America is merely potential. Scarcity will persist as long as the
United States feels itself obligated to help the undeveloped nations through the stages of economic growth from the conditions of a traditional society toward an "age of high mass consumption." Rostow's analysis of societies which have attained
high mass consumption is, however, similar to the descriptions
of Patten and Galbraith. He notes, for instance, that in the
United States, England, and Canada in the 1950's, the "balance
of attention" shifted from "supply to demand, from problems
of production to problems of consumption and of welfare in
the widest sense." Moreover, Rostow is concerned about the

possibility of "secular spiritual stagnation" in an age of abundance unless men increase their consumption of what Patten called "aesthetic" goods. Like Patten and Galbraith, he is a moralist as well as an economist. He values the "adventure of seeing what man can and will do when the pressure of scarcity is removed, when men can operate at the "full stretch of our moral commitment, our energy, and our resources." [21]

The difference between Galbraith and Rostow is substantial, despite their wide area of agreement. Their points of view are conditioned by divergent intellectual heritages. Galbraith's mode of reasoning is primarily deductive. Although he is ironical about the "conventional wisdom" that results from adherence to the doctrines and methods of classical economics, most of his work is within the classical tradition. Like John Maynard Keynes, also a product of the classical style, Galbraith is more comfortable with logic than with historical and sociological data. [22]

Rostow's intellectual forebears, however, are the German historical economists and their American students of social and economic development. Over the past forty years, students of economic development have had an ambivalent attitude toward the concept of a transition from scarcity to abundance. On the one hand, they recognized the potential abundance of the developed nations; on the other, they feared the narrowing nationalism implicit in the declaration that abundance characterized the world—when, in actuality, the majority of people still struggled for subsistence. This ambivalence is reflected in the work of such scholars as Colin Clark and Eugene Staley. It is significant that, of those who believed that Patten's concept of an "economy of plenty" was of "seminal" importance, the only economist whose works are still studied is Joseph Schumpeter, himself a seminal thinker on economic development. [23]

It is probably more important for the state of contemporary thought about abundance that Schumpeter, in his own work, never utilized Patten's insights. In a sense, Patten encompassed in his own mind the two different kinds of thinking later evident in Galbraith and Rostow. Because he tried to be at the same time

"English" and "German," deductive and historical, he could not speak directly to the more specialized economists of a later generation. Students of development found his theoretical excursions irrelevant; theorists probably considered tiresome his concern for the complexities of the past and the present.

The present state of thinking about the implications of abundance seems to require men who share Patten's determination to use both logic and evidence. As the concept of abundance has become part of the conventional wisdom, there has been a lack of restraint among converts to the new frame of reference. As the existence of abundance, actual or potential, becomes "obvious," in the way the persistence of scarcity was self-evident a century ago, there has been an abundance of *ad hoc* opinions and a scarcity of disciplined research. Two schools of thought have developed. One group, which agrees with Galbraith that social thought should be based on the assumption of abundance, searches for efficient ways of supplying incomes or claims on abundant goods to the minority of Americans and the majority of other peoples who do not participate in the affluent society, and making available new ways of using leisure to those who do. The other group, which accepts Rostow's doctrine that abundance is merely an exciting possibility, emphasizes the need to provide work, rather than income, for the unemployed, the threat of scarcity from the misuse of natural resources, and the danger that the possibility of abundance may become a new justification for the preservation of the *status quo* in economic organization.[24]

The contemporary uncertainty about the implications of abundance is reflected in the work of the sociologist David Riesman. In 1950, Riesman and two associates at the University of Chicago published *The Lonely Crowd*, in which they assumed that the United States "is rapidly, if unevenly, becoming an affluent society." According to Riesman, the "primary problem for the future will be what to do with the surplus of time and resources on our hands." During the next decade, Riesman wrote numerous essays on this theme. Without examining the complex issues of economic theory involved in the concept of abundance, he attempts to analyze the effects of abundance on American society. He manages to agree with every other student of abundance, no matter what his views. Our era, for instance, is one of "abundance," "potential abundance," a "taste of abundance," and "relative abundance." At some points he emphasizes the pressing need to make leisure creative; at others, he gives priority to making work creative. He frequently writes as if the United States were his only concern; yet, just as often, he is a fervent internationalist, eager to help developing nations. In the collection of essays published in 1964 as *Abundance for What?* Riesman makes almost every point about abundance and restraint that has been made in social thought from Patten's first book to the present day.[25]

Yet Riesman is more than a superficial popularizer, more than a new Harriet Martineau spreading, and thinning, the word about a new way of viewing economic life. *The Lonely Crowd* was the first attempt to examine systematically the effects on the attitudes of individuals of a change from a production to a consumption orientation. His conclusion that men have lost their "social freedom and their individual autonomy in seeking to become like each other" in an economy of abundance echoes Simon Patten's fears about the results of an unrestrained embracing of affluence by the American middle class. Unlike Patten, however, Riesman and his associates sought empirical evidence of the effects of affluence on individuals.[26]

Just as few economists have examined the implications of Riesman's conception of the transition from "inner-directed" to "other-directed" personalities, Riesman has not benefited from philosopher Herbert Marcuse's 1955 book, *Eros and Civilization*. Marcuse argues that a condition of abundance should modify the concept of "reality" by which actions and feelings are judged. Sigmund Freud's definition of reality, which Marcuse labels the "performance principle," was relevant to an age of scarcity, when men had to struggle to subsist. That struggle, as well as the utility of the performance principle, is ending. The restraint and repression of desires necessary for existence in the age of scarcity are irrelevant to an era which possesses the "means for fulfilling human needs with a minimum of toil." When men define their standard of living in terms of "automobiles, television sets, airplanes, and tractors," they are using an outmoded definition of reality. Marcuse would measure the "level of living" by the extent of "universal gratification of the basic human needs, and the freedom from guilt and fear." Concerned, like Patten, with basing morality on joy rather than fear, Marcuse calls for a "struggle against any constraint on the free play of human faculties, against toil, disease, and death." [27]

Where Patten could use economics, history, sociology, biology, and psychology to explore the implications of abundance, men like Galbraith, Rostow, Riesman, and Marcuse are insulated from each other's thinking. There are connections between the concepts of public squalor, of the stages of economic growth, of other-directedness, and of a changing reality principle which could be of service in the formulation of programs for education, labor, economic growth, and social welfare. Most economists avoid the issues of abundance because the concept involves a degree of subjectivity which threatens their efforts to create a "value-free" science. But even though the assumption of abundance requires a normative answer to the question, "How much is enough?" the answers to questions posed for research do not necessarily have to rest on subjective judgments. Similarly, the refusal of men like Riesman and Marcuse to examine in detail the economic causes and implications of abundance, which leads them to oversimplify such issues as consumers' choice, economic growth, and the costs of labor, suggests that the present boundaries separating the various social and behavioral sciences may be inappropriate.

The concept of abundance is now the first principle of American social policy. In the 1930's, Franklin D. Roosevelt alternated between the assumption of scarcity, reflected in the crop-restriction program and his longing for a balanced budget, and the assumption that the United States could produce enough goods to provide a decent standard of living for the one-third of a nation who were ill-fed, ill-clothed, and ill-housed. In the mid-1960's, Lyndon B. Johnson eliminated from his own pronouncements the ambivalence of Roosevelt's vision. Addressing the Democratic National Convention in the summer of 1964, he declared, "This nation . . . has man's first chance to build a great society, a place where the meaning of man's life matches the marvels of man's labor." Five months later, in his State of the Union address, Johnson assumed that America is in the "midst of abundance." Men, freed from the "wants of the body," could seek fulfillment of the "needs of the spirit." The pioneering vision of Simon Patten has become public policy. The next step, the development of programs for action based on the assumption of abundance, lies ahead.[28]

The vision of abundance, of enough to go around, has been part of the spiritual heritage of Western man for thousands of years. In biblical times, men dreamed of a land of milk and honey. In subsequent centuries, utopian writers looked back to a golden age behind them or forward to a golden age ahead. Yet deep in the Judaeo-Christian heritage is the belief that, because of Adam's sin, men must accept scarcity on this earth. An economy of abundance was destroyed when the first mortals were expelled from Eden for lack of appropriate restraint.

In the eighteenth and nineteenth centuries, however, changes in technology and in the organization of production provided new grounds for optimism. The theory of economics was created to explain and justify this optimism. In the early nineteenth century, when the problems of industrialism became more obvious, pessimism became the dominant tone of economic thought. Yet even Thomas Malthus, whose arguments persuaded many men of the inevitability of scarcity, believed that moral restraint could lead to a "great actual population and a state of society in which abject poverty and dependence are comparatively but little known." [29]

The optimism which had sustained social science in the eighteenth century has been reasserted in our time by American scholars whose work was foreshadowed in the ideas of Simon Patten. America, a land to which many utopians have, for four centuries, transferred their hopes, was the first nation to develop an economy which gave substance to the dream of an age of plenty. America was also a land where the creation of abundance was dependent on the tenacity of restraints against powerful feelings. Hard, disciplined work was required to transform the prairie sod into acres of wheat and corn. Industrial wealth was created at vast cost to the health and welfare of employers and workers. Simon Patten realized that the restraints which had enabled men to produce enough to go around were not appropriate in an age of abundance. It was no longer necessary to disregard joy, health, and sympathy and concentrate on the struggle for subsistence. The sudden removal of old restraints might, however, destroy the economy of abundance. The long age of scarcity had conditioned men to seize, in their rare moments of affluence and leisure, the pleasures that were available. It was necessary to call upon science, social and natural, for new restraints which would enable men to enjoy and perpetuate the age of abundance.

The discovery of abundance has given the world of the mid-twentieth century new grounds for both hope and concern. It remains to be seen whether we will be able to create those restraints, attuned to a new view of economic reality, which will enable us to transform the human condition.

Notes

The titles of frequently cited periodicals have been abbreviated as follows:

AEA Bull.	*Bulletin of the American Economic Association*
AEA Pubs.	*Publications of the American Economic Association*
AER	*American Economic Review*
AJS	*American Journal of Sociology*
ASS Pubs.	*Publications of the American Sociological Society*
CC	*Charities and the Commons*
EJ	*Economic Journal*
ER	*Educational Review*
IJE	*International Journal of Ethics*
Ind	*The Independent*
Jahrbücher	*Jahrbücher für Nationalökonomie und Statistik*
JPE	*Journal of Political Economy*
Mon	*The Monist*
Moody's	*Moody's Magazine*
Na	*The Nation*
NR	*New Republic*

PSM	*Popular Science Monthly*
PSQ	*Political Science Quarterly*
QJE	*Quarterly Journal of Economics*
Sci	*Science*, New Series
Sur	*The Survey*
YR	*Yale Review*

A Note on the Author's Assumptions

1. Roy Harrod, *The Life of John Maynard Keynes* (London, 1951), 193–194. On the relationship between abstractions and reality in economics, cf. Joseph Schumpeter, *History of Economic Analysis* (New York, 1954), 41–42: "Analytic work begins with material provided by our vision of things, and this vision is ideological almost by definition. It embodies the picture of things as we see them."

2. The interpretation of the history of religious toleration presented here is derived from Wilbur K. Jordan, *The Development of Religious Toleration in England* (Cambridge and London, 1932–1940), 4 vols.

Introduction. The Context of Scarcity, 1750–1880

1. For the image and the anti-image see Howard Mumford Jones, *O Strange New World* (New York, 1964), chs. i–ii. The best introductions to the origins of economics as a discipline are Joseph Schumpeter, *History of Economic Analysis* (New York, 1954), and O. H. Taylor, *A History of Economic Thought* (New York, 1960).

2. D. H. Macgregor, *Economic Thought and Policy* (London, 1949), 1–30, and John R. Commons, *Institutional Economics* (New York, 1934), *passim*, are the best surveys of the concept of scarcity in eighteenth- and nineteenth-century economic thought.

3. Most popular histories of economic thought divide the classical economists into optimists and pessimists. Probably the most influential exponents of this view were Charles Gide and Charles Rist, *History of Economic Doctrines* (Paris, 1913; Boston, 1914).

4. This point of view in favor of ambiguity is taken by Schumpeter, Taylor, Mark Blaug, *Ricardian Economics* (New Haven, 1958), Gertrude Himmelfarb in her Introduction to *On Population*

by Thomas Robert Malthus (New York, 1960), and T. W. Hutchison, *A Review of Economic Doctrines, 1870–1929* (Oxford, 1953).

5. Blaug, 5, 12–14, 64–66, 93, 105; cf. Patrick Colquohoun, *Treatise on Indigence* (London, 1806), 7–8.

6. Himmelfarb, xxvii, 549, 583–594; Blaug, 32–33.

7. Blaug, 8; Hutchison, 7; Calvin Woodward, "Reality and Social Reform: The Transition from Laissez-Faire to the Welfare State," *Yale Law Journal*, LXXVII (Dec., 1962), 286–328.

8. Malthus, 131; James Mill, *An Essay on Government* (London, 1820; New York, 1955), 60. For an economist's view of Mandeville, see Simon N. Patten, *The Development of English Thought* (New York, 1898), 204ff; cf. Harry K. Girvetz, *The Evolution of Liberalism* (New York, 1963), ch. i.

9. Hutchison, 79, 325; cf. T. W. Hutchison, *Positive Economics and Policy Objectives* (Cambridge, Mass., 1964), 86: "In applying any model to explain or predict an actual historical case, the economist has to select or 'weigh' what he considers to be the actually important forces at work."

10. Blaug, 26, 190; Frank W. Taussig, "Stationary State," in Henry Higgs, ed., *Palgrave's Dictionary of Political Economy* (London, 1926), 466; cf. B. J. Horton, ed., *Dictionary of Modern Economics* (Washington, 1948), 314.

11. *Principles of Political Economy* (London, 1848, and subsequent editions), Bk. iv, ch. vi, sec. 2; Hutchison, *Positive Economics*, 140; Blaug, 189–190.

12. Hutchison, *Review*, 53; Blaug, 92–93, 117–118, 190–191; George Lichtheim, *Marxism: An Historical and Critical Study* (New York, 1961), 211.

13. Hutchison, *Review*, 136; Jack C. Myles, "German Historicism and American Economics" (unpublished dissertation, Princeton University, 1956), chs. i–ii.

14. Lichtheim, 179, 189, 372; Karl Marx, *Critique of the Gotha Program* (Moscow, 1947), 26–27, 33.

15. Karl Marx, *Capital* (New York, 1906), 11–26.

16. Hutchison, *Review*, 11–13, 27; Blaug, 214.

17. Hutchinson, *Review*, 29–30, 140; Blaug, 229; R. S. Howey, *The Rise of the Marginal Utility School, 1870–1889* (Lawrence, Kan., 1960), *passim*.

18. George J. Stigler, "The Early History of Empirical Studies of Consumer Behavior," *JPE*, LXII (April, 1954), 95–113; John Roscoe Turner, *The Ricardian Rent Theory in Early American Economics* (New York, 1921), *passim*.

Chapter I. Illinois and Germany, 1852–1885

1. Rexford Guy Tugwell, "Notes on the Life and Work of Simon Nelson Patten," *JPE*, XXXI (April, 1923), 159; Jennie M. Patten, *History of the Somonauk United Presbyterian Church* (Chicago, 1928), 17–19, 36–37, 44.

2. Tugwell, 161; Jennie Patten, *History*, 64, 213–214.

3. Tugwell, 174.

4. Howard Mumford Jones, *O Strange New World* (New York, 1964), 196, 215.

5. Jennie Patten, *History*, 276, 213, 284; Tugwell, 158.

6. Patten, *History*, 210, 287; Tugwell, 165.

7. State of Illinois, *Journal of the House of Representatives*, 19th General Assembly, sess. beginning Jan. 1, 1855 (Springfield, 1855), 37, 68, 395–396, 414; 21st General Assembly, sess. beginning Jan. 3, 1859 (Springfield, 1859), 32, 215, 259, 291, 691–694, 757.

8. Simon N. Patten, *Mud Hollow: From Dust to Soul* (Philadelphia, 1922), 255–256; cf. Jane Addams, *The First Twenty Years at Hull House* (New York, 1910), 23–42. William Patten was active as an army recruiter during most of the Civil War and went to war himself, as a captain in the 156th Illinois Volunteers, in March, 1865 (J. W. Vance, *Report of the Adjutant General of the State of Illinois* [Springfield, 1886], 453). After the war, William Patten was elected to the state senate, where he served four years.

9. Patten, *Mud Hollow*, 255.

10. Jennie Patten, *History*, 249–250; Simon Patten, *Mud Hollow*, 320.

11. *Register of the Thirty-First Session of the Rock River Annual Conference of the Methodist Episcopal Church* (Chicago, 1871), 23; *Twelfth Annual Catalogue of Jennings Seminary at Aurora, Kane County, Illinois* (Aurora, 1870), *passim*. For Patten's grades and curriculum, see "Statement of Scholarship, Simon N. Patten, Student, G. W. Quereau, Principal, Jennings Seminary, Aurora," June 12, 1873, Central Records Department, Northwestern University, Evanston, Ill.; Northwestern University, Registrar's Office, "Northwestern Students Records, 1859–1886," 26; Northwestern University, *Catalogue of the Northwestern University for the Academic Year 1873–74* (Racine, 1873), 62; Arthur Herbert Wilde, *Northwestern University: A History, 1855–1905* (New York, 1905), I, *passim*.

12. The first legend can be found in Edward T. Devine, *When Social Work Was Young* (New York, 1938), 11, and in John Rutherford Everett, *Religion in Economics* (New York, 1956), 99–103, the second in Tugwell, 170.

13. Simon N. Patten, Philadelphia, Pa., to Richard T. Ely, Oct. 22, 1909, Ely Papers, State Historical Society of Wisconsin, Box 13. Joseph Johnson, the friend who urged Patten to join him in Germany, and who later recalled that he himself "did not like the German economists," probably did not write of intellectual matters, and Patten had not yet met Edmund James, who might have gone into detail about Johannes Conrad and the German approach to social science (Joseph F. Johnson, New York, to Henry W. Farnam, n.d. but probably 1906, Farnam Papers, Yale University Library).

14. G. Stanley Hall, *Life and Confessions of a Psychologist* (New York, 1923), 219–221; Richard T. Ely, *Ground under Our Feet* (New York, 1938), 37; Joseph Dorfman, "The Role of the German Historical School in American Economic Thought," *AER*, XLV (May, 1955), 18, 23.

15. Charles Franklin Thwing, *The American and the German University* (New York, 1928), *passim;* Edmund J. James, "University Reform in Germany," ms., n.d., James Papers, University of Illinois Archives, *passim.*

16. Ely, *Ground, passim;* Frank W. Taussig, "College Graduates in Germany," *Na*, XI (April 2, 1885), 275–276; Tugwell, 177; William H. Allen to the author; Eugene Seligman, Heidelberg, Ger., to Edwin R. A. Seligman, June 24, 1879, Seligman Papers, Columbia University Library.

17. Patten, Freiburg im Breisgau, Ger., to Giddings, March 24, 1898, Giddings Papers, Columbia University Library.

18. Karl Diehl, "Johannes Conrad," *Jahrbücher*, CIV (1915), 737–740, 742. For Conrad's later estimation of Patten's work, see his *Grundriss zum Studium der Politischen Ökonomie* (Jena, Ger., 1896), 3, 4, 7, and Devine, 13.

19. Johannes Conrad, *Liebig's Ansicht von der Bodenschöpfung und ihre Geschichtliche, Statistische, und Nationalökonomische Begründung* (Jena, 1864), 123–124, 126, 138, 140–141, 150.

20. Jack C. Myles, "German Historicism and American Economics" (unpublished dissertation, Princeton University, 1956), chs. i, ii; William J. Ashley, "Roscher's Programme of 1843," *QJE*, IX (Oct., 1894), 100, 102–103.

21. Myles, ch. i; T. W. Hutchison, *A Review of Economic Doc-*

trines, 1870–1929 (Oxford, 1953), 4, 130–136; R. S. Howey, *The Rise of the Marginal Utility School, 1870–1889* (Lawrence, Kan., 1960), *passim*.

22. Myles, 60–75; Hutchison, *Review*, 130–132; Henry R. Seager, "Economics at Berlin and Vienna," *JPE*, I (March, 1893), 236–262; Henry Grossman, "The Evolutionist Revolt against Classical Economics," *JPE*, LI (Oct., Dec., 1943), 381–396, 506–522.

23. Hutchison, *Review*, 21, 180; Myles, 64; cf. Gunnar Myrdal, *The Political Element in the Development of Economic Theory* (Cambridge, Mass., 1954), 4; cf. Joseph Schumpeter, *History of Economic Analysis* (New York, 1954), 811–815; cf. Anne Ashley, *The Social Policy of Bismarck* (London, 1912).

24. Seager, 243; Ely, 114; Schumpeter, 867; Julien Benda, *La Trahison des Clercs* (Paris, 1927).

25. Diehl, 742, 750; Simon N. Patten, *Das Finanzwesen der Städte und Staate der Vereinigten Staaten* (Jena, Ger., 1878).

26. Patten, Philadelphia, Pa., to Ely, Oct. 22, 1909, Ely Papers, Box 73; cf. Patten, Philadelphia, Pa., to Farnam, n.d., Farnam Papers.

27. Ely, 121–126; cf. Anna Haddow, *Political Science in American Colleges and Universities* (New York, 1939).

28. Tugwell, 177–179.

29. *Ibid.*, 180; Ely, 169; Devine, 11. The fact that Patten began his teaching career in elementary and secondary schools does not indicate that he lacked direction in his career. There was no formal academic ladder in the 1880's. Hundreds of eminent scholars of the period also started as teachers in grammar or high schools.

30. Patten, Philadelphia, Pa., to Ely, Feb. 20, 1900, Ely Papers, Box 8. Patten and Ely had discussed the problems involved in publishing the book in 1885 (Patten, Sandwich, Ill., to Ely, July 18, 1885, Ely Papers, Box 1).

31. Simon N. Patten, *The Premises of Political Economy* (Philadelphia, 1885), 10, 14.

32. *Ibid.*, 21–32, 59–60.

33. *Ibid.*, 72–86. Earlier American economists, particularly George Tucker and Henry C. Carey, had attacked the law of diminishing returns. These men were not, however, trained in the conventions of economic debate. Moreover, the history of American economic thought seems to have been discontinuous. Patten may have read Henry Carey before he wrote *The Premises*, but he had a low opinion of him, and it is probable that Patten did not know anything about George Tucker until many years later. For earlier attacks

on the law of diminishing returns see John Roscoe Turner, *The Ricardian Rent Theory in Early American Economics* (New York, 1921), 104–107; Henry W. Spiegel, *The Rise of American Economic Thought* (New York, 1960), 110; Arnold W. Green, *Henry Charles Carey: Nineteenth Century Sociologist* (Philadelphia, 1951), *passim*.

34. Green, 46, 53, 56, 59, 64. Patten had not studied marginal-utility analysis when he wrote *The Premises*. He apparently did not discover the work of Karl Menger, W. S. Jevons, and John Bates Clark until 1886 (Patten, Morton Grove, Ill., to John Bates Clark, Nov. 1, 1886, Clark Papers, Columbia University Library). In 1901, Patten told Ely, "I still hold the same views on the doctrines advanced in my *Premises*, though it is easy to see how new material could modify some of the conclusions," and noted that the "marginal utility theory of value" had "modified the scope of the science and altered its content" (Patten, Philadelphia, Pa., to Ely, March 6, 1901, Ely Papers, Box 35).

35. Patten, *The Premises*, 17–20.

36. *Ibid.*, 188–191.

37. *Ibid.*, 216–217.

38. *Ibid.*, 221, 234, 236–237, 241. Sumner was bitterly opposed to the implications of German economics. In 1907, for instance, he declared, "I cannot see that German economists have ever won any doctrine by their methods and I think that it is fallacious to try to deduce doctrines from history. . . . I have largely lost faith in economics as a discipline. . . . It is complicated with history, politics, and ethics and cannot get standing ground as a science" (William Graham Sumner, Fisher's Island, Me., to Farnam, June 29, 1907, Farnam Papers).

39. Patten, *The Premises*, 244. Since *The Premises* appeared before the German-trained economists had established any journals, the book received no public notice from men qualified to review it. Patten later declared that the book was poorly received. There are numerous references to it in American writings on economics in the 1890's, but most of Patten's colleagues seem to have read *The Premises* after they had studied his later work (Ely, Madison, Wis., to Patten, Feb. 23, 1901; Patten, Philadelphia, Pa., to Ely, Feb. 20, March 16, 1901, Ely Papers, Boxes 28, 34, 35). There was, however, one German review of *The Premises* (E. Leser, *Jahrbücher*, XIV [1887], 267–274). Leser declared that Patten was presenting "new truths of general significance."

Chapter II. Professionalism and Social Change, 1885–1910

1. Simon N. Patten, Philadelphia, Pa., to Richard T. Ely, Oct. 22, 1909, Jan. 26, 1910, Ely Papers, State Historical Society of Wisconsin, Boxes 74–75; cf. Henry W. Farnam, New Haven, Conn., to Ely, Feb. 8, 1910, Edmund J. James, Urbana-Champaign, Ill., to Ely, Dec. 11, 1909, Edwin R. A. Seligman, New York, N.Y., to Ely, Nov. 16, 1909, March 14, 1910, Ely Papers, Boxes 74–75.

2. Patten to Ely, Oct. 22, 1909, Patten, Sandwich, Ill., to Ely, July 18, 1885, Ely Papers, Box 1; John Bates Clark, Northhampton, Mass., to Henry Carter Adams, Jan. 24, 1888, Clark Papers, Columbia University Library; Andrew D. White, Ithaca, N.Y., to Ely, July 6, 1885, Franklin H. Giddings, Holyoke, Mass., to Ely, Nov. 2, 1886, James, Philadelphia, Pa., to Ely, Oct. 15, 1886, Frank W. Taussig, Cambridge, Mass., to Ely, Oct. 10, 1886, Ely Papers, Boxes 1–2; Arthur T. Hadley, Berlin, Ger., to Farnam, May 8, 1879, Farnam Papers, Yale University Library; Thomas M. Cooley, "Diary," n.p., n.d., Cooley Papers, Michigan Historical Collections; Henry C. Adams, Ithaca, N.Y., to James K. Angell, March 26, 1886, Adams Papers, Ann Arbor, Mich.; Henry C. Adams, "The Position of Socialism in the Historical Development of Political Economy," *Penn Monthly*, X (April, 1879), 294.

3. Patten to Ely, Oct. 22, 1909; Alfred W. Coats, "The Political Economy Club: A Neglected Episode in American Economic Thought," *AER*, LI (Sept., 1961), 625, 634; "The First Two Decades of the American Economic Association," *AER*, L (Sept., 1960), 556–557.

4. On the sociology of professions see Howard S. Becker, "The Nature of a Profession," *Yearbook of the National Society for the Study of Education*, LXI (Chicago, 1962); Everett C. Hughes, *Men and Their Work* (Glencoe, Ill., 1958).

5. Joseph Dorfman, *The Economic Mind in American Civilization* (New York, 1946), III, *passim*; Charles A. Barker, *Henry George* (New York, 1955).

6. See below, Ch. IX. See also Richard T. Ely, "The American Economic Association, 1885–1909," *American Economic Association Quarterly*, XI (April, 1910), 68; *Ground under Our Feet* (New York, 1938), 125, 133; Jack C. Myles, *German Historicism and American Economics* (unpublished dissertation, Princeton University, 1956), 135–136.

7. Albion W. Small, *The Origins of Sociology* (Chicago, 1924),

245; Eugen von Philippovich, "The Verein für Sozialpolitik," *QJE,*
V (Jan., 1891), 227.

8. Philippovich, "The Verein," 232; Joseph Schumpeter, *History
of Economic Analysis* (New York, 1954), 802, 804; cf. Eugen von
Philippovich, "The Infusion of Socio-Political Ideas into the Literature of German Economics," *AJS,* XVIII (Sept., 1912), 145–199.

9. Coats, "The Political Economy Club," 631, 634; Myles, 135,
154.

10. Ely, "The American Economic Association," 55–61; *Ground,*
134–140. Ely's interpretation was a compromise, to avoid dispute
among his colleagues in 1910, rather than a documented historical
study. In 1909, when Ely was preparing his history of the first
twenty-five years of the Association, Patten and James disputed his
initial claim to full credit as founder. The dispute never became
public, because Ely agreed to give Patten and James greater importance in his history; Patten disliked controversy and tried to
smooth over the differences, and James's illness prevented him from
searching for more accurate data about what had happened a quarter-
century earlier. Ely first told James, "I more than anyone else must
be regarded as the founder." James had reminded Ely that they and
Patten had "discussed the matter" in Baltimore in February, 1883.
Patten persuaded James to let the matter rest, but agreed that "Ely's
assumption that he set the ball rolling should be disputed if he
makes it in his paper." When Ely agreed to place more emphasis
on the role of Patten and James in founding the Association, Patten
persuaded James that it was "a great gain to have our platform
thus accepted as the starting point." Ely finally admitted to James
that he "was influenced by" him in 1884 and 1885. Ely was extremely emotional about his priority in the A.E.A. He almost refused to present his paper, for example, because his old enemies,
J. Laurence Laughlin of Chicago and Arthur T. Hadley of Yale,
were scheduled to participate in the twenty-fifth anniversary cele-
bration (James, Urbana-Champaign, Ill., to Ely, Nov. 29, 1909, Ely,
Madison, Wis., to James, Dec. 1, 17, 1909, Ely, Madison, Wis., to
Davis R. Dewey, Dec. 4, 1909, Ely Papers, Box 74; Patten, Philadelphia, Pa., to James, Dec. 13, 22, 1909, James Papers, University
of Illinois Archives; James, Urbana-Champaign, Ill., to Ely, March
4, 1905, Patten, Sandwich, Ill., to Ely, July 18, 1885, Ely Papers,
Boxes 1, 57).

11. Ely, *Ground,* 296; James and Patten, "Society for the Study
of National Economy," copy of original draft, 1, James Papers.

12. Ely, *Ground,* 297–299; James and Patten, 2–3.

13. James and Patten, "Society for the Study of National Economy," typescript with corrections, 1, 2, 4, 5, James Papers.

14. Ely, Baltimore, Md., to Seligman, June 9, 23, 1885, Seligman Papers, Columbia University Library; White, Ithaca, N.Y., to Ely, June 24, 1885, Patten to Ely, July 18, 1885, Ely Papers, Box 1. The ten economists who attended the first meeting were James, Ely, Henry C. Adams, Edward W. Bemis, Clarence Bowen, John B. Clark, Davis R. Dewey, Washington Gladden, Edwin R. A. Seligman, and Andrew D. White. Francis A. Walker, Lyman Abbott, William W. Folwell, Franklin H. Giddings, Albert Shaw, and Woodrow Wilson, though not present at the meeting, became officers or committee members during the first year. Patten, Albert Bolles, Henry B. Gardner, E. R. L. Gould, J. W. Jenks, L. C. Powers, and Stuart Wood were in the first published list of members but did not attend the first meeting or serve on any committees during the first year (Thomas N. Carver, Cambridge, Mass., to Seligman, Dec. 23, 1909, Secretary's Files, A.E.A., Evanston, Ill.).

15. Coats, "The First Two Decades," 558–559; Patten, Philadelphia, Pa., to Ely, Feb. 17, 1893, Ely Papers, Box 11; Francis A. Walker, Boston, Mass., to Seligman, April 25, 1887, Seligman Papers; John H. Gray, "The German Economic Association," *Annals*, I (Jan., 1891), 515; F. Y. Edgeworth, "The British Economic Association," *EJ*, I (March, 1891), 1–14.

16. Ely, Madison, Wis., to Jeremiah W. Jenks, Sept. 27, 1894, Secretary's Files, A.E.A.; Ely, Madison, Wis., to Theodore Roosevelt, Dec. 15, 1914, Ely Papers, Box 95; Patten, Philadelphia, Pa., to Ely, March 29, 1889, Secretary's Files, A.E.A.; Patten, Philadelphia, Pa., to William W. Folwell, Oct. 27, 1890, Folwell Papers, Minnesota Historical Society; Winthrop Daniels, Princeton, N.J., to Patten, Jan. 13, 1908; Winthrop Daniels, Princeton, N.J., to Gifford Pinchot, Dec. 1, 1908, Secretary's Files, A.E.A.; "Note," *Economic Bulletin*, I (June, 1908), 107.

17. Annual Dinner, Dec. 30, 1908, Secretary's Files, A.E.A.; Simon N. Patten, "The Making of Economic Literature," *Economic Bulletin*, I (Jan., 1909), 290–300, reprinted in Simon N. Patten, *Essays in Economic Theory* (New York, 1924), 244, 247. Edwin R. A. Seligman was critical of Patten's address and worried about a "streak of pessimism running through the whole address" (Seligman, New York, N.Y., to Daniels, Jan. 15, 1909, Secretary's Files, A.E.A.).

18. *The Wharton School: Its First Fifty Years* (Philadelphia, 1931), *passim;* Minutes, Wharton School Faculty Meetings, July, 1888, University of Pennsylvania Archives.

19. *The Wharton School,* 12; Edward P. Cheyney, *History of the University of Pennsylvania* (Philadelphia, 1940), *passim;* Roland P. Falkner, "Recollections of Early Days of the Wharton School," typescript dated April 30, 1931, n.p.; Albert S. Bolles, Williamstown, Mass., to Emory Johnson, May 6, 1931, University of Pennsylvania Archives. See also James, John B. McMaster, Robert E. Thompson, Philadelphia, Pa., to William Pepper, Feb. 1, 1888; James, Philadelphia, Pa., to Pepper, May 11, 1888; Patten, Chicago, Ill., to Jesse Y. Burke, June 8, 1888; Patten, Philadelphia, Pa., to Burke, April, 1891, Archives General File, University of Pennsylvania Archives.

20. *The Wharton School,* 13, 17; "On the Library," Minutes, Wharton School Faculty Meetings, Feb. 21, 1890; William Romaine Newbold, "History of the Graduate School," *Old Penn,* XI (March–April, 1913), 808ff, *passim;* Minutes, Faculty of Philosophy, 1888–1895, *passim;* Minutes, Wharton School Faculty Meetings, 1889–1895, *passim;* Minute Books of the American Academy of Political and Social Science, 1889–1895, Philadelphia, Pa., I; James, Philadelphia, Pa., to Clark, n.d., probably 1890, Clark Papers, Columbia University Library; Patten, Philadelphia, Pa., to Folwell, Feb. 21, 1890, Folwell Papers; James, Philadelphia, Pa., to Fred M. Taylor, Nov. 14, Dec. 9, 1892, Taylor Papers, Michigan Historical Collections.

21. James H. S. Bossard, "Robert Ellis Thompson—Pioneer Professor in Social Science," *AJS,* XXXV (Sept., 1929), 239–249; Robert Ellis Thompson, "Laveleye and the *Kathedersozialisten,*" *Penn Monthly,* VII (May, 1876), 390, 394; Patten, Philadelphia, Pa., to Ely, Nov. 30, Dec. 13, 1888, Secretary's Files, A.E.A.; Robert Ellis Thompson, Philadelphia, Pa., to Joseph Wharton, April 2, 1892, Cyrus Adler, Philadelphia, Pa., to Wharton, May 23, 1892, Archives General File.

22. James departed in the summer of 1895 after a bitter dispute with the provost, William Pepper, and the Board of Trustees (James, Philadelphia, Pa., to Pepper, Dec. 10, 1894, Archives General File; James, "Diary," Jan. 1–18, 1895, James Papers). In 1899, Patten told Henry Carter Adams, "We are going through a sort of crisis here." See Patten, Philadelphia, Pa., to Adams, Jan. 10, 1899, Adams Papers, Ann Arbor, Mich.; Henry R. Seager, Philadelphia, Pa., to Jenks, Oct. 24, 1895, Secretary's Files, A.E.A.; Minutes, Wharton School Faculty Meetings, 1895–1909, *passim;* Seager, Philadelphia, Pa., to Giddings, Nov. 2, 1897, Secretary's Files, A.E.A.

23. Considerable correspondence between these European scholars and Americans can be found in the Ely, Clark, James, Seligman,

and Ward papers. T. W. Hutchison, in "Insularity and Cosmopolitanism in Economic Ideas, 1870–1914," *AER*, XLV (May, 1955), Suppl., 9, notes: "Towards the end of the eighties and through the nineties we come to the peak decade in the flow and interchange of ideas in the neoclassical period. . . . All these advances are carried through by a wide international exchange of ideas." The rising status of American university programs in social science was noted by scholars at the time. See, for example, Victor Branford, "The Organization of Economic and Political Studies in American Universities," *EJ*, XII (Dec., 1902), 535–537; Henry C. Adams, "Political Science in German Universities," *Michigan Alumnus*, V (Jan., 1899), 135–138.

24. Alfred W. Coats, "American Scholarship Comes of Age: The Louisiana Purchase Exposition, 1904," *Journal of the History of Ideas*, XXII (July–Sept., 1961), 404–417, is the best study of the Congress. Yet Coats's thesis that the conference was the "direct product of a Germanic passion for pure scholarship which was scarcely representative of American life" neglects the facts that, despite Hugo Münsterberg's Hegelian list of subjects to be discussed, the Congress permitted American scholars and their European teachers and colleagues to exchange ideas about social policy as well as about pure scholarship and that none of the Americans seem to have given much thought to Münsterberg's grandiose plan. The Americans were secure enough in their own creative work not to worry about where Germanic influence ended and American intellectual life began. George Haines and Frederick H. Jackson, in "A Neglected Landmark in the History of Ideas," *Mississippi Valley Historical Review*, XXXIV (Sept., 1947), 201–220, seem to have missed the implications of the Congress when they declare that the "direction of the Congress fell, apparently without explicit intention, into the hands of men who had strong German-American interest." For Patten's participation in the Congress, see Patten, Philadelphia, Pa., to Albion W. Small, Sept. 2, 1904, Small Papers, University of Chicago Library.

Chapter III. The Standard of Living, 1885–1891

1. Simon N. Patten, *The Stability of Prices* (Baltimore, 1888), 33, 48–50, 55.

2. Mark Blaug, *Ricardian Economics: A Historical Study* (New Haven, 1958), 23, 28, 122–126.

3. T. W. Hutchison, *Review of Economic Doctrines, 1870–1929* (Oxford, 1953), 44, 141.

4. Patten, *Stability*, 48, 36, 42–43, 61, 58.

5. *Ibid.*, 58, 63–64.

6. *Ibid.*, 58; cf. Simon N. Patten, *The Principles of Rational Taxation* (Philadelphia, 1890), 7–10.

7. Patten, *Stability*, 63–64, 11, 62.

8. Ibid., 62–63, 58–59. A German reviewer declared, "Die Schrift ist für weitere Kreise bestimmt. Dies hat wohl den Verf. davon abgehalten, in den im Titel derselben angegebenen Gegenstand tiefer einzudringen" (J. L., "The Stability of Prices," *Jahrbücher*, LV [1890], 98–99). Alfred Marshall, the leading English economist of the period, considered Patten's work on stable prices to be as important as the work of Eugen Böhm-Bawerk, Friedrich Wieser, John Bates Clark, and Francis A. Walker (Marshall, *The Principles of Economics* [London, 1961], 462).

9. Blaug, 176, 179–180; Mary Jean Bowman, "The Consumer in the History of Economic Doctrine," *AER*, XLI (May, 1951), Suppl., 1–18.

10. Hutchison, 14–16; George J. Stigler, "The Early History of Empirical Studies of Consumer Behavior," *JPE*, LXII (April, 1954), 95–113; R. S. Howey, *The Rise of the Marginal Utility School, 1870–1889* (Lawrence, Kan., 1960), *passim;* Eugen Böhm-Bawerk, "The Austrian Economists," *Annals*, I (Jan., 1891), 362–384.

11. Hutchison, 114; Stigler, *passim;* Howey, *passim.*

12. John Ruskin, *Unto This Last* (London, 1862), 144, 156; Bowman, 11–12, notes the technical concerns of professional economists which Ruskin ignored.

13. Alfred W. Coats, *Methodological Controversy as an Approach to the History of American Economics* (unpublished dissertation, The Johns Hopkins University, 1953), *passim;* Joseph Dorfman, "The Role of the German Historical School in American Economic Thought," *AER*, XLV (May, 1955), 27; Edward F. Schroeder, *The Marginal Utility Theory in the United States of America* (Nymegen, Neth., 1947), *passim.* Howey, in *The Rise*, 140, notes that Patten's "Die Bedeutung der Lehre vom Grenznutzen," *Jahrbücher* LVII (1891), 481–534, was one of the earliest monographs on marginal utility published in Germany. The only American economist before Patten to deal with consumption was Amasa Walker, in *The Science of Wealth* (Boston, 1866). Walker's essay, "Importance of a Right of Consumption," is reprinted in Henry W.

Spiegel, ed., *The Rise of American Economic Thought* (New York, 1960), 137–142.

14. Simon N. Patten, "The Effect of the Consumption of Wealth on the Economic Welfare of Society," in Richard T. Ely, ed., *Science Economic Discussion* (New York, 1889), 135. *Science Economic Discussion* consists of contributions to a debate among American economists on methodology and the role of the state in economic life. Patten's essay had two purposes: to set forth his theory of consumption and to help Ely, Henry C. Adams, and Edwin R. A. Seligman refute Simon Newcomb, Arthur T. Hadley, and Frank W. Taussig.

15. Patten, "The Effect," 124–126.

16. *Ibid.*, 130–131.

17. Simon N. Patten, *The Consumption of Wealth* (Philadelphia, 1889), 31, 37.

18. *Ibid.*, 45, 64, 67–68.

19. *Ibid.*, 24.

20. *Ibid.*, 24; Patten, "The Effect," 130–132.

21. Patten, *Consumption*, 24.

22. *Ibid.*, 25–29, 52, 69.

23. *Ibid.*, 54, 57.

24. *Ibid.*, 68–70. The phrase "socialization of consumption," which admirably described Patten's program and which he used in his later writings on the subject, was coined by William Smart, a Scottish economist, in "The Effects of the Consumption of Wealth on Distribution," *Annals*, III (Nov., 1892), 290. Smart based his ideas on Patten's arguments.

25. Patten, *Rational Taxation, passim.*

26. *Ibid.*, 7; Joseph Dorfman, *The Economic Mind in American Civilization* (New York, 1946–1959), II, *passim;* see above, Ch. I.

27. Simon N. Patten, *The Economic Basis of Protection* (Philadelphia, 1890), *passim.* Patten, List, and Carey were compared in Leo S. Rowe, review of *American Protectionism* by Ugo Rabbeno, *Annals*, IV (Nov., 1893), 476–480.

28. See Epilogue.

29. Patten, *Protection*, 90, 113, 137–138, 143. *The Economic Basis of Protection* attracted notice from scholars in the United States, England, France, and Italy. It was later translated into French and Italian. For comments on the book by Henry Carter Adams, John Bates Clark, John R. Commons, and Frank W. Taussig see below, Ch. VII. Arthur T. Hadley, *Economics* (New York, 1896), 438–439, argued that tariffs, in fact, inhibited the development of

varied consumption. Richmond Mayo-Smith considered it a "weak" book, but had considerable respect for Patten (Mayo-Smith, New York, N.Y., to Edwin R. A. Seligman, July 22, 1890, Seligman Papers, Columbia University Library). Three anonymous American reviewers gave the book a rough reception. A writer in *Na*, LI (July 17, 1890), 57–58, accused Patten of corrupting the minds of students at the Wharton School. *PSM*, XXXVII (Sept., 1890), 703–704, complained that Patten included few facts and figures. A writer in *Sci*, XV (May 16, 1890), 306–307, called the book "a mass of confusion." An English economist, C. Bastable, in *EJ*, I (Sept., 1891), 596–599, declared that Patten had merely reworked the doctrines of List and Carey. M. Courcelle-Seneuil, in the *Journal des Economistes*, VI (May, 1891), 299–303, blasted Patten as a member of the historical school and criticized his inclusion of moral and political considerations in economic theory. Charles Gide, in the *Revue d'Economie Politique*, V (March, 1891), 410–412, was disturbed by the fact that Patten, despite his German training, used deductive arguments. Later, Gide and Charles Rist, in *The History of Economic Doctrines* (Boston, 1914), 285–286, criticized Patten's nationalistic bias. Another Frenchman, Paul Cauwes, in the Preface to the French translation of Patten's book (Paris, 1899), i–xiii, defended Patten against the strictures of his countrymen. An Italian, Luigi Cossa, in *An Introduction to the Study of Political Economy* (London and New York, 1893), 479, called Patten's defense of protectionism "specious." Another Italian economist, Ugo Rabbeno, in *The American Commercial Policy* (London, 1895), 384–410, attacked Patten root and branch.

30. Simon N. Patten, "Can Economics Furnish an Objective Standard for Morality?" *Journal of Speculative Philosophy*, XXII (Sept., 1892), 322–332, reprinted in Patten's *Essays in Economic Theory* (New York, 1924), 137–142. The article appeared four years after Patten wrote it. His thought had changed considerably in these years, and he was embarrassed by its publication. As he told Edward A. Ross, "The latter part of the article is defective as it was written several years ago and was in Dr. [William T.] Harris' hands four years awaiting the revival of his magazine [*The Journal of Speculative Philosophy*]" (Patten, Philadelphia, Pa., to Ross, Nov. 17, 1892, Ross Papers, State Historical Society of Wisconsin).

31. Patten emphasized the necessity of fighting "with nature for food" ("Can Economics," 140). Many examples of Patten's efforts to assert agrarian values can be found in his writings of the 1890's. For instance, discussing city government at a meeting of the Ameri-

can Academy of Political and Social Science on November 17, 1893, he declared, "Our residence regions might be called condensed farms" ("Minutes of the Proceedings," *Annals*, IV [May, 1894], 263).

32. Simon N. Patten, "Another View of the Ethics of Land Tenure," *International Journal of Ethics*, I (April, 1891), 354–370. Patten criticized both Henry George's and John Bates Clark's resolution of the paradox of the existence of poverty in the midst of progress. George, he argued, exaggerated the seriousness of the problem. Clark's desire for a system of perfect competition disregarded the fact that nature, as well as man, "helps in the production of wealth" and led to the conclusion that laborers had no "right to share in the natural resources of the country" (*ibid.*, 362–364). Charles A. Barker, in *Henry George* (New York, 1955), 557–558, notes that "Patten rejected George's program, yet spoke in a more friendly way than Clark did of his ethics."

33. Simon N. Patten, "The Economic Causes of Moral Progress," *Annals*, III (March, 1893), 124–149, reprinted in *Essays*, 171, 179.

34. *Ibid.*, 167–169, 172. According to Patten, morality depended on two "underlying conditions," the size of complements of pleasures and the equality of the pleasures, and two "active instincts," the ejection of discordant elements and the "correct" calculation of pleasures. Contemporary moralists and criminologists wrongly emphasized the fear of punishment. Crime could be eliminated by applying Patten's economic theory: "Three solid meals a day break down the sympathy with theft, destructive revenge and other crimes against property and good order" (*ibid.*, xx, 174–175).

Chapter IV. The Problems of Welfare, 1892–1896

1. Simon N. Patten, *The Theory of Dynamic Economics* (Philadelphia, 1892), reprinted in Simon N. Patten, *Essays in Economics* (New York, 1924); quotations from pp. 121, 123.

2. *Essays*, 55–57, 81, 97–125.

3. *Ibid.*, 61–62, 66; for Marx see George Lichtheim, *Marxism: An Historical and Critical Study* (New York, 1961), 176ff. Patten introduced diagrams and geometric logic for the first time in his career. With these new tools, he analyzed the dynamic aspect of the marginal increment of consumption, the distribution of subjective and objective values, the minimum shares in distribution, and retail prices. It is difficult to reproduce the complexity of Patten's eco-

nomics in summary form. An explication can be found in James Lane Boswell, *The Economics of Simon Nelson Patten* (Philadelphia, 1933).

4. Patten, *Essays*, 97–100.

5. *Ibid.*, 127, 113, 116.

6. *Ibid.*, 127. For reviews of *The Theory of Dynamic Economics* by John Bates Clark, John A. Hobson, and John R. Commons, and for discussion of a controversy on several doctrines in which Patten, Clark, Eugen Böhm-Bawerk, and Alfred Marshall participated, see below, Ch. IX. Arthur T. Hadley, reviewing for the *PSQ*, VII (Sept., 1892), 562–563, claimed that Patten confused "subjective" and "objective" rent and criticized him for assuming that "articles which have the same value have the same marginal utility to different consumers." Patten replied to Hadley in "Some Explanations Relating to *The Theory of Dynamic Economics*, *QJE*, VII (Jan., 1893), 177–187.

Robert Meyer, a member of the Austrian school, attacked Patten in "Die Zunehmende Mannigfaltigkeit der Consumption," *Zeitschrift für Verwaltung, Sozialpolitik und Volkswirtschaft*, II (1893), 358–418. Meyer rejected Patten's theory of progress toward a harmonious variety of consumption. Patten, he contended, had reversed the order of economic events. Varied consumption was the result, not the cause, of progressive economic development. Proper analysis required that problems due to changing patterns of consumption be separated from those of changing needs and costs. New consumer goods increased the variety of consumption only when they replaced goods previously in use. Meyer concluded, however, that Patten, by pointing out that the setting of economic goals required cooperation between social and natural scientists and politicians, had made a notable contribution. Patten's utilitarianism was attacked by Henry W. Stuart, "The Hedonistic Interpretation of Subjective Value," "Subjective and Exchange Value," *JPE*, IV (Dec., 1895, June, 1896), 64–84, 352–385. Patten received considerable newspaper publicity for the book. The Spokane *Spokesman*, Jan. 15, 1893, declared, "Dr. Patten sets forth the theory and principles in accordance with which many of the problems now puzzling legislators and breeding agitators must finally be solved," and *The Week*, Toronto, Jan. 20, 1893, admonished students of political economy "to give good heed to the contents of this pamphlet" (Alumni Records File, University of Pennsylvania Archives).

7. Patten dealt with these problems throughout the 1890's. For a summary and explication of his publications on psychology, abun-

dance, and education see Daniel M. Fox, "Simon N. Patten: Moralist of American Abundance" (unpublished dissertation, Harvard University, 1964).

8. Simon N. Patten, "The Economy of Memory in the Study of Arithmetic," *Education*, IX (Sept.–Oct., 1888), 6–13, 79–86; "The Educational Value of College Studies," *ER*, I (Feb., 1891), 110–120; "The Educational Value of Political Economy," *AEA Pubs.*, V (Nov., 1890), 1–32; "Economic Aspects of Technical Education," *AEA Pubs.*, VI (Jan., 1891), 119–121.

9. Simon N. Patten, "The Importance of Economic Psychology to Teachers," *Sixty-Third Annual Meeting of the American Institute of Instruction* (Boston, 1892), 11, 20–21; "Economics in Elementary Schools," *Annals*, V (Jan., 1895), 478–482, 489; "The Teaching of Economics in Secondary Schools," *AEA Pubs.*, X (March, 1895), 119–138; cf. "An Economic Measure of School Efficiency," *ER* (May, 1911), 467–477.

10. Simon N. Patten, "University Training for Businessmen," *ER*, XXIX (March, 1905), 217–233; "The Place of University Extension," *University Extension*, II (Feb., 1894), 263–264, 275. Patten's first recorded use of the term "social work" was in the latter article. The first record of one of his students' using the term is in Samuel M. Lindsay's "Social Work at the Krupp Factories," *Annals*, III (Nov., 1892), 330–362. For claims regarding Patten's originality in coining the term, see below, Ch. VI.

11. "The Place," 275, 281, 291.

12. On nutrition see Elmer V. McCollum, *A History of Nutrition* (Boston, 1957); Johannes Conrad, *Liebig's Ansicht von der Bodenerschöpfung und ihre Geschichtliche, Statistische und Nationalökonomische Begründung* (Jena, Ger., 1864).

13. Minutes, Faculty of Philosophy, 1888–1895, 1895–1910; Minutes, Wharton School Faculty Meetings, 1889–1895, 1895–1912, University of Pennsylvania Archives.

14. J. Russell Smith to the author, interview, Swarthmore, Pa., Sept. 10, 1962.

15. Solomon S. Huebner to the author, interview, Merion, Pa., Sept. 11, 1962; Scott Nearing to the author, interview, Boston, Mass., Jan. 5, 1963; Frances Perkins to the author, interview, New York, N.Y., Dec. 28, 1962.

16. Smith, Huebner, Nearing, Perkins interviews; letter from Walter S. Tower, Carmel, Calif., to the author, Nov. 22, 1962.

17. William H. Allen to the author, interview, New York, N.Y., Sept. 14, 1962; Smith, Huebner, Perkins interviews.

18. Edward T. Devine, "The New Basis of Civilization: Patten," *CC*, XVIII (May 4, 1907), 1935; Edward T. Devine, *When Social Work Was Young* (New York, 1938); Samuel M. Lindsay, *Recollections of Theodore Roosevelt* (Winter Park, Fla., 1955); Rexford G. Tugwell, "Notes on the Life and Work of Simon Nelson Patten," *JPE*, XXXI (April, 1923), 153–208.

19. *The Economic Basis of Protection* (Philadelphia, 1891), 144.

20. *The Theory of Social Forces* (Philadelphia, 1896), 5, 48.

21. *Ibid.*, 7–9.

22. *Ibid.*, 20, 6, 26, 40.

23. *Ibid.*, 31, 37, 47. For the relationships among American psychologists in the period see Edwin G. Boring, *History, Psychology and Science* (New York, 1963), 132–133, 163–168; cf. William James, *The Principles of Psychology* (New York, 1890), I, 30, II, 283, 321; cf. James M. Baldwin, *Handbook of Psychology* (New York, 1889, 1891), II, 201, 257, 302; James M. Baldwin, *Elements of Psychology* (New York, 1893), *passim;* Donald Broadbent, *Behavior* (New York, 1961), 56–57. Patten argued in favor of Baldwin's contention that pain arises in motor currents in "Overnutrition and Its Consequences," *Annals*, X (July, 1897), 37, and discussed impulse and desire in Baldwin's terms in *The Theory of Prosperity* (New York, 1901), 184. Patten always learned a great deal from oral discussion and may have been stimulated by James M. Cattell, who was professor of psychology at the University of Pennsylvania from 1888 to 1891. Another man who may have influenced Patten's psychological theorizing was Edwin Grant Conklin, who was a member of the department of biology at the University of Pennsylvania from 1896 to 1898. Conklin's "The Relation of the Psychic Life to the Nervous System," *Scientific American Suppl.*, LIV (Sept. 13, 20, 1902), 22330–22332, 22343, contained several doctrines which Patten also held.

24. Patten, *Social Forces*, 47.

25. *Ibid.*, 51–52.

26. *Ibid.*, 51–53.

27. *Ibid.*, 75, 77, 122.

28. *Ibid.*, 51–54, 64–70.

29. *Ibid.*, 64–70.

30. *Ibid.*, 78–79.

31. *Ibid.*, 81, 84–85.

32. *Ibid.*, 92–93.

33. *Ibid.*, 93–94; cf. Reinhard Bendix, *Max Weber: An Intellectual Portrait* (New York, 1960), *passim.*

34. Patten, *Social Forces*, 86, 98–99, 138–140, 142–143, 148.

35. *Ibid.*, 92–93; Simon N. Patten, "The Formulation of Normal Laws," *Annals*, VII (May, 1896), 443, 449.

36. Patten, *Social Forces*, 151; cf. John Ruskin, *The Political Economy of Art* (London, 1857), *Unto This Last* (London, 1862). For reviews by Lester F. Ward and Franklin H. Giddings of *The Theory of Social Forces* see below, Ch. IX. William Caldwell, a philosopher at the University of Chicago, reviewed the book in *IJE*, VII (April, 1897), 345–353. Caldwell noted that Patten had affinities with Schopenhauer, the only other modern philosopher to found a "whole system of philosophy upon the will or the motor tendencies of man." Caldwell, however, criticized Patten for seeking social progress in the development of social forces rather than in the "piecemeal construction of social ideals out of impressions and cognitions." Patten replied to Caldwell in "The Theory of Social Forces: An Explanation," *IJE*, VII (July, 1897), 492–496, that he did not want to minimize the importance of "sensory nerves" but merely wanted to argue that motor nerves developed before sensory. Lester F. Ward, in *Glimpses of the Cosmos* (New York, 1918), VI, 4–5, agreed with Caldwell's attack on Patten. Another notable review was written by C. R. Henderson of the University of Chicago for *The Dial*, XX (May 1, 1896), 277. Henderson, the only academic man besides Patten who had a significant influence on social work in the early twentieth century, disliked Patten's "biological" psychology and ignored the economic points in his argument. He admitted, however, that Patten's book was an improvement over the "superficial criticism of Comte."

37. Simon N. Patten, "Overnutrition and Its Social Consequences," *Annals*, X (July, 1897), 44–46; Edward A. Ross, *Social Control* (New York, 1901), was the first book-length statement of Ross's doctrine. Ross had, however, discussed the concept in various articles and probably in conversation with Patten. For the relationship between Ross and Patten, see below, Ch. IX.

38. "Overnutrition," 49–50, 51, 53.

Chapter V. Authority and Action, 1897–1903

1. Simon N. Patten, Philadelphia, Pa., to Edward A. Ross, Nov. 24, 1892, Ross Papers, State Historical Society of Wisconsin.

2. The University of Pennsylvania granted Patten a leave of

absence, without salary, for one year (*Minutes of Trustees,* XIII, 1892–1900, 460, University of Pennsylvania Archives). Patten sailed for Europe in May, 1897. He spent the summer in Scotland and the next academic year at Oxford and Freiburg im Breisgau.

3. Patten, Edinburgh, Scot., to Franklin H. Giddings, Aug. 27, 1897; Patten, Freiburg im Breisgau, Ger., to Giddings, March 24, 1898; Patten, Edinburgh, Scot., to Giddings, July 25, 1898, Giddings Papers, Columbia University Library.

4. Simon N. Patten, *The Development of English Thought* (New York, 1899), vi, 43.

5. On Engels and Marx see George Lichtheim, *Marxism: An Historical and Critical Study* (New York, 1961), 244ff; Henry T. Buckle, *History of Civilization in England* (London, 1857), I, 211–213, 850–853. Patten's reason for dealing with England paralleled Buckle's: "The conditions and circumstances isolating England for many centuries have made English thought more normal and more uniform than that of her continental neighbors. The advantages of England's insular position are too well known to require restatement" (Patten, *English Thought,* vi–vii). Buckle, Benjamin Kidd, and Thorold Rogers, the historian of English prices, were the only writers Patten cited in *English Thought.*

6. *English Thought,* 43–44.

7. *Ibid.,* 52–54.

8. *Ibid.,* 54–55, chs. iii–v. Patten seems to have believed that his interpretation of the history of thought was adequate until he reached Adam Smith. After that point, he realized, "it broke down" (Henry R. Seager, "Professor Patten's Theory of Prosperity," *Annals,* XIX [March, 1902], 244). The historical narrative in *The Development of English Thought* is a curious combination of insight and fantasy. The discussion of the antecedents of English thought, for instance, begins with some questionable theories about the different qualities of northern and southern races. Yet Patten's emphasis on the socialistic element in early Christianity is provocative (*English Thought,* 70–77). Patten approached Max Weber's thesis of the relation between the Protestant ethic and the spirit of capitalism. Calvinism, he declared, "flourished in an age when industrial success and scientific knowledge were intimately connected with religious thought and the Calvinist succeeded because he had a better knowledge of his environment and more industrial energy than his opponents" (*ibid.,* 94, 124, 201, 251, 261). Patten's effort to give his social theory historical validity had questionable success. Although he convincingly presented the historical background of

overnutrition, his argument about the development of strong and weak appetites seems fantastic (*ibid.*, 99, ch. ii).

9. *Ibid.*, 19–21; Reinhard Bendix, *Max Weber: An Intellectual Portrait* (New York, 1960), *passim;* Simon N. Patten, "The Failure of Biologic Sociology," *Annals*, IV (May, 1894), 942.

10. *English Thought*, 94, 124, 201, 251, 261.

11. *Ibid.*, 396.

12. *Ibid.*, 23–31, 47.

13. *Ibid.*, 28–30, 390, 376. Patten (*ibid.*, 374) specifically criticized the utopianism of Edward Bellamy in *Looking Backward* (Boston, 1887).

14. *English Thought*, 268, 271, 302, 375, 385, 389.

15. Walter E. Weyl described Patten, noting "his smile. His long arms and legs. The sallow face. The heavy, high jaw. The contortions. The gentle methods of argument" ("Diary," April 19, 1913, Weyl Papers, Rutgers University Library).

16. Patten, *English Thought*, 401–402, 407–408. Patten claimed in *The Social Basis of Religion* (New York, 1911), vi, that he did not learn of James's pragmatism until 1910. On Comte see W. M. Simon, *European Positivism in the Nineteenth Century* (Ithaca, N.Y., 1963), 28, 108–109. *The Development of English Thought* attracted more critical attention than any of Patten's previous books. Charles M. Andrews, in the *American Historical Review*, V (Jan., 1900), 330–332, recommended it to all students of "continental or English history," because the "explanations he advances have never perhaps been so lucidly or convincingly presented before." Sidney Ball, in the English *Economic Review*, X (Jan. 15, 1900), 114–118, criticized Patten's "perverse and unprofitable ingenuity" but concluded that it was a "thoughtful and strenuous book." Charles De Garmo, in *ER*, XVII (May, 1899), 484–488, declared that Patten's interests "are as broad as human life itself, and upon each of its important departments he throws a light that amounts to illumination." Karl Diehl, in an essay-review for *Jahrbücher*, III (1900), 681–690, gave the book unstinted praise and summarized Patten's thought over the previous decade. Warner Fite, in "Professor Patten's Psychological Doctrines," *JPE*, VII (June, 1899), 384–391, accused Patten of preserving the outdated faculty psychology by overemphasizing the influence of the environment on human development. C. R. Henderson, reviewing the book in *The Dial*, XXVIII (June 1, 1900), 436–437, denied that styles of art could be explained largely by economic conditions. C. M. Hill, reviewing for *JPE*, VII (Sept., 1899), 554–563, declared

that despite numerous flaws, the book "ought to have been written." Munroe Smith, in "Patten's Study of English Thought," *PSQ*, XV (March, 1900), 112–119, praised some of Patten's theories as "plausible" but had an "impression of unreality, of an excursion into some scientific dreamland." R. M. Wenley, reviewing for *Sci*, IX (May 9, 1899), 713–715, praised the book's "frankness, originality, and great brilliance." For a review by Thorstein B. Veblen, see below, Ch. IX. Several anonymous reviewers had mixed feelings about the book. A critic in *Na*, LXIX (July 6, 1889), 12–13, called the book "persistently and almost wantonly intelligent." A reviewer in *The Outlook*, LXII (June 3, 1899), 311–312, was bothered by Patten's "exaggerated estimate of the influence of environment." A critic in the English *Spectator*, LXXXIII (Sept. 16, 1899), 381–382, misunderstood many of Patten's ideas but concluded that the book was "interesting and suggestive." The Chicago *Tribune* (n.d., quoted in a publisher's advertisement in Simon Patten, *Heredity and Social Progress* [New York, 1903], n.p.), declared, "It is decidedly one of the best written and most thoughtful of recent books." Justice Oliver Wendell Holmes had considerable affection for the book and mentioned it several times in his correspondence with Sir Frederick Pollock and Harold Laski (Mark DeW. Howe, ed., *Holmes-Pollock Letters* [Cambridge, Mass., 1941], 118, 237, 261; *Holmes-Laski Letters* [Cambridge, Mass., 1953], I, 4, 5, 138–139, 926).

17. Patten, Philadelphia, Pa., to Charles Hull, Oct. 13, 1899, March 16, 1900, Secretary's Files, A.E.A., Evanston, Ill.; Patten, Chester, Pa., to Richard T. Ely, Sept. 5, 1900, Ely Papers, State Historical Society of Wisconsin, Box 31. Patten's only publication while he was working on the book was a review of Franklin H. Giddings' *Elements of Sociology*, in *Annals*, XIII (March, 1899), 375–377.

18. Calvin Woodward, "Reality and Social Reform: The Transition from Laissez-Faire to the Welfare State," *Yale Law Journal*, LXXII (Dec., 1962), 286–328.

19. *The Theory of Prosperity* (New York, 1902), 1–3, 94; Asa Briggs, *A Study of the Work of Seebohm Rowntree* (London, 1961), 33–34. Briggs notes that when Rowntree visited the United States in 1921, he received his warmest welcome at the University of Pennsylvania. It is possible that this reception was in some measure a result of the work of Patten and his students, who dominated the Wharton School faculty (*ibid.*, 167).

20. *Prosperity*, 31, 194–195. For an introduction to Ostwald's theories see Ostwald's *Natural Philosophy* (New York, 1910).

21. *Prosperity*, 46, 63, 73, 84. Patten's arguments on monopoly

and free competition brought him into sharp conflict with John Bates Clark, whose views later became the theoretical basis for the antitrust activities of the administrations of Theodore Roosevelt, William Howard Taft, and Woodrow Wilson. Patten dealt in detail with Clark's views (*ibid.*, 107–132). For the relationship between Patten and Clark see below, Ch. IX.

22. *Prosperity*, 60–63.

23. *Ibid.*, 88, 94, 138–140.

24. *Ibid.*, 152, 156, 162–163.

25. *Ibid.*, 164–165.

26. *Ibid.*, 174, 175, 211, 214.

27. *Ibid.*, 216–229.

28. *Ibid.*, 224, 226, 237.

29. *Ibid.*, 174–175, 176, 191, 202, 204, 206–207; cf. Patten's review of *Principles of Western Civilization* by Benjamin Kidd, in *Annals*, XIX (May, 1902), 461–463. *The Theory of Prosperity* was, in general, well received, although not as the major breakthrough Patten had hoped it would be. In 1912, when Patten referred to the reception of the book as "disappointing" (*The Reconstruction of Economic Theory* [Philadelphia, 1912], in *Essays in Economic Theory* [New York, 1924], 273), he apparently had his own intentions, rather than the comments or reviewers, in mind. Henry B. Gardner, in *YR*, XI (Feb., 1903), 409–412, considered Patten's attack on the limits of reason as a tool for engineering social reform the "most suggestive portion of the work," but noted some "confusion" in Patten's arguments about the distribution of wealth. Alvin S. Johnson, in "Patten's Theory of Prosperity," *PSQ*, XVII (June, 1902), 313–319, ably summarized Patten's views and probed into a number of flaws in Patten's logic. The most thorough review was Henry Seager's "Professor Patten's *Theory of Prosperity*," *Annals*, XIX (March, 1902), 239–255. Seager surveyed all of Patten's work since 1885 and welcomed him back to the field of economic theory. Sarah E. Simons, in *AJS*, VIII (July, 1902), 122–129, criticized Patten for "blurring" Lester Ward's distinction between feeling and function but concluded that the book deserved the "attention of every thinker on social subjects." Anonymous reviewers treated Patten with respect. A writer in *Na*, LXXV (July 24, 1902), 74–75, compared Patten favorably with Adam Smith and approved of Patten's solutions to economic problems. A writer in *The Independent*, LIV (Oct., 1902), 2365–2367, declared that "Professor Patten is always to be reckoned with seriously." A writer in *Gunton's Magazine*, XXIX (Jan., 1903), 76–81, attacked Patten for using

marginal-utility theory. Foreign reviews were favorable. Sidney Ball, in the *Economic Review*, XII (Oct., 1902), 501–502, declared that the book was "original and ingenious." Three German writers focused on Patten's program of social reform, of which they approved, though with some reservations about Patten's optimism: Georg Brodnitz, *Jahrbücher*, III (1906), 398–401; Johann von Komorzynski, *Zeitschrift für Sozialwissenschaft*, VII (1904), 279–286; Wilhelm Lexis, *Jahrbücher für Gesetzgebung, Verwaltung und Volkwirtschaft im Deutschen Reich*, XXVII (1903), 338–342. A notable later analysis of Patten's arguments in *The Theory of Prosperity* appeared in Benjamin M. Anderson, *Social Value* (New York, 1911), 42, 175, 197–198.

30. *Heredity and Social Progress* (New York, 1903), 1–5, 27.

31. *Ibid.*, 45, 86, 91, 130, 184, 188–189, 194, 205. *Heredity and Social Progress* was the only book in which Patten attempted to cite all his sources: August Weismann, *Essays upon Heredity and Kindred Biological Problems* (Oxford, 1889–1892); Patrick Geddes and J. Arthur Thomson, *The Evolution of Sex* (London and Melbourne, 1889); William James, *Principles of Psychology* (New York, 1890); Paolo Mantegazza, *Physiognomy and Expression* (New York, 1891); Theodule A. Ribot, *The Psychology of the Emotions* (Paris, 1896; London, 1897).

32. *Heredity*, 207–209. Patten knew that he had not solved the problems of progress. He was aware, for instance, of the inadequacy of his biological speculations: the epigraph of the book was T. H. Huxley's statement, "Next to being right in the world, the best of all things is to be clearly and definitely wrong, because you will come out somewhere (*ibid.*, vi). Most of Patten's critics, however, did not agree that Patten had "come out somewhere." Three biologists accused Patten of purveying nonsense: Gary N. Calkins, *PSQ*, XVIII (Sept., 1903), 539–541; Charles H. Judd, *YR*, XIII (Aug., 1904), 221–222; Guy M. Whipple, *ER*, XXVII (March, 1904), 309–312. Economists were more favorable. J. Paul Goode, in *Annals*, XXII (Sept., 1903), 366–369, declared that the "great question is answered. Progress starts with a surplus and not in a deficit." R. S. Marett, in *Economic Review*, XII (Oct. 15, 1903), 498–501, declared that there was a "touch of genius" about everything Patten wrote. Anonymous reviewers in *Gunton's Magazine*, XXV (Aug., 1903), 167–170, and *Na*, LXXVI (June 11, 1903), 483, were critical of specific doctrines but impressed by the scope and insight of Patten's work. Edward T. Devine, in *Charities*, XI (Oct. 3), 1903, 316–318, forecast Patten's influence on social work in the next decade. He

discussed the relevance of Patten's doctrines for social workers—particularly the implication that the Americanization of immigrants and the improvement of the lot of Negroes could proceed rapidly in a surplus economy. See below, Ch. VI. An interesting analysis of *Heredity and Social Progress* appeared in Lucius Moody Bristol's *Social Adaptation* (Cambridge, Mass., 1921), 236–244.

33. Rexford G. Tugwell, "Notes on the Life and Work of Simon Nelson Patten," *JPE*, XXXI (April, 1923), 198.

Chapter VI. An Active Pragmatist, 1904–1914

1. Paul U. Kellogg, in "As We Find Ourselves," *Survey*, LXXIV (May, 1938), 136, noted that "it was Dr. Patten who gave social work its name." Edward T. Devine was not certain "whether Patten actually used the phrase 'social work' earlier than anyone else," but he believed that Patten was mainly responsible for its adoption by the profession (Devine, New York, N.Y., to James H. S. Bossard, n.d., quoted in Bossard, "Sociology at the University of Pennsylvania," mimeographed, n.d. but probably 1930, 7, University of Pennsylvania Archives; Frank J. Bruno and Louis Towley, *Trends in Social Work, 1874–1956* [New York, 1957], 137).

2. *University Courier*, Jan. 24, 1893, n.p., Wharton Clipping Book; Bossard, "Sociology," 10, University of Pennsylvania Archives; Edward T. Devine, *When Social Work Was Young* (New York, 1938), 20, 11. Shelby M. Harrison, later director of the Russell Sage Foundation, recalled "one instance where Devine was considering resigning from a fairly important post in social welfare —because of some disagreements in policy; wrote Patten about it; Patten counseled deliberate further consideration, which advice Devine took; and in the end decided against resigning" (Harrison, New York, N.Y., to the author, Aug. 18, 1962); cf. Roy Lubove, *The Progressives and the Slums* (Pittsburgh, 1963), 194.

3. Devine, New York, N.Y., to Richard T. Ely, Nov. 23, 1903, Ely Papers, State Historical Society of Wisconsin, Box 50; cf. Devine, New York, N.Y., to Charles McCarthy, Dec. 19, 1909, McCarthy Papers, State Historical Society of Wisconsin, Box 2; Edward T. Devine, *Misery and Its Causes* (New York, 1909), 11, 24, 250; *The Normal Life* (New York, 1917), 131, 140, 173, 195; cf. "At the Bar of Judgment," *Sur*, XXIV (April 23, 1910), 25–26; cf. "Social Ideals Implied in Present American Programs of Voluntary Philanthropy," *AJS*, XVIII (May, 1914), 784–795.

4. William H. Allen, "Reminiscences," 30, Oral History Research Office, Columbia University; Frances Perkins to the author, interview, New York, N.Y., Dec. 28, 1962.

5. *The New Basis of Civilization* (New York, 1907), 10; Bossard, "Sociology," 7.

6. *New Basis*, 37, 44.

7. *Ibid.*, 57, 61, 85.

8. *Ibid.*, 68, 70–71.

9. *Ibid.*, 76; cf. Raymond Williams, *Culture and Society, 1780–1950* (New York, 1960).

10. *New Basis*, 153, 158, 195.

11. *Ibid.*, 126, 129, 130, 135–137, 103–107, 178, 185; cf. Daniel M. Fox, *Engines of Culture* (Madison, 1963), chs. i, ii, iv.

12. *New Basis*, 185, 192, 205, 211–212, 219–220.

13. *Ibid.*, 178, 211–220. The reviews of *The New Basis of Civilization* were generally favorable. Edward T. Devine, in *CC*, XVIII (May 4, 1907), 135–136, called Patten the "ablest exponent of the new view of philanthropy." George E. Vincent, in *PSQ*, XXII (Dec., 1907), 741–743, criticized Patten's "contemptuous dismissal of the Malthusian doctrine" but praised the general message of the book. An anonymous reviewer in the New York *Times Review of Books*, June 1, 1907, 347, emphasized the concept of the surplus economy and Patten's advocacy of city planning and public welfare. Another anonymous reviewer, in *The Outlook*, LXXXVI (Aug. 10, 1907), 765–767, charged that Patten minimized the importance of the church and the home, but concluded that the book was "both attractive and constructive."

14. For Devine and Perkins, see above, nn. 3, 4, 13. Miss Wald paraphrased Patten in a call to philanthropists to accept the "challenge of this new civilization" ("Family Rehabilitation," speech, Oct. 16, 1913, Wald Papers, New York Public Library); see also Mary R. Richmond, *The Good Neighbor* (Philadelphia, 1907), 17; cf. Benjamin C. Marsh, *Lobbyist for the People* (Washington, D.C., 1954), 13–14; cf. Lubove, *The Progressive and the Slums*, 231.

15. Muriel W. Pumphrey, *Mary Richmond and the Rise of Professional Social Work in Baltimore: The Foundation of a Creative Career* (unpublished dissertation, New York School of Social Work, 1956), 250, 273, 448, 454.

16. "Who Is the Good Neighbor?" *CC*, XIX (Feb. 29, 1908), 1642–1646. Lubove, in *The Progressives and the Slums*, 200, notes: "The trend toward professional social work was inexorable, despite Mary Richmond's firm belief in the real or potential value of vol-

unteer service. The complex social problems of the twentieth century and the ideal of 'scientific philanthropy' promulgated by the charity organization societies imposed demands upon social workers, in terms of time, skill, and training which the volunteers could not always satisfy"; see also Zilpha D. Smith, "The Good Neighbor Again," *CC*, XX (May 16, 1908), 230–232.

17. Edward T. Devine, "Neighborliness and Personal Service vs. Citizenship and Improved Conditions," *CC*, XX (Feb. 28, 1908), 1636; "What We Believe," *CC*, XX (Sept. 5, 1908), 636; *Misery and Its Causes*, 162–163.

18. The name of the magazine was changed from *Charities and the Commons* to *The Survey* in 1910.

19. Patten's sharpest statement of his earlier position was in "The Economic Basis of Prohibition," *Annals*, II (July, 1891), 59–68; cf. James H. Timberlake, *Prohibition and the Progressive Movement* (Cambridge, Mass., 1963).

20. "Prohibition and Social Psychology," *McClure's Magazine*, XXXI (Aug., 1908), 438–444; Edward T. Devine, "Better American Inspired than America Sober," *CC*, XX (Sept. 5, 1908), 695.

21. "Better an Inspiration of Oxygen than of Alcohol," *CC*, XXI (Sept. 21, 1908), 299–300; "The Social Basis of Prohibition," *CC*, XXI (Nov. 19, 1908), 707–708.

22. "Social Basis," 706–707.

23. William H. Allen to the author, interview, New York, N.Y., Sept. 14, 1962, Scott Nearing to the author, interview, Boston, Mass., Jan. 5, 1963, J. Russell Smith to the author, interview, Swarthmore, Pa., Sept. 10, 1962, Margaret Mead to the author, interview, New York, N.Y., April 6, 1963; "Patten Divorced: Strange Views of Marital Life," Hartford *Times*, May 27, 1909, n.p., "Patten Divorced," Philadelphia *Press*, May 27, 1909, 1, Alumni Records File, University of Pennsylvania Archives. Patten seems never to have directly mentioned his marriage after 1908. The "Diary of Matrimonial Disputes," which his wife accused him of keeping, has not survived, and its existence is denied by his surviving colleagues and friends (Allen and Nearing to the author). The only reference to the divorce in Patten's later writings was an oblique passage in *Mud Hollow* (Philadelphia, 1922), 370.

24. *American Examiner*, n.p., n.d., Alumni Records File, University of Pennsylvania Archives; Simon N. Patten, "Young Wives in Industry," *Ind.*, LVII (Dec. 1, 1904), 1244–1249; "New Adjustments for Women," *Ind.*, LXI (Sept. 20, 1906), 674–681. Patten's opinions on working women received wide coverage in the press:

New York *Times*, April 11, 1904; *Harper's Weekly*, April 23, 1904; Lincoln, Neb., *State Journal*, May 15, 1904; Louisville, Ky., *Evening Post*, Jan. 31, 1905; New York *World*, Jan. 31, 1905, Feb. 1, 1905, Alumni Records File, University of Pennsylvania Archives. Patten continued his attack on the consumption habits of middle-class women in an interview with the Philadelphia *Public Ledger*, Nov. 3, 1907; cf. Boston *Courier*, Nov. 9, 1907; Atlanta *Constitution*, n.d., Alumni Records File, University of Pennsylvania Archives. See also Simon N. Patten, "Shall Woman Be a Tool or a Partner?" *Twentieth Century Magazine*, VI (July, 1912), 256–257; "Extravagance as a Virtue," *Current Opinion*, LIV (Jan. 1913), 51–52; "The Standardization of Life and Its Results," New York *Times*, April 13, 1913, Sect. V, 8. Patten's exhortations to working girls drew considerable adverse comment: Cleveland *Leader*, Dec. 15, 1912, Toledo *Blade*, n.d., New York *World*, April 17, 1913, Archives General File, University of Pennsylvania Archives; Gustave Stickley, "Borrowed Plumes," *Craftsman*, XXIII (Jan., 1913), 489; cf. Simon N. Patten, "The Standardization of Family Life," *Annals*, XLVIII (July, 1913), 81–90; *The Development of English Thought* (New York, 1898), 76–77, 132–133, 252–255, 269.

25. "The Conflict Theory of Distribution," *YR*, XVII (Aug., 1908), 238, reprinted in *Essays in Economic Theory* (New York, 1924), 228, 231. Patten had ignored the depression of the 1890's, perhaps because he considered it only a minor setback in the transition from a scarcity to a surplus economy. His reputation and public activities in the first decade of the twentieth century made it impossible for him to ignore the crisis of 1907 without appearing to be either evasive or a defender of the *status quo*. In 1907, he told a reporter that Wall Street was "losing its grip" on the nation and that, in self-defense, New York bankers were "locking up" the nation's wealth. Congress, he declared, should increase the currency and compel country banks to keep a larger percentage of their money in their own vaults (Philadelphia *North American*, Jan. 21, 1907, Alumni Records File, University of Pennsylvania Archives); cf. J. A. Hobson and A. F. Mummery, *The Physiognomy of Industry* (London, 1890); cf. Simon N. Patten, "The Principles of Economic Interference," *Sur*, XXII (April 3, 1909), 14–16.

26. "Immigration Control: Construction vs. Distribution," *Sur*, XXV (Feb. 18, 1911), 866. In this article, Patten, for the first time, advocated tariff reform—not free trade, but the lowering of those tariffs which caused industrial stagnation (*ibid.*, 867).

27. Simon N. Patten, *The Social Basis of Religion* (New York,

1911), vi–xiv; "The Method of Science: A Reply," *Sci*, XXXIII (April 14, 1911), 580.

28. Simon N. Patten, "Ideals of Progress," *Sur*, XXVI (June 3, 1911), 388–389, 391–392. Patten did not indicate whether he meant equality of opportunity, income, and status, or equality before the law. His first reference to Nietzsche was in *New Basis*, 84, where he attacked the concept of the superman.

29. *Social Basis*, 181, 220.

30. *Ibid.*, 217–219. The religion of joy, which would replace the discipline of fear, would modify the structure of capitalism (*ibid.*, 216). The social program of the religion of joy was similar to the social gospel preached by many Protestant clergymen of this generation. Patten declared, for example, "If laborers remain outside the church, if immigrants are not assimilated into our national life . . . a slow but certain death awaits the church" (*ibid.*, 211). *The Social Basis of Religion* excited more controversy than any of Patten's writings since *The Development of English Thought*. The French sociologist Emile Durkheim, reviewing in *L'Année Sociologique*, XII (1913), 79–80, declared with some embarrassment that although the "title of the book and the name of its author oblige us not to pass it by in silence . . . it suffers from an entirely subjective construction, which has no element related to observation of the facts." Raffaele Pettazone, of the University of Rome, reviewing in *Scientia*, XV (May, 1914), 474–475, was mildly critical of Patten's ignorance of Durkheim's work on religious sociology. American reviewers were harsher. Thomas N. Carver, in *AER*, I (Dec., 1911), 792–794, attacked Patten for not realizing that the "truest altruism" required the elimination of the unfit, but concluded that "no book of recent times has discussed more fundamental problems, or discussed them more satisfactorily or intelligently." Patten replied to Carver in "Theories of Progress," *AER*, II (March, 1912), 61–68. Frances F. Bernard, reviewing for *AJS*, XVIII (Sept., 1912), 264–265, accused Patten of exaggerating the importance of poverty and ignoring the "prevalence of immorality and vice among the well-to-do." James T. Shotwell, in *PSQ*, XXVII (March, 1912), 152–154, called attention to egregious historical errors in the book. Reviewers in religious journals objected to Patten's emphasis on the connection between sin, misery, and poverty. An anonymous writer in the *Expository Times*, of Edinburgh, Scotland, XXII (June, 1912), 417, claimed that individual salvation was more important than the welfare of the community. E. Albert Cook, in the *American Journal of Theology*, XVI (April, 1912), 312–315, asserted that no amount

of economic progress could prevent sin without the "faith and feelings of true religion." C. S. Gardner, in *Review and Expositor: A Baptist Quarterly*, IX (April, 1912), 281–282, distorted Patten's logic to imply that "those who have adequate incomes are without sin." William Brenton Greene, Jr., in the *Princeton Theological Review*, IX (July, 1911), 471–474, declared that, despite Patten's efforts to "undermine" the historical basis of Christianity, sin was the cause of misery. An anonymous Catholic writer commented sarcastically that Patten's admission that the "church is not entirely superfluous in the world today . . . is quite a concession for a professor in a state university" (Cleveland *Catholic Universe*, Aug. 11, 1911, Alumni Records File, University of Pennsylvania Archives). There is no record of any leading social-gospel minister's reviewing the book.

31. Simon N. Patten, *The Reconstruction of Economic Theory* (Philadelphia, 1912), 60–61.

32. *Ibid.*, 61–63, 80, 94. B. M. Anderson, reviewing *The Reconstruction* in *PSQ*, XXVIII (March, 1913), 123–129, attacked Patten's application of the terms pluralism and monism to economic theory and pointed out a number of inconsistencies and contradictions in Patten's theories of price and distribution. Despite his criticism, Anderson concluded that Patten's general doctrines were "significant and timely." Cf. Benjamin M. Anderson, New York, N.Y., to Roswell C. McCrea, Nov. 22, 1912, McCrea Papers, in possession of Joseph Dorfman, Columbia University. Henry W. Farnam, professor of economics at Yale, defended German economists and treated Patten's models of economic trends as if they were meant to be inductive statements about American realities. Farnam pointed out how much work in historical economics had been done at the Wharton School, argued that abundance and advances in technology did not diminish the need for toil, decried Patten's criticism of thrift and deplored his support of trade unions. He concluded that Patten was more concerned with the "philosophy" than with the "science" of economics ("Notes on Professor Patten's *Reconstruction of Economic Theory*," Dec., 1912, Farnam Papers, Yale University Library). Albion W. Small, in *AJS*, XVIII (Jan., 1913), 580–583, attacked Patten's "disparagement of German economists," his "snobbery toward Karl Marx," and his attack on nonpragmatic sociologists. Small claimed, however, that the concept of the "creative economy" was a major contribution to sociological analysis and concluded that "we may forgive much in a thinker who frequently returns from his wanderings with trophies like this." Cf. Albion

W. Small, Chicago, Ill., to Edward A. Ross, Nov. 18, 1912, Ross Papers, State Historical Society of Wisconsin. Charles Horton Cooley, a University of Michigan sociologist, expressed views similar to those expounded in *The Reconstruction*, though without mentioning Patten, in "Political Economy and Social Process," *JPE*, XXVI (April, 1918), 366–374.

33. *Reconstruction*, 62; Simon N. Patten, *Heredity and Social Progress* (New York, 1903), 30, 247; *Product and Climax* (New York, 1909), 42, 56, 58.

34. "The Laws of Social Attraction," *PSM*, LXXIII (Oct., 1908), 354–360; cf. "The Evolution of a New Woman," *Annals*, LVI (Nov., 1914), 111–121.

35. "The Laws of Environmental Influence," *PSM*, LXXIX (Oct., 1911), 396–402. Patten was not sure of himself. He ended the article with a question: "Are social traits acquired or natural?" (*ibid.*, 402); see also Simon N. Patten, "Types of Men," *PSM*, LXXX (March, 1912), 273–279.

36. Simon N. Patten, "The Genesis of Personal Traits," *PSM*, LXXXIII (Aug., 1913), 149–152. It is impossible to determine when Patten first read Freud. His knowledge of Freudian theory seems more profound than what he could have acquired from reading or hearing about Freud's lectures in the United States, published as *Über Psychoanalyse* (Leipzig, 1910). Moreover, in 1919, Patten noted that "Freud is a man with a cure who seems to be trying harder to be an evolutionary philosopher than to be a physician" ("An Analysis of Mental Defects," *Mon*, XXX (Jan., 1920), 107. This was before Freud had written his major speculative works. It is possible that Patten had read one of Freud's early attempts to probe the broader implications of psychoanalysis, "Das Interesse an der Psychoanalyse," *Scientia*, XIV (Sept., Nov., 1913), 240–250, 340–368. *Scientia* was an international, multilingual journal of social and natural science which appears to have been read by American scholars. Moreover, one of Patten's books, *The Social Basis of Religion*, was sympathetically reviewed by *Scientia* just a few months after Freud's articles were published. Patten retained an inconsistent commitment to associationist psychology. He declared, for example, that the "mechanisms of repression" were caused by the "association of ideas" and were thus "post-natal in origin" ("The Genesis," 156).

37. Patten's criticism of eugenics was immediately applicable to the problems of immigration and Americanization. Americans were not a "race with a heredity, but a culture with a unity." The ex-

clusion of "foreign elements" would narrow American culture. The old American stock attempted to "keep things immobile and static," while the new immigrants from southern and eastern Europe provided the "dynamic force" for adjustment to the emerging environment of abundance. Eugenics was irrelevant to the problems of adjustment to new conditions, since in each generation language, traditions, and habits of thought must be "reimposed" by education rather than by manipulating the "germ-plasm" ("Becoming American," *Open Court*, XXIX [July, 1915], 385–393). Patten contradicted this view, however, in "Economic Zones and the New Alignment of National Sentiment," *Sur*, XXXIII (March 6, 1915), 613, when he declared that "eugenics is giving us a stronger man and a vigorous woman." In *Culture and War* (New York, 1916), 51, he reasserted his preference for environmental change. In 1918, however, he returned to ambiguity when he told a newspaper reporter that the United States would not be a "dumping ground" for "undesirable" people after the war, without specifying whether undesirability was a result of heredity or environment ("The Best Will Come Over," Cleveland *Plain Dealer*, Dec. 22, 1918, Alumni Records File, University of Pennsylvania Archives).

38. Simon N. Patten, "Social Reform and Politics," *Sur*, XVIII (April 27, 1912), 173–174; J. Russell Smith and Scott Nearing to the author; Roswell C. McCrea, in Leo S. Rowe *et al.*, "Memorial Addresses on the Life and Services of Simon N. Patten," *Annals*, CVII (May, 1923), Suppl., 353. Patten's students—William Draper Lewis, Samuel M. Lindsay, and Henry Seager, for example—were leading members of the Progressive Party (Lindsay, *Recollections of Theodore Roosevelt* [Winter Park, Fla., 1955], *passim*).

39. Simon N. Patten, "The Relation of Voluntary to Political Action," *Sur*, XXIX (Jan. 4, 1913), 421–422; "Wanted: a New Kind of Social Worker," *Sur*, XXIX (Nov. 2, 1912), 116; "Social Hymns," *Sur*, XXIX (Dec. 7, 1912), 275. Patten wrote social poetry himself in order to provide models for more talented poets to follow. The national hymn, "America," became "My country 'tis in thee/ Thy ceaseless energy/ Evokes our best." This and other songs were published in Simon N. Patten, *Advent Songs* (New York, 1917) and *Songs of America* (New York, 1917). Clippings in the Alumni Records File, University of Pennsylvania Archives, indicate that the press across the nation was appalled by Patten's poetry.

40. "The Reorganization of Social Work," *Sur*, XXX (July 5, 1913), 468–469.

41. *Ibid.*, 471–472.

42. "New Year Resolutions," *Sur*, XXXI (Dec. 27, 1913), 361.

43. Simon N. Patten, "Theories of Progress," *AER*, II (March, 1912), 68.

Chapter VII. War and Social Reform, 1914–1918

1. Philadelphia *Inquirer*, Dec. 11, 1898, Alumni Records File, University of Pennsylvania Archives; cf. Simon N. Patten, *The Development of English Thought* (New York, 1898), 393.

2. *Inquirer*, Dec. 11, 1908; Simon N. Patten, "A Revision of American Policies," *Annals*, LIV (July, 1914), 193, 195.

3. "A Revision," 194, 196–197, 200; cf. Simon N. Patten, "Territorial Expansion," *University Lectures* (Philadelphia, 1915), 197–209; cf. William E. Leuchtenberg, "Progressivism and Imperialism: The Progressive Movement and American Foreign Policy," *Mississippi Valley Historical Review*, XXXIX (Dec., 1952), 498.

4. Patten, *Heredity and Social Progress* (New York, 1903), 202–203; cf. "The Relation of Sociology to Psychology," *Annals*, VIII (Nov., 1896), 450; "The World's Peace in the Making," *World's Work*, XXIII (Dec., 1911), 155–156; cf. Edward M. Burns, *David Starr Jordan: Prophet of Freedom* (Stanford, Calif., 1953), 78–106.

5. Norman Angell, *The Great Illusion* (London, 1910); Patten, "The World's Peace," 156; Joseph Schumpeter, *The Sociology of Imperialisms* (New York, 1951), 14, 90, 125.

6. Simon N. Patten, "Responsibility for the War," *NR*, I (Nov. 14, 1914), 21–22; "Causes and Issues of the War," Milwaukee *Free Press*, Nov. 24, 1914, n.p., Alumni Records File, University of Pennsylvania Archives. Graham Wallas, the English political scientist, replied to Patten in "United States of Europe," *NR*, I (Jan. 2, 1915), 24. Wallas sympathized with Patten's hope for a united Europe but denied that unity could be achieved by conquest and asserted that the "traditional policy of Germany and Austria-Hungary would be unfitted for its achievement." Recalling the Zaverne incident, Wallas denied that the Germans represented the "antiracist" point of view.

7. "Economic Zones and the New Alignment of National Sentiment," *Sur*, XXXIII (March 6, 1915), 612–613. Patten applied his concept of amalgamation to the idea of a united Europe, which he had broached the previous autumn in "The Unnatural Boundaries of European States," *Sur*, XXIV (April 3, 1915), 24–27, 31–32.

Economic progress made "larger states inevitable." He proposed that Europe be divided into "economic zones, each of which would be self-sufficing."

8. "Economic Zones," 612–613.

9. *Culture and War* (New York, 1916), 10, 14, 18–23, 26. Patten's concept of "ceaseless flow" seems similar to the doctrines of his French contemporary, Henri Bergson. There is no evidence, however, that Patten ever read Bergson or any other French writers. On Ostwald's attitude toward social change see Friedrich Hayek, *The Road to Serfdom* (Chicago, 1963), 173.

10. *Culture and War*, 27, 34, 38, 40.

11. *Ibid.*, 43–44.

12. *Ibid.*, 43–45, 47.

13. *Ibid.*, 48, 50, 53–61. Patten concluded that "we must have a world religion or no religion" (*ibid.*, 61).

14. Philadelphia *Inquirer*, Nov. 11, 1914, Alumni Records File, University of Pennsylvania Archives; Simon N. Patten, "Economic Fallacies that Favor War," *Moody's*, XVIII (Jan., 1915), 13–17.

15. Simon N. Patten, "The War and the Stock Market," *Moody's*, XVIII (March, 1915), 113–115; "The Future of the Stock Market," *Moody's*, XVIII (April, 1915), 161–163. Although Patten's view of the problems raised by the war was becoming increasingly complex, he still had more faith in German than in Anglo-American wisdom. "A reasonable compromise," he declared, could be "effected at any time if England were willing" (Philadelphia *Public Ledger*, Jan. 17, 1915, Alumni Records File, University of Pennsylvania Archives).

16. "The Financial Menace to America of the European War," *Annals*, LX (July, 1915), 123–124, 127, 129. In this article, Patten made his closest approach to an underconsumption theory of depressions: "People cut down their present consumption in favor of future consumption, through the fear of future want. Any new conditions diminishing the fear of future want will check the tendency to save and cause an increase of present consumption. The diminution of fear means a rising rate of interest. . . . Industrial progress is thus from a state where fears are static while risks are diminishing to a condition in which fears are diminishing and risks are static" (*ibid.*, 25).

17. "A Slump in Morality," *NR*, IV (Sept. 11, 1915), 155; "The Morality of Force," *NR*, IV (Oct. 16, 1915), 286.

18. "The Day of Financial Reckoning," *Moody's*, XIX (Jan., 1916), 37–39.

19. "Taxation after the War," *Annals*, LXIV (March, 1916), 210–214; cf. Philadelphia *North American*, Oct. 13, 1915, Alumni Records File, University of Pennsylvania Archives.

20. "The Basis of National Security," *Annals*, LXVI (July, 1916), 2, 4–5.

21. *Ibid.*, 10–11; "War Impoverishing Us, Says Patten," Philadelphia *Public Ledger*, Nov. 27, 1916, 7; "Dr. Patten Advocates Alliance with Britain on the Seas," New York *Times*, April 29, 1916, 11.

22. "The Basis," 11. Edward T. Devine seems to have expressed Patten's ideas on the war to the social workers in the peace movement (Paul U. Kellogg, "Notes Taken at the Cosmopolitan Club," July 8, 1915; cf. Patten, Philadelphia, Pa., to Kellogg, Feb. 17, 1917, *Survey* files, New York School of Social Work).

23. Philadelphia *Daily Pennsylvanian*, Feb. 28, 1917, Alumni Records File, University of Pennsylvania Archives; " U. S. Now Ready for War, Avers Patten," Philadelphia *Public Ledger*, March 13, 1917, 4.

24. Membership card, "Wisconsin Loyalty League," Ely Papers, State Historical Society of Wisconsin, Box 111; John Bates Clark, New York, N.Y., to William W. Folwell, March 13, 1917, Folwell Papers, Minnesota State Historical Society; Franklin H. Giddings, New York, N.Y., to Kellogg, Feb. 13, 1915, *Survey* files. American social scientists were not strikingly different in their attitudes toward the war from their colleagues in other countries. As early as 1911, for example, Eugen von Philippovich, a leading Austrian economist, told E. R. A. Seligman that "no economist in Austria or Hungary" would be "inclined to play a role in the peace movement." He did not think it "possible to throw a bridge over the deeper contrasts between nations and states" (Philippovich, Vienna, Austria, to Seligman, Nov. 11, 1911, Seligman Papers, Columbia University Library). See also Edmund J. James, Urbana-Champaign, Ill., to Johannes Conrad, Oct. 24, 1914, to Count J. von Bernstoff, Aug. 31, 1914, to Marie Krukenberg, May 11, 1915, Sept. 6, 1915, to Dr. Else Westen-Conrad, June 7, 1915; "Open Letter to the President of the United States" by James, n.d., probably 1915; Gifford Pinchot, New York, N.Y., to William Draper Lewis, Nov. 29, Dec. 20, 1915; Lewis, Philadelphia, Pa., to James, Nov. 5, 1915; Albert Shaw, New York, N.Y., to James, Feb. 19, 1916, James Papers, University of Illinois Archives. Cf. Merle E. Curti, "The American Scholar in Three Wars," *Journal of the History of Ideas*, III (June, 1942), 241–264.

25. Scott Nearing to the author, interview, Boston, Mass., Jan. 5, 1963; Margaret Mead to the author, interview, New York, N.Y., April 6, 1963; Lightner Witmer, *The Nearing Case* (New York, 1915), xii–xiii, 54–55, 116; Scott Nearing, *Social Religion* (New York, 1913), 20; *Educational Frontiers* (New York, 1925), 12.

26. Minutes of Trustees, XVI, Oct. 11, 1915, 264, University of Pennsylvania Archives; Nearing to the author, interview; Witmer, *Nearing Case, passim;* "Report of the Committee of Inquiry on the Case of Prof. Scott Nearing," *Bulletin of the American Association of University Professors,* II (May, 1916), 157–158; Arthur O. Lovejoy, Baltimore, Md., to Ely, June 29, 1915, Ely Papers, Box 98. Patten's views on academic freedom were not shared by many of his fellow economists. Ely, for example, also believed that a distinction should be made between "what is said in the classroom and what is said outside," but he felt that "there must always be certain restrictions upon freedom of utterance" (Ely, Madison, Wis., to Seligman, Dec. 18, 1914, Seligman Papers, Columbia University Library). Henry Carter Adams, who, like Ely, had been involved, before the turn of the century, in a controversy over the political implications of teaching the new economics, believed by 1915 that "nine times out of ten" academic-freedom disputes were the "fault of the man rather than of the institution" (H. C. Adams, Ann Arbor, Mich., to Allyn A. Young, April 26, 1915, Secretary's Files, A.E.A.).

27. Board of Trustees, University of Pennsylvania, to Patten, April 4, 1917, Archives General File; Eric F. Goldman, *John Bach McMaster, American Historian* (Philadelphia, 1943), 60; "Dr. Patten Will Leave U. of P. at End of This Year," Philadelphia *Public Ledger,* April 6, 1917, 1.

28. "Dr. Jordan on 'The Present Crisis,'" *Old Penn,* XV (April 6, 1917), 421; Minutes, Wharton School Faculty Meeting, April 16, 1917; Minutes of Trustees, XVII, June 11, 1917, 11. In his only public criticism of the trustees, Patten claimed that his retirement raised "anew the question of free speech, and is akin to the case of Dr. Scott Nearing, who virtually was forced out of the Wharton School" ("Ousts Pacifist Professor," New York *Times,* April 7, 1917, 13). The war issue forced a sort of selective perception on many of Patten's contemporaries. Joseph Willits, later dean of the Wharton School, recalled, for instance, "In 1917 . . . I didn't realize that he was retired because of his opposition to the American entry into the war. . . . I thought he had been retired at the earliest possible opportunity but I didn't realize there was a particular cause" (letter from Joseph Willits, New York, N.Y., to the author, Oct. 31, 1962).

29. "American Academy of Political and Social Science Discusses Problems of Present World War," Philadelphia *Public Ledger*, April 21, 1917, 16.

30. "Peace Without Force," *Annals*, LXXII (July, 1917), 31–40, reprinted in *Essays in Economic Theory* (New York, 1924), 350–356; "Problems of War Finance," *YR*, VII (Oct., 1917), 73.

31. "Problems," 85–88; "Liquidation Taxes," *Annals*, LXXV (Jan., 1918), 169, 175, 177. Patten's views on taxes were shared by Professor Frank W. Taussig of Harvard University, who was an adviser to President Woodrow Wilson. In 1919, Taussig recommended to Wilson "remodelling of the tax system, with income, excess profits, and estate taxes as the mainstays of the future" (quoted in Redvers Opie, "Frank William Taussig," *EJ*, L (June–Sept., 1940), 19.

32. "Mandeville in the Twentieth Century," *AER*, VIII (March, 1918), 88–98, reprinted in *Essays*, 461, 364. Edwin R. A. Seligman, in "Who Is the Twentieth Century Mandeville?" *AER*, VIII (March, 1918), Suppl., 339–349, attacked Patten's views on finance. He accused Patten of suffering lapses of both logic and understanding. Patten, he asserted, confused long-term production credit with short-term consumption credit; by a chain of illogic Patten held that while consumption credit might be socially useful, public production credit was dangerous. Seligman noted that Patten was thus led to "take back not a few of the statements which form a large part of the solid contributions he has made to economic science."

33. "The Tomorrow of Finance," *Annals*, LXXVI (March, 1918), 268–270.

34. "The Fallacy of Price Bidding," *Annals*, LXXVIII (July, 1918), 129–143, reprinted in *Essays*, 369–371.

35. *Essays*, 373–375.

36. *Ibid.*, 375.

37. "Making National Debts National Blessings," *Annals*, LXXXII (March, 1919), 40–49.

38. *Ibid.*, 49–51.

39. "The Failure of Liberal Idealism," *Freeman*, I (July 14, 21, 1920), 418–421, 444–446, reprinted in *Essays*, 376–385. Although Patten said to Scott Nearing in 1917, "Hurrah for the Russian Revolution," Nearing believes Patten was referring to the overthrow of Czarist despotism rather than to the Bolshevik revolution (Scott Nearing, *Educational Frontiers*, 186; Nearing to the author, interview).

Chapter VIII. Materialism, Collectivism, and Abundance,
1917–1922

1. For the generalizations about scientific materialism in this chapter I am heavily indebted to Donald H. Fleming, Introduction to *The Mechanistic Conception of Life* by Jacques Loeb (Cambridge, Mass., 1964).

2. Fleming, xi.

3. *Ibid.*, xx. Franklin H. Giddings, one of Patten's closest friends, was on the Bryn Mawr faculty when Loeb taught there. For the relationship between Patten and Giddings see below, Ch. IX.

4. Simon N. Patten, "The Mechanism of Mind," *Annals*, LXXI (May, 1917), 204–207, 214. For Patten's initial acquaintance with Freud's work see the hypothesis stated in Ch. VI, n. 36.

5. "The Track of Evolution," *Scientific Monthly*, V (Oct., 1917), 351, 358. For the German materialists' involvement with the science of nutrition see Fleming, ix.

6. "The Divided Self," *Mon*, XXIX (April 1919), 228, 230, 237; "The Genesis of Consciousness," *Mon*, XXIX (July, 1919), 435, 445, 447; "Wish and Will," *Mon*, XXX (Jan., 1920), 131–132, 133–135, 137, 139–140; Fleming, xvi, xxx. Patten may have derived some of his ideas about tropisms, reflexes, and instincts from Maurice Parmelee's *The Science of Human Behavior, Biological and Physiological* (New York, 1913), which was brought to the attention of economists by Wesley C. Mitchell, in "Human Behavior and Economics: A Survey of Recent Literature," *QJE*, XXIX (Nov., 1914), 1–47.

7. "An Analysis of Mental Defects," *Mon*, XXX (Jan., 1920), 107, 109, 111, 124–125. Since shock and fear arise from external events, Patten considered Freud's theory of the Oedipus complex too complicated: "Back of every hate are two things, a shock and a fear. The effect of this on parents and children is that discipline is enforced by the parent of the same sex while there is a laxness of discipline between parent and child of the opposite sex. . . . But there is more than this; parents use their children of the opposite sex to arouse their own sex feelings. . . . That elements of the father and mother complexes arise in this way can be explained without the use of [Freud's] subconscious philosophy" (*ibid.*, 109).

8. "Back Sliding on Social Work," *Sur*, XLIV (June 5, 1920), 339.

9. *Ibid.*, 338, 342–343.

10. *Ibid.,* 343.

11. "The Failure of Liberal Idealism," *Freeman,* I (July 14, 21, 1920), 418–421, 444–446, reprinted in *Essays in Economic Theory* (New York, 1924), 376–385.

12. *Essays,* 376–379, 381.

13. *Ibid.,* 378, 381, 385; Fleming, xii.

14. *Mud Hollow: From Dust to Soul* (Philadelphia, 1922), 378, 381.

15. *Ibid.,* 14, 62, 114, 163, 193.

16. *Ibid.,* 61, 71.

17. *Ibid.,* 90, 98, 105.

18. *Ibid.,* 75, 94, 98, 100

19. *Ibid.,* 156, 159, 161

20. *Ibid.,* 125, 194, 223–225.

21. *Ibid.,* 227.

22. *Ibid.,* 230–231, 383, 235, 239, 249, 252–253, 302–303.

23. *Ibid.,* 267, 270–271, 278, 279–281, 284, 288–289, 291–293.

24. *Ibid.,* 298, 308, 340, 365, 357, 363–364.

25. *Ibid.,* 383–384. *Mud Hollow* did not excite much attention when it appeared. Joseph Willits, a former student of Patten, reviewing for the *Annals,* CIII (Sept., 1922), 151–153, made the best possible case for the book: "Prophecy can scarcely be expected to be worked out into a logical, consistent and detailed philosophy, but rather must devote itself to outlining new territory for human thinking." William Leiserson, reviewing in *Sur,* XLVIII (Aug. 15, 1922), 627, declared that the second section of the book was one of the most valuable contributions to a "study of civilization in the United States" in recent years. An anonymous reviewer in the "Literary Review," New York *Evening Post,* July 29, 1922, Sect. II, 842, praised the book: "Nobody will bother about whether to place it with fiction or philosophy or sociology who once comes under the spell of this study of the soul." A reviewer in the "Book Review," New York *Times,* May 28, 1922, 16, called the book a "puzzle" and asserted that the "characters are abnormal or subnormal, and their actions are strangely incomprehensible." A reviewer in the London *Times Literary Supplement,* XXI (June 1, 1922), 366, called the novel a "maze of quasi-philosophical and metaphysical jargon."

26. Joseph Willits to the author, interview, New York, N.Y., June 6, 1962, Alfred H. Williams to the author, interview, Philadelphia, Pa., Dec. 27, 1962, Raymond T. Bye to the author, interview, Moylan, Pa., Sept. 13, 1962; letter from Matthew W. Black,

Philadelphia, Pa., to the author, June 27, 1962; Edward T. Devine, New York, N.Y., to Edmund J. James, Nov. 6, 1918, James Papers, University of Illinois Archives; Walter E. Weyl, "Diary," June 28, 1918, Weyl Papers, Rutgers University Library; Willits, review of *Mud Hollow*, 152; Francis Tyson, Pittsburgh, Pa., to Paul U. Kellogg, June 5, 1922, *Survey* files, New York School of Social Work; Philadelphia *Public Ledger*, June 23, 1922, Philadelphia *Bulletin*, July 25, 1922, New York *Times*, July 25, 1922, New York *World*, Aug. 27, 1922, Alumni Records File, University of Pennsylvania Archives. Patten was buried from the Presbyterian church in Philadelphia where he had worshiped regularly since 1887. The honorary pallbearers included the entire Wharton School faculty and such old friends as Henry R. Seager, Samuel M. Lindsay, Joseph French Johnson, Edward T. Devine, and William H. Allen. Several months after his death, Patten's friends organized two memorial meetings, at which he was eulogized (Richard T. Ely *et al.*, "Memorial to Former President Simon N. Patten," *AER*, XIII [March, 1923], Suppl., 259–293; Leo S. Rowe *et al.*, "Memorial Addresses on the Life and Services of Simon N. Patten," *Annals*, CVII [May, 1923], 335–367).

27. *The New Science* (Ithaca, N.Y., 1948), 70, 93, 330.

Chapter IX. The Communication of Abundance, 1890–1920

1. John B. Clark, review of *The Economic Basis of Protection* by Simon N. Patten, in *Annals*, II (Oct., 1890), 340–341; "Patten's Dynamic Economics," *Annals*, III (July, 1892), 30, 34, 44. Before Clark's review was published, Patten told him that he would hold his opinion "in high esteem" (Patten, Philadelphia, Pa., to Clark, April 6, 1892, Clark Papers, Columbia University Library). Clark's review of *Dynamic Economics* started a debate on various technical aspects of economic theory in the *Annals* in which four leading economic theorists, Eugen Böhm-Bawerk, Alfred Marshall, Clark, and Patten participated: Patten, "Cost and Utility," "Cost and Expense"; Clark, "The Surplus Gains of Labor"; Marshall, "Consumer's Surplus"; Böhm-Bawerk, "The Ultimate Standard of Value," *Annals*, III (Jan., March, May, 1893), 409–428, 607–617, 618–621, 703–735, V (Sept., 1894), 149–208. Cf. John B. Clark, *Essentials of Economic Theory* (New York, 1907), X, 42–44, 558; Frank W. Taussig, "Recent Literature on Protection," *QJE*, VII (Jan., 1893), 173–176; David Kinley, Urbana, Ill., to Richard T. Ely, May 22,

1900, Ely Papers, State Historical Society of Wisconsin, Box 30. A number of Patten's contemporaries were gradually converted to his doctrines. Arthur T. Hadley of Yale University, for example, refused at first to review *The Consumption of Wealth* because of his "radical disagreement" with it (Hadley, New Haven, Conn., to Edwin R. A. Seligman, July 1, 1889, Seligman Papers, Columbia University Library). By 1896, however, in *Economics* (New York, 1896), 70, Hadley accepted most of Patten's arguments on consumption. See also E. R. A. Seligman, *Essays in Economics* (New York, 1925), 150. For a detailed statement of the relationship between Patten and these men, as well as other economists, and for a summary of the correspondence among them see Daniel M. Fox, "Simon N. Patten: Moralist of American Abundance" (unpublished Ph.D. dissertation, Harvard University, 1964), ch. vii.

2. Edmund J. James, Urbana-Champaign, Ill., to W. Pohlmann, Nov. 6, 1906, James Papers, University of Illinois Archives; Ely, Madison, Wis., to Patten, Nov. 20, 1899, Oct. 8, 1903, Ely Papers, Boxes 27, 49; Charles Bullock, "Notes Taken at the University of Wisconsin, 1892–95," ms., Bullock Papers, Harvard University Archives; Ely, "A Decade of Economic Theory," *Annals*, XV (March, 1902), 247–249; C. F. Adams, Jr., Richard T. Ely, Franklin H. Giddings, and William T. Harris, "Discussion of Patten's 'The Educational Value of Political Economy,'" *AEA Pubs.*, VII (March, 1891), 104–113; Franklin H. Giddings, Springfield, Mass., to Lester F. Ward, June 23, 1887, Ward Papers, Brown University Library; Giddings, Northampton, Mass., to Seligman, Aug. 26, 1890, Seligman Papers; Franklin H. Giddings, review of *Principles of Economics* by Alfred Marshall, in *Annals*, I (Oct., 1890), 334–336; cf. Giddings, "Theory of Capital,"*QJE*, IV (Jan., 1890), 205; Giddings, "Utility, Economics, and Sociology," *Annals*, V (Nov., 1894), 398–404; Giddings, *The Principles of Sociology* (New York, 1896), 41, 51, 405–406; Patten, Philadelphia, Pa., to Ely, Oct. 12, 1903, Ely Papers, Box 49.

3. Clark, New York, N.Y., to Ely, May 2, 1902, quoted in Joseph Dorfman, *The Economic Mind in American Civilization* (New York, 1949), III, 187.

4. On professionalism see above, Ch. II. Patten's professional activities are treated in detail in Fox, ch. v. Among Patten's contributions to the discussion of the traditional disputed questions were "Malthus and Ricardo," *AEA Pubs.*, IV (Sept., 1889), 9–34; "The Interpretation of Ricardo," *QJE*, VII (April, 1893), 323–353; and "The Scope of Political Economy," *YR*, II (Nov., 1893), 364–387.

5. Simon N. Patten, *The Development of English Thought* (New York, 1898), 396. Patten was criticized for not attempting to be politically neutral in a presidential address to the British Economic Association in 1898 (James Bonar, "Old Lights and New in Economic Study," in R. L. Smyth, ed., *Essays in Economic Method, 1860–1913* [London, 1962], 165–186); cf. T. W. Hutchison, *A Review of Economic Doctrines 1870–1929* (Oxford, 1953), 63.

6. Hutchison, *A Review*, 88–92, viii–ix; T. W. Hutchison, *Positive Economic and Policy Objectives* (Cambridge, Mass., 1964), 142; cf. George J. Stigler, "The Nature and Role of Originality in Scientific Progress," *Economica*, XXII (Nov., 1935), 293–302.

7. R. S. Howey, *The Rise of the Marginal Utility School* (Lawrence, Kan., 1960); Hutchison, *A Review*, 18–19; Joseph Dorfman, "The Background of Institutional Economics," in *Institutional Economics* (Berkeley, 1963), 36–37.

8. Hutchison, *Positive Economics*, 18–38; cf. Mark Blaug, *Ricardian Economics: An Historical Study* (New Haven, 1958), 187, 215.

9. Hutchison, *Positive Economics*, 40, 43. Wesley C. Mitchell's *The Backward Art of Spending Money and Other Essays* (New York, 1937), contains many ideas quite similar to Patten's. Yet Mitchell had very little regard for Patten's work (Joseph Dorfman to the author, interview, New York, N.Y., Sept. 12, 1962). On Ely see above, n. 2. On Commons see Epilogue.

10. Hutchison, in *A Review*, 424–425, discusses the leading concerns of economists in the period.

11. On Keynes see Epilogue.

12. Hutchison, *A Review*, 100, 114, 272, 303–306.

13. Hutchison, *Positive Economics*, 40.

14. Hutchison, *A Review*, 246; Gustav Cassel, *Fundamental Thoughts in Economics* (London, 1925), 183, 106; D. H. Macgregor, *Economic Thought and Policy* (London, 1949), 1, 3, 4.

15. Hutchison, *A Review*, 119–128; John A. Hobson, *The Economics of Distribution* (New York, 1900), 331.

16. "The Subjective and Objective View of Distribution," *Annals*, IV (Nov., 1893), 378–403; review of *The Theory of Dynamic Economics* by Simon N. Patten, in *EJ*, II (Dec., 1892), 688–690; *The Evolution of Modern Capitalism* (London, 1893), 341–342.

17. Ely, Madison, Wis., to James T. Young, April 1, 1900, Ely Papers, Box 29; Hobson, review of *Dynamic Economics*, 690, "The Subjective and Objective View," 400, *Imperialism* (London, 1902), *passim*.

18. V. I. Lenin, *Imperialism: The Highest Stage of Capitalism* (Zurich, 1916), in *Collected Works* (New York, 1942), XIX, 83, 91, 173–175. Hobson did not mention Patten in his autobiography, *Confessions of an Economic Heretic* (London, 1938), although he did speak of other Americans, notably E. A. Ross and Thorstein Veblen. Patten's influence on Hobson is ignored in two recent publications dealing with him: E. E. Nemmers, *Hobson and Underconsumption* (Amsterdam, 1956), and Harvey J. Levin, "Standards of Welfare in Economic Thought," *QJE*, LXX (Feb., 1956), 117–138. Hobson did, however, utilize ideas which he may have derived from Patten in his later work, for example, in *Work and Wealth* (New York, 1914), vii, and in *Poverty in Plenty* (New York, 1931), 85.

19. Walter E. Weyl, "Diary," May 18, 1912, Weyl Papers, Rutgers University Library; Walter E. Weyl, *The New Democracy* (New York, 1912), 163, 166, 235. For Weyl's biography see Charles Forcey, *Crossroads of Liberalism* (New York, 1961). Weyl was an undergraduate at the Wharton School from 1890 to 1892 and a graduate student in 1893–1894 and from 1895 to 1897. He received grades of "distinction" in all of Patten's courses and spent one year studying with Johannes Conrad at Halle (Student Records, 1890–1894, 1896–1898, University of Pennsylvania Archives).

20. Weyl, *The New Democracy*, 259–260. Unlike Weyl, however, Patten did not finally predicate his reform program on a stable or declining population curve (Patten, "The Revival of Economic Orthodoxy," *PSM*, LXXXI [Sept., 1912], 249).

21. For details about Veblen's life, see Joseph Dorfman, *Thorstein Veblen and His America* (New York, 1934).

22. *Ibid.*, 68; Thorstein Veblen, *The Place of Science in Modern Civilization and Other Essays* (New York, 1919), *passim*; Hutchison, *A Review*, 264–267.

23. Thorstein Veblen, review of *The Development of English Thought* by Simon N. Patten, in *Annals*, XIV (July, 1899), 125, 127, 129, 131; David M. Potter, *People of Plenty* (Chicago, 1954), 174; David Riesman, *Abundance for What?* (New York, 1964), 160.

24. The controversies among economists and sociologists in the 1890's are summarized in Fox, ch. v. Patten's most widely read contributions to the debate were "The Failure of Biologic Sociology," *Annals*, IV (May, 1894), 919–947, and "The Relation of Economics to Sociology," *Annals*, V (Jan., 1895), 577–583.

25. Albion W. Small *et al.*, "The Relation of Sociology to Economics," *AEA Pubs.*, X (March, 1895), 107–109. Writing to Edward

A. Ross in 1894, Patten declared, "It is remarkable the hold sociology seems to have . . . but I am at least one economist who proposes to die game" (Patten, Philadelphia, Pa., to Ross, Oct. 8, 1894, Ross Papers, State Historical Society of Wisconsin). See also C. W. A. Veditz, "Organization of the American Sociological Society," *AJS*, XI (Jan., 1906), 555–563.

26. On Ward see Charles Hunt Page, *Class and American Sociology: From Ward to Ross* (New York, 1940); Lester F. Ward, review of *The Theory of Social Forces* by Simon N. Patten, in *AJS*, I (March, 1896), 636–637.

27. Lester F. Ward, "L'Economie de la Douleur et l'Economie du Plaisir," *Annales de l'Institut International de Sociologie*, IV (July, 1897), 89–134. Ward read the paper in a rough English translation on August 28, 1897, at the University of Chicago. See Ward's *Glimpses of the Cosmos* (New York, 1918), VI, 47; *Outlines of Sociology* (New York, 1899), 168, 205; *Pure Sociology* (New York, 1903), 98, 105, 243, 283, 284, 288. In *Applied Sociology* (Boston, 1906), 285, Ward used Patten's statement from *The Theory of Social Forces* (Philadelphia, 1896), 125, that the "end of morality is the best utilization of the environment" as one of several epigraphs to the final chapter. The other epigraphs were taken from Comte, Cuvier, and Francis Bacon.

28. Ward, review of *Theory of Social Forces*, 635, 638–639.

29. Ward, *Glimpses of the Cosmos*, IV, 180–189, 445; cf. *Psychic Factors in Civilization* (Boston, 1892), 266–271.

30. Patten, Philadelphia, Pa., to Ward, April 23, 1897; cf. Patten, Edinburgh, Scot., to Ward, July 29, 1897, Ward Papers. See also Patten, "The Failure of Biologic Sociology," 924–927, 933; "The Organic Concept of Society," *Annals*, V (Nov., 1894), 405–407.

31. Patten, Philadelphia, Pa., to Ross, April 27, Nov. 24, Dec. 17, 1892, July 23, 1893; Ross, Madison, Wis., to R. H. Garner, March 4, 1915; Patten, Philadelphia, Pa., to Ross, March 2, April 25, Oct. 8, 1894, Dec. 2, 1896; Patten, Eustis, Me., to Ross, July 4, 1905, Ross Papers. Another source of dispute between Patten and Ross may have been claims to primacy of authorship for the phrase "race suicide." Ross first used the term in 1901, in "The Causes of Race Superiority," *Annals*, XVIII (July, 1901), 88. Lester F. Ward, in "Eugenics, Euthenics and Eudemics," *AJS*, XVIII (May, 1913), 751, claimed that Ross's article made the first use of the term. Ross claimed primacy for himself in *The Social Trend* (New York, 1922), 17. Yet Patten had used the phrase in *The Development of English Thought* (New York, 1898), 385, and Rexford G. Tugwell, in

"Notes on the Life and Work of Simon Nelson Patten," *JPE*, XXXI (April, 1923), 201, claims that Patten used the term first. Dr. Julius Weinberg, who has done extensive research for a biography of Ross, believes that Ross probably coined the term, though he had been stimulated to think in terms of "race suicide" by Francis A. Walker as early as 1891 (Weinberg, Detroit, Mich., to the author, Feb. 28, 1963); cf. John Higham, *Strangers in the Land* (New Brunswick, N.J., 1955), 147. But neither Patten nor Ross ever indicated that the phrase, which was popularized by Theodore Roosevelt, came from Walker.

32. *Social Control* (New York, 1901), 34, 314–315; Ross, Madison, Wis., to Philip E. Keller, Feb. 25, 1937, Ross Papers. Cf. Don Martindale, *The Nature and Types of Sociological Theory* (Boston, 1960), 321–324.

33. The personal relationship between Patten and Giddings is revealed in letters in the Giddings Papers, Columbia University Library, for instance: Patten, Estes Park, Col., to Giddings, Aug. 19, 1895; Patten, Philadelphia, Pa., to Giddings, Oct. 29, 1898, May 21, 1897, Sept. 9, 27, 1901. Patten attacked Giddings' sociology in "The Relation of Economics to Sociology." Giddings replied in "Utility, Economics and Sociology" and "Sociology and the Abstract Sciences," *Annals*, V (Nov., 1894, March, 1895), 398–404, 756–765. For other points of intellectual divergence between the two men see Franklin H. Giddings, *Principles of Sociology* (New York, 1896), 41, 51, 405–406; *Inductive Sociology* (New York, 1901); 38–39, 232, 240, 243; "The Economic Ages," *PSQ*, XVI (June, 1901), 196, 218–220. See also Simon N. Patten, *Essays in Economic Theory* (New York, 1924), 275–276; cf. Martindale, 318–319.

34. Simon N. Patten, *The Development of English Thought*, *passim*.

Epilogue. The Triumph of Abundance, 1920–1965

1. Allen G. Gruchy, *Modern Economic Thought: The American Contribution* (New York, 1947), 408; Rexford G. Tugwell, "Experimental Economics," in R. G. Tugwell, ed., *The Trend of Economics* (New York, 1924), 374, 377, 409; *The Industrial System and the Governmental Arts* (New York, 1933), 4, 228; Gruchy, 442. Tug-

well's career is presented in detail in Bernard Sternsher, *Rexford Tugwell and the New Deal* (New Brunswick, N. J., 1964).

2. Henry A. Wallace, *Statesmanship and Religion* (New York, 1934), 6, 94, 97, 131, 138. Wallace recalls that Tugwell "tried to get me interested in Patten. . . . Rex looked on him as a truly great man" (letter from Wallace, South Salem, N.Y., to the author, March 6, 1963).

3. Herbert C. Hoover, *The Challenge to Liberty* (New York, 1934), 42, 86, 102, 123–124, 177–180.

4. On the medical materialists see Donald H. Fleming, Introduction to *The Mechanistic Conception of Life* by Jacques Loeb (Cambridge, Mass., 1964). For later scientific opinion see below, nn. 19 and 24.

5. Stuart Chase, *The Economy of Abundance* (New York, 1934), 28; John Dewey, *Liberalism and Social Action* (New York, 1935), 58, 50. Chase seems to have derived more from Patten than any of the others did, although Patten is only quoted once in his book. Most of the Patten influence on him seems to have come through Scott Nearing and Rexford Tugwell. Chase recalls, "I read a bit of Patten in my salad days, but he never made the impression on me that Veblen did or H. G. Wells, or even Scott Nearing. I went to Russia with Rexford Tugwell in 1927, and Rex was a devoted disciple of Simon Patten and quoted him at every opportunity" (letter from Chase, Georgetown, Conn., to the author, March 25, 1963).

It should be said that many Socialists took up the age-of-plenty theme in this period—notably Harold Laski in England and Norman Thomas in the United States. See, for example, Norman Thomas, *Human Exploitation* (New York, 1934); Harold Laski, *Reflections on the Revolution of Our Time* (London, 1940). But, unlike Patten and the others treated in this study, the Socialists believed that the age of plenty required a massive redistribution of wealth rather than a mere rethinking and reordering of the means of producing and consuming wealth.

6. Extrapolating from Patten's thought, it seems likely that he would have argued that the harnessing of energy and the improvement of industrial techniques were sufficiently well handled by capitalists within the existing institutional fabric of American society. He was more concerned with what was produced and how goods were consumed than with the improvement of production and the application of technology to all social institutions. Moreover, he was satisfied with orthodox monetary theories and would

have resisted the Technocrats' desire to replace the specie standard with units based on energy.

7. *The General Theory of Employment, Interest and Money* (London, 1936), 30–31, 377.

8. *Ibid.*, 377, 378; letter to the London *Times*, Sept. 13, 1938.

9. *The Economic Consequences of the Peace* (London, 1919), 21; *Essays in Persuasion* (London, 1931), 334–335, 364–367.

10. *Essays in Persuasion*, 334; John R. Commons, *The Distribution of Wealth* (New York, 1893), 4–5, 116, 121, 131, 169.

11. *The Legal Foundations of Capitalism* (New York, 1924), 135; *Institutional Economics* (New York, 1934), 201, 886.

12. *Institutional Economics*, 259, 284, 621, 628.

13. *Ibid.*, 773, 794, 893.

14. *Ibid.*, 774; Keynes, *Essays in Persuasion*, 334–335.

15. Keynes, *General Theory, passim; Essays in Biography* (London, 1933).

16. Letter from Keynes to William Beveridge, March 17, 1942, quoted in Beveridge, *Power and Influence* (New York, 1955), 309; Beveridge, *Social Insurance and Allied Services* (London, 1942), 165–166; Friedrich A. Hayek, *The Road to Serfdom* (Chicago, 1963), 98, 188, 192–193; Keynes's comments are quoted in Hayek's book—I have not located the original source.

17. Colin Clark, *The Conditions of Economic Progress* (London, 1940), 3–4; *ibid.* (3d ed.; London and New York, 1957), "Preface to the Second Edition," dated 1947, x–xiv; Hayek, 98.

18. Clark, 3d ed., x, xi, 5, 492–494. It does not seem that Clark was influenced by Simon Patten. He does, however, rely heavily on an article by Allyn Young, "Increasing Returns and Economic Progress," *EJ*, XXXVIII (Dec., 1928), 527–542. Young, who taught at Harvard, was familiar with Patten's work.

19. D. H. Macgregor, *Economic Thought and Policy* (London, 1949), 2, 17–19, 166–167. Among the authors who embraced the assumption of abundance were Edward H. Carr, in *The Conditions of Peace* (London, 1942); James B. Carey, secretary-treasurer of the Congress of Industrial Organizations, in a speech of June 16, 1943, quoted in Eugene Staley, *World Economic Development* (Montreal, 1944), 20–21 (Staley himself was rather equivocal); Percival and Paul Goodman, in *Communitas* (Chicago, 1947); Lancelot Hogben, in *Science for the Citizen* (London, 1938); Roderick Saidenberg, in *Post-Historic Man* (Chapel Hill, N.C., 1950); Bernhard J. Stern, in "Social Aspects of Technology," *Annals*, CCXLII (Nov., 1945), 46–52. A number of prominent scholars questioned the opti-

mists in these years. To name a few: A. L. Bowley, "Production and Efficiency," *Journal of the Royal Statistical Society*, CII (April, 1939), Part I, 1–16; Charles Galton Darwin, *The Next Million Years* (London, 1952); George O'Brien, *The Phantom of Plenty* (Dublin, 1948).

20. John K. Galbraith, *The Affluent Society* (Boston, 1958), 120, 123, 143, 151, 209, 291, 295, 356; *American Capitalism: The Concept of Countervailing Power* (Boston, 1952), 108. For the similarities in the two men's backgrounds see Galbraith's *The Scotch* (Boston, 1964).

21. *The Stages of Economic Growth* (Cambridge, Eng., 1960), 80–81, 73, 91, 166–167.

22. The intent of this paragraph is neither to denigrate the classical style nor to suggest that Galbraith and Keynes were uninfluenced by institutional and historical economics. I am merely characterizing their emphases, not entering into the professional debates of economists.

23. Joseph Schumpeter, *History of Economic Analysis* (New York, 1954), 875–876. Schumpeter was familiar with Patten's work from the beginning of his own career; see, for example, "Die Neuere Wirtschaftstheorie in den Vereinigten Staaten," *Jahrbücher für Gesetzgebung, Verwaltung, und Volkswirtschaft*, XXXIV (1910), 49–51. The ambivalence about abundance among development economists is also reflected in the work of Eugene Staley. See, for example, his *World Economic Development* (Montreal, 1944), 2, 11, 22, 29; cf. Barbara Ward, *Toward a World of Plenty?* (Toronto, 1964).

24. A few recent books which explore the problems of abundance, potential or actual: Adolf A. Berle, *The American Economic Republic* (New York, 1963); Harrison Brown, James Bonner, and John Weir, *The Next Hundred Years* (New York, 1961); Kenneth Boulding, *The Meaning of the Twentieth Century* (New York, 1964); Gunnar Myrdal, *Challenge to Affluence* (New York, 1964); Bernard D. Nossiter, *The Mythmakers: An Essay on Power and Wealth* (Boston, 1964); Gerald Piel, *Science in the Cause of Man* (New York, 1962); Robert Theobald, *The Challenge of Abundance* (New York, 1961).

I do not intend specific criticism of any of these books. Each, however, tends to fall into one of the two groups I have characterized. Moreover, there is a lack of historical perspective in all these books, stemming in part from the assumption that, except for some utopians, nobody examined the problems of emerging abundance before the Second World War, or, in some instances, before Professor Galbraith.

25. David Riesman, with Nathan Glazer and Reuel Denney, *The Lonely Crowd* (New Haven, 1950; New York, 1956), *passim;* David Riesman, *Abundance for What?* (New York, 1964), xiii, 47, 49, 110, 120, 171, 182–183, 291–292, 107. The problem raised by talking about potential and actual abundance at the same time has been well stated by David Potter, *People of Plenty* (Chicago, 1954), 84: "A vital distinction separates mere potential abundance—the copious supply of natural resources—and actual abundance—the availability to society of a generous quota of goods ready for use. . . . To say that physical plenty is conducive to social plenty—that the potential precedes the actual—is not at all the same as to say that every potentiality will become an actuality or even that the growing actuality will remain within the limits indicated by the potentiality from which it sprang."

26. Riesman, *The Lonely Crowd*, 349; cf. *Faces in the Crowd* (New Haven, 1952).

27. *Eros and Civilization* (New York, 1962), 1, 12, 13, 16, 32, 34, 84–85, 139, 143.

28. On Roosevelt see Potter, 120; Franklin D. Roosevelt, *Looking Forward* (New York, 1933), 49; Basil Rauch, ed. *The Roosevelt Reader* (New York, 1957), *passim.* For Lyndon Johnson see "Transcript of the President's Acceptance Speech," New York *Times*, Aug. 29, 1964, 6; "Text of the President's Message to Congress on the State of the Union," New York *Times*, Jan. 5, 1965, 16. John F. Kennedy occasionally used the abundance frame of reference, for instance in his letter transmitting his first antipoverty bill to Congress, quoted in Ben H. Bagdikian, *In the Midst of Plenty* (New York, 1964), i. But Kennedy, unlike Johnson, did not use abundance as the central assumption behind his program.

29. Quoted in Gertrude Himmelfarb, Introduction to *On Population* by Thomas Robert Malthus (New York, 1960), xxx.

A Note on Sources

The sources used in preparing this study fall into three general categories: those relating to the climate of opinion in social science in which the abundance frame of reference developed; those relating directly to Simon N. Patten; and those relating to the general intellectual, social, and economic history of the period.

I would like to thank the following institutions which have granted me permission to publish excerpts from letters and manuscript materials in their possession: American Economic Association, letters in the Secretary's Files; Brown University Library, Lester Ward Collection; Columbia University Libraries, John Bates Clark, Franklin H. Giddings, and Edwin Seligman collections; Oral History Research Office of Columbia University, William H. Allen oral history memoir; University of Illinois Archives, Edmund J. James Papers; Michigan Historical Collections of the University of Michigan, Henry C. Adams Papers; Minnesota Historical Society, William W. Folwell Collection; New York Public Library, Lillian Wald Papers; University Archives of the University of Pennsylvania, Archives General, Alumni Records, and Wharton School Files; State Historical Society of Wisconsin, Richard T. Ely and Edward A. Ross papers; Yale University Library, Farnam Family Papers.

A number of general works on the history of economic thought were useful for this study. Joseph Schumpeter's *History of Economic Analysis* (New York, 1954) is probably the most perceptive study of the complexity of professional economics. O. H. Taylor's *A History of Economic Thought* (New York, 1960) is a sophisticated attempt to place economic thought in the context of general economic development. Mark Blaug's *Ricardian Economics: A Historical Study* (New Haven, 1958) is an outstanding monograph on the history of classical economics in England. R. S. Howey's *The Rise of the Marginal Utility School* (Lawrence, Kan., 1960) is a trenchant study of an international revolution in economic thought. T. W. Hutchison's *A Review of Economic Doctrines, 1870–1929* (Oxford, 1953) is a sophisticated survey of the field. Hutchison's article "Insularity and Cosmopolitanism in Economic Ideas, 1870–1914" (*AER*, XLV [May, 1955], Suppl., 1–16) is of considerable importance for understanding the complexity of international relations among economists in the period. His recent book, *Positive Economics and Policy Objectives* (Cambridge, Mass., 1964), is a penetrating study of methodological controversy among economists over the past century. Articles by Mary J. Bowman, J. J. Spengler, and George Stigler cited in my notes were extremely useful.

A great deal of impressive scholarly work has been done on the history of American economic thought in this period. Joseph Dorfman's volumes, *The Economic Mind in American Civilization*, III (New York, 1949) and *Thorstein Veblen and His America* (New York, 1934), are still the best guide. The best study of the influence of German education on American economists is Jack C. Myles's "German Historicism and American Economics" (unpublished Ph.D. dissertation, Princeton University, 1956). Dorfman's article "The Role of the German Historical School in American Economic Thought" (*AER*, XLV [May,

1955], Suppl., 17–28) contains some stimulating insights. A number of works by the English historian Alfred W. Coats were extremely valuable. His "Methodological Controversy as an Approach to the History of American Economics" (unpublished Ph.D. dissertation, The Johns Hopkins University, 1953) is the best study of American economic logic in Patten's generation. Professor Coats has graciously provided access to a more recent version of this study, soon to appear as a book. A number of Coats's articles cited in my notes have shed considerable light on the profession of economics in the period and have suggested lines for further investigation. Allen G. Gruchy's *Modern Economic Thought: The American Contribution* (New York, 1947) contains some useful material, although it is heavily biased in defense of the institutional school.

The history of sociology and psychology needs considerable work. Don Martindale's *The Nature and Types of Sociological Theory* (Boston, 1960) is a trenchant contribution to the history of sociological doctrines. John Madge's *The Origins of Scientific Sociology* (New York, 1963) does not live up to the promise of its title but contains several excellent chapters, particularly on methodology in the past generation. The best history of the sociological profession is still Albion W. Small's *The Origins of Sociology* (Chicago, 1924). Luther L. and Jessie Bernard's *Origins of American Sociology* (New York, 1943) and Howard W. Odum's *American Sociology* (New York, 1951) and *American Masters of Social Science* (New York, 1927) are useful catalogues of names and ideas. *The History and Prospects of the Social Sciences* (New York, 1925), edited by Harry Elmer Barnes, contains several excellent essays, notably Kimball Young's "Social Psychology." William T. O'Connor's *Naturalism and the Pioneers of American Sociology* (Washington, D.C., 1942) and Charles Hunt Page's *Class and American Sociology* (New York, 1940) are occasionally perceptive but do not use unpublished documents and ignore the intellectual context in which sociology developed. Edwing G. Boring's *A History of Experimental Psychology* (New York, 1950) is still the standard source. Fay B. Karpf's *American Social Psychology* (New York, 1932) is a useful guide to ideas and men which has not been superseded.

The history of social science must be studied in terms of men as well as of ideas. Various Europeans contributed to the development of the concept of a transition to abundance—notably Wilhelm Roscher, Johannes Conrad, Eugen Böhm-Bawerk, Karl Marx, John Stuart Mill, and Herbert Spencer. The writings of such American contemporaries of Patten as Henry Carter Adams, John Bates Clark, John R. Commons, Richard T. Ely, Franklin H. Giddings, Edward A. Ross, William Graham Sumner, Francis A. Walker, and Lester F. Ward reveal the intellectual atmosphere in which Patten's thought matured. An important source for the views of Patten and his German-trained colleagues is *Science Economic Discussion* (New York, 1887), by Richard T. Ely and others, a symposium in which the new economists refuted their more conservative colleagues. The autobiographies of a number of Patten's contemporaries shed light on the intellectual context of the period, particularly those of William H. Allen, Richard T. Ely, John R. Commons, Edward T. Devine, G. Stanley Hall, John A. Hobson, Alvin S. Johnson, Emory R. Johnson, David Kinley, Benjamin C. Marsh, John A. Ryan, Edward A. Ross, and Rexford G. Tugwell.

A number of biographies of American social scientists provided useful background for this study—particularly Charles A. Barker's *Henry George* (New York, 1955), Alfred Bornemann's *J. Laurence Laughlin* (Washington, D.C., 1940), Edward M. Burns's *David Starr Jordan* (Stanford, Calif., 1953), Joseph Dorfman's *Thorstein Veblen and His America* (New York, 1934), Edward A. Fitzpatrick's *McCarthy of Wisconsin* (New York, 1944), Patrick W. Gearty's *John A. Ryan* (Washington, D.C., 1953), Arnold W. Green's *Henry Charles Carey* (Philadelphia, 1951), Eric F. Goldman's *John Bach McMaster* (Philadelphia, 1943), L. G. Harter's *John R. Commons* (Corvallis, Ore., 1962), James Leiby's *Carroll Wright and Labor Reform* (Cambridge, Mass., 1960), James P. Munroe's *Francis A. Walker*

(New York, 1923), Muriel Pumphrey's "Mary Richmond" (unpublished D.S.W. dissertation, New York School of Social Work, 1956), and Julius Weinberg's "Edward A. Ross" (unpublished Ph.D. dissertation, University of Michigan, 1963).

Neither Patten nor any members of his immediate family left any papers. Documents about Patten's parents and his childhood environment can be found in Jennie M. Patten's *History of the Somonauk United Presbyterian Church* (Chicago, 1928). Rexford G. Tugwell's "Notes on the Life and Work of Simon N. Patten" (*JPE*, XXXI [April, 1923], 153–208) is a useful source of anecdotes about Patten's early life, many of them told to Tugwell by Patten himself.

The Jennings Seminary Papers provide background on the curriculum and faculty of the secondary school Patten attended. His final-report sheet from Jennings and his grade records at Northwestern University are in the Registrar's Files, Northwestern University Archives. Patten's only surviving comments on his years in Germany date from the middle years of his life and are in letters preserved in the papers of Richard T. Ely and Edwin R. A. Seligman. The life and thought of Patten's teacher in Germany, Johannes Conrad, are ably presented in an essay by Karl Diehl. Richard T. Ely's *Ground Under Our Feet* (New York, 1938) contains revealing anecdotes about Patten as a young scholar.

There is little information about Patten's career between 1879 and 1887. Tugwell is the best source on this period, although he notes that Patten did not like to speak about these years. Ely's *Ground Under Our Feet* and Edward T. Devine's *When Social Work Was Young* (New York, 1938) present anecdotal material. Later recollections of the efforts of Patten and Edmund James to establish an association of economists in these years can be found in the James and Ely papers.

Patten's activities at the Wharton School are reflected in various documents in the University of Pennsylvania Archives— particularly in the Archives General, Alumni Records, and Wharton School Faculty files. His activities in the American

Economic Association are recorded in correspondence in the Secretary's Files. Data about his life and work are contained in letters in the Henry Carter Adams, Richard T. Ely, Henry W. Farnam, William W. Folwell, Franklin H. Giddings, Edmund J. James, Roswell C. McCrea, Edward A. Ross, Edwin R. A. Seligman, Albion W. Small, and Frederick J. Turner papers. Some of his activities as a theoretician of social work are recorded in *The Survey* files, the Paul U. Kellogg Papers, and Devine's autobiography. Anecdotes about Patten in this period can be found in Tugwell's essay and in memorial essays read at meetings of the American Economic Association and the American Academy of Political and Social Science. William H. Allen, Raymond T. Bye, Matthew W. Black, Joseph Dorfman, Solomon S. Huebner, Alvin S. Johnson, William E. Lingelbach, Margaret Mead, Scott Nearing, Ernest M. Patterson, S. Howard Patterson, Frances Perkins, J. Russell Smith, Alfred H. Williams, and Joseph Willits provided useful anecdotal material in interviews with the author. Harry Elmer Barnes, Stuart Chase, Shelby M. Harrison, Rexford G. Tugwell, Henry A. Wallace, and Walter S. Tower recalled details about Patten's life and thought in letters to the author.

An exhaustive chronological bibliography of Patten's writings was compiled by James Boswell, in *The Economics of Simon Nelson Patten* (Philadelphia, 1934). Only a few additional articles were found in the course of my study. Patten's most significant articles appeared in the *Annals of the American Academy of Political and Social Science*. From 1888 to 1903, Patten contributed articles to most of the leading American periodicals, as well as to a few European journals, devoted to economics and sociology. After 1905, he wrote more articles for *Charities and the Commons*—later *The Survey*—the social workers' magazine, and for more popular periodicals like *The Independent*, the *New Republic, Popular Science Monthly*, and *Science* than for scholarly journals. Most of his newspaper articles can be found in the Alumni Records File, University of Pennsylvania Archives.

The most significant contemporary analyses of Patten's work were written by Benjamin M. Anderson, John Bates Clark, Franklin H. Giddings, John A. Hobson, Ugo Rabbeno, Henry R. Seager, Thorstein Veblen, and Lester F. Ward. The articles are cited in the Bibliography, below.

Boswell's monograph, though the best summary of Patten's economic theories, ignores his social thought and does not trace changes in Patten's ideas during his career. John R. Everett's *Religion in Economics* (New York, 1946) goes beyond available sources to romanticize Patten's life. Moreover, Everett's analysis of Patten's thought seems to be based on a small sample of Patten's writings. The chapter on Patten in David Noble's *The Paradox of Progressive Thought* (St. Paul, Minn., 1958) contains perceptive insights. Noble, however, distorts some of Patten's ideas in order to argue his thesis about American thought in the period: He regards Patten as a follower of Auguste Comte, despite Patten's frequent attacks on Comte, and misreads Patten's concept of "stalwartism" as a glorification of the American middle class. The chapter on Patten in Sidney Fine's *Laissez-Faire and the General Welfare State* (Ann Arbor, Mich., 1958) is generally accurate and suggestive. Another excellent summary of Patten's ideas is in the third volume of Joseph Dorfman's *The Economic Mind in American Civilization*.

A number of works help place social science and the life of Simon Patten in the context of an age. Koppel S. Pinson, in *Modern Germany* (New York, 1954), Samuel P. Hays, in *The Response to Industrialism* (Chicago, 1957), and Arthur M. Schlesinger, Sr., in *The Rise of the City* (New York, 1933) describe the changes in German and American society during the period. Annie Ashley's *The Social Policy of Bismarck* (London, 1912) is still the best survey of the content of German social legislation and its influence on the social policy of other nations in the late nineteenth and early twentieth centuries.

The history of higher education in this period is treated in several works. The best description of German universities is still Johannes Conrad's *The German Universities for the Last*

Fifty Years (Glasgow, 1885). Charles W. Thwing's *The American and the German University* (New York, 1928) is a useful comparative study. Fredrick Rudolph's *The American College and University* (New York, 1962) is an instructive general history. Anna Haddow's *Political Science in American Colleges and Universities, 1636–1900* (New York, 1939) contains useful data. Richard Hofstadter and Walter Metzger's *The Development of Academic Freedom in the United States* (New York, 1955) is a valuable study of the intellectual climate in American universities. Edward P. Cheyney's *History of the University of Pennsylvania* (Philadelphia, 1940) and various pamphlet and typescript materials in the University of Pennsylvania Archives illuminate the history of Patten's immediate academic environment.

There are many outstanding works on the intellectual and social currents of the period. The essays in *Paths of American Thought* (Boston, 1964), edited by Morton White and Arthur M. Schlesinger, Jr., contribute to an understanding of the complexity of intellectual history. The influence of Darwinism on Western and, more particularly, American thought is ably treated by Bert J. Loewenberg, in "Darwinism Comes to America, 1859–1900" (*Mississippi Valley Historical Review*, XXVIII [Dec., 1941], 339–368), by Richard Hofstadter, in *Social Darwinism in America* (Boston, 1960), and by Philip Wiener, in *Evolution and the Founders of Pragmatism* (Cambridge, Mass., 1939). American intellectuals' attitudes toward racism and immigration are discussed by John Higham, in *Strangers in the Land* (New Brunswick, N.J., 1955) and by Barbara M. Solomon, in *Ancestors and Immigrants* (Cambridge, Mass., 1956). William E. Leuchtenberg's "Progressivism and Imperialism" (*Mississippi Valley Historical Review*, XXXIX [Dec. 1952], 483–504) contains several suggestive ideas about the relation between progressivism and imperialism. Bernard Semmel's *Imperialism and Social Reform* (London, 1960) implicitly raises some interesting questions about American attitudes, although it deals entirely with European sources. Similarly, William Simon's recent work, *European Positivism in the Nineteenth Century* (Ithaca, N.Y., 1963), is useful for students of American intellectual history. Donald Fleming's Introduction to *The Mechanistic Conception of Life* by Jacques Loeb (Cambridge, Mass., 1964) is a brilliant survey of the history of scientific materialism in Europe and the United States.

The best general history of American philanthropy is Robert Bremner's *American Philanthropy* (Chicago, 1960). The history of American social work is chronicled by Frank J. Bruno in *Trends in Social Work, 1874–1956* (New York, 1957). Some of the dilemmas of social workers in the years around the turn of the century are examined by Roy Lubove in *The Progressives and the Slums* (Pittsburgh, 1962) and *The Professional Altruist* (Cambridge, Mass., 1965). The best survey of changing attitudes toward poverty in Europe and the United States is Calvin Woodward's "Reality and Social Reform: The Transition from Laissez-Faire to the Welfare State" (*Yale Law Journal*, LXII [Dec., 1962], 286–328). David Owen's *English Philanthropy, 1660–1960* (Cambridge, Mass., 1964) and Asa Briggs's *A Study of the Work of Seebohm Rowntree* (London, 1961) describe the international context in which late nineteenth- and early twentieth-century social reform occurred. James H. Timberlake, in *Prohibition and the Progressive Movement* (Cambridge, Mass., 1963), Lawrence Cremin, in *The Transformation of the School* (New York, 1961), E. V. McCollom, in *A History of Nutrition* (Boston, 1957), and Raymond C. Callahan, in *Education and the Cult of Efficiency* (Chicago, 1964), probe areas of reform to which the abundance frame of reference was relevant. Charles Forcey's *The Crossroads of Liberalism* (New York, 1961) is a study of three men who were deeply influenced by Patten's generation of social scientists. Louis Hartz's *The Liberal Tradition in America* (New York, 1955) is a useful corrective for the impulse to emphasize the radicalism of any American thinker at the expense of his liberalism.

There are no secondary works which deal with the concept of a transition from an age of scarcity to an age of abundance.

David Potter's *People of Plenty* (Chicago, 1954) examines the influence of abundance on American national character but treats the intellectual history of the concept only in passing. Herbert Marcuse's *Eros and Civilization* (Boston, 1955) examines the psychological implications of the transition. The most significant sources for understanding contemporary thought on abundance are John K. Galbraith's *The Affluent Society* (Boston, 1958), David Riesman's *The Lonely Crowd* (New Haven, 1950), and *Abundance for What?* (New York, 1964), and Walt W. Rostow's *The Stages of Economic Growth* (Cambridge, Eng., 1960).

Bibliography

MANUSCRIPTS

Adams, Henry Carter, Papers, 1880–1920, Michigan Historical Collections.

Allen, William H., Reminiscences, Oral History Collection, Columbia University Library.

American Academy of Political and Social Science, Minutes, 1889–1922, Philadelphia, Pa.

American Economic Association, Secretary's Files, 1885–1920, Evanston, Ill.

Bullock, Charles, Papers, 1890–1920, Harvard University Archives.

Clark, John Bates, Papers, 1880–1922, Columbia University Library.

Ely, Richard T., Papers, 1880–1922, State Historical Society of Wisconsin.

Farnam, Henry W., Papers, 1878–1920, Yale University Library.

Folwell, William W., Papers, 1880-1920, Minnesota Historical Society.

Giddings, Franklin H., Papers, 1890–1902, Columbia University Library.

James, Edmund J., Papers, 1885–1922, University of Illinois Archives.

Jennings Seminary, Catalogues and Visitors' Reports, 1869–1873, Garrett Biblical Institute.

Kellogg, Paul U., Papers, 1912–1922, New York School of Social Work.

McCarthy, Charles F., Papers, 1905–1914, State Historical Society of Wisconsin.

McCrea, Roswell C., Papers, 1905–1910, in possession of Joseph Dorfman, New York, N.Y.

Northwestern University Archives, Registrar's Files, 1875–1877.

Ross, Edward A., Papers, 1890–1910, State Historical Society of Wisconsin.

Seligman, Edwin R. A., Papers, 1878–1922, Columbia University Library.

Small, Albion W., Papers, 1904, University of Chicago Library.

Survey Associates Files, 1910–1922, New York School of Social Work.

Taylor, Fred M., Papers, 1890–1900, Michigan Historical Collections.

Turner, Frederick J., Papers, 1892, 1897, Huntington Library.

University of Pennsylvania Archives: Archives General, Alumni Records, and Wharton School Files, 1882–1922.

Weyl, Walter E., "Diary," Rutgers University Library.

PRINTED SOURCES

The titles of frequently cited periodicals have been abbreviated as follows:

AEA Bull.	*Bulletin of the American Economic Association*
AEA Pubs.	*Publications of the American Economic Association*
AER	*American Economic Review*
AJS	*American Journal of Sociology*
ASS Pubs.	*Publications of the American Sociological Society*
CC	*Charities and the Commons*
EJ	*Economic Journal*
ER	*Educational Review*
IJE	*International Journal of Ethics*
Ind	*The Independent*
Jahrbücher	*Jahbücher für Nationalökonomie und Statistik*
JPE	*Journal of Political Economy*
Mon	*The Monist*
Moody's	*Moody's Magazine*
Na	*The Nation*
NR	*New Republic*

PSM   *Popular Science Monthly*
PSQ   *Political Science Quarterly*
QJE   *Quarterly Journal of Economics*
Sci   *Science*, New Series
Sur   *The Survey*
YR   *Yale Review*

Books and Monographs by Simon N. Patten

Advent Songs. New York, 1916.
The Consumption of Wealth. Philadelphia, 1889, 1901.
Culture and War. New York, 1916.
The Development of English Thought. New York, 1898.
The Economic Basis of Protection. Philadelphia, 1890, 1900.
The Educational Value of Political Economy. Baltimore, 1890.
Essays in Economic Theory, ed. Rexford G. Tugwell. New York, 1924.
Das Finanzwesen der Staaten und Städte der Nordamerikanischen Union. Jena, Ger., 1878.
Heredity and Social Progress. New York, 1903.
Mud Hollow: From Dust to Soul. Philadelphia, 1922.
The New Basis of Civilization. New York, 1907–1921.
The Premises of Political Economy. Philadelphia, 1885.
The Principles of Rational Taxation. Philadelphia, 1890.
Product and Climax. New York, 1909.
The Reconstruction of Economic Theory. Philadelphia, 1912.
The Social Basis of Religion. New York, 1911.
Songs of America. New York, 1917.
The Stability of Prices. Baltimore, 1888.
The Theory of Dynamic Economics. Philadelphia, 1892.
The Theory of Prosperity. New York, 1902.
The Theory of Social Forces. Philadelphia, 1896.

Articles by Simon N. Patten

"An Analysis of Mental Defects," *Mon*, XXX (Jan., 1920), 107–125.
"Another View of the Ethics of Land Tenure," *IJE*, I (April, 1891), 354–370.
"Are Pensions for College Teachers a Form of Socialism?" *Sci*, XXVII (May 22, 1908), 822–824.

"An Attempt to Define Socialism," with John Martin *et al.*, *AEA Bull.*, IV (April, 1911), 347–367.

"The Background of Economic Theories," *ASS Pubs.*, VII (1912), 126–130.

"Back Sliding on Social Work," *Sur*, XLIV (June 5, 1920), 338–343.

"The Basis of National Security," *Annals*, LXVI (July, 1916), 1–11.

"Becoming American," *Open Court*, XXIX (July, 1915), 385–393.

"Die Bedeutung der Lehre vom Grenznutzen," *Jahrbücher*, LVII (Oct., 1891), 481–534.

"The Beginning of Utility," *Annals*, V (Sept., 1894), 257–260.

"Better an Inspiration of Oxygen than of Alcohol," *CC*, XXI (Nov. 21, 1908), 299–300.

"Can Economics Furnish an Objective Standard for Morality?" *Journal of Speculative Philosophy*, XXII (Sept., 1892), 322–332.

"The Church as a Social Institution," *Ind*, LXXI (July 20, 1911), 131–133.

"The Conflict Theory of Distribution," *YR* (Aug., 1908), 156–184.

"A Contribution to the Theory of Railway Rates," *AEA Pubs.*, VI (March, 1891), 56.

"Contributions to Economic Theory," with John B. Clark *et al.*, *AEA Pubs.*, VIII (March, 1892), 77–103.

"Cosmic Processes," *Mon*, XXX (July, 1920), 406–442.

"Cost and Expense," *Annals*, III (May, 1893), 703–735.

"Cost and Utility," *Annals*, III (Jan., 1893), 409–428.

"The Crisis in American Home Life," *Ind*, LXVIII (Feb. 17, 1910), 342–346.

"The Day of Financial Reckoning," *Moody's*, XIX (Jan., 1916), 37–39.

"The Decay of State and Local Governments," *Annals*, I (July, 1890), 26-42.

"Distribution by a Law of Rent," with Alvin Johnson *et al.*, *AEA Pubs.*, IV (Feb., 1903), 154–172.

"The Divided Self," *Mon*, XXIX (April, 1919), 223–237.

"Economic Aspects of Technical Education," *AEA Pubs.*, VI (Jan., 1891), 115–122.

"The Economic Basis of Prohibition," *Annals*, II (July, 1891), 59–68.

"The Economic Causes of Moral Progress," *Annals*, III (March, 1893), 129–149.

"Economic Dynamics," with M. Pantaleoni *et al.*, *AEA Pubs.*, XI (April, 1910), 112–135.

"Economic Fallacies that Favor War," *Moody's*, XVIII (Jan.,1915), 13–17.

"The Economic Interpretation of History," *CC*, XX (May 16, 1908), 228–229.

"An Economic Measure of School Efficiency," *ER*, XLI (May, 1911), 467–477.

"Economic Psychology," *Journal of Education*, XLIV (Dec. 17, 1896), 412–413.

"Economic Zones and the New Alignments of National Sentiment," *Sur*, XXXIII (March 6, 1915), 612–613.

"Economics in Elementary Schools," *Annals*, V (Jan., 1895), 461–489.

"The Economy of Memory in the Study of Arithmetic," *Education*, IX (Sept., Oct., 1888), 61–74, 79–86.

"Education Through Activity," *CC*, XII (Aug. 6, 1904), 790–793.

"The Educational Value of College Studies," *ER*, I (Feb., 1891), 105–120.

"The Effect of the Consumption of Wealth on the Economic Welfare of Society," in R. T. Ely *et al., Science Economic Discussion* (New York, 1886), 123–135.

"The Evolution of a New Woman," *Annals*, LVI (Nov., 1914), 111–121.

"Extravagance as a Virtue," *Current Opinion*, LIV (Jan., 1913), 51–52.

"Facts about the Accounts of Learned Societies," *Sci*, XXXVII (March 7, 1913), 371.

"The Failure of Biologic Sociology," *Annals*, IV (May, 1894), 919–947.

"The Failure of Liberal Idealism," *Freeman*, I (July 14, 21, 1920), 418–421, 444–446.

"The Fallacy of Price Bidding," *Annals*, LXVIII (July, 1918), 129–143.

"The Financial Menace to America of the European War," *Annals*, LX (July, 1915), 123–129.

"The Formulation of Normal Laws," *Annals*, VII (May, 1896), 426–449.

"The Fundamental Idea of Capital," *QJE*, III (Jan., 1889), 128–203.

"The Future of the Stock Market," *Moody's*, XVIII (April, 1915), 161–163.

"The Genesis of Consciousness," *Mon*, XXIX (July, 1919), 432–447.

"The Genesis of Personal Traits," *PSM*, LXXXIII (Aug., 1913), 157–159.

"The German Way of Thinking," *Forum*, LIV (July, 1915), 18–26.

"Hymn Writing," *Sur*, XXXI (Jan. 3, 1914), 403–404.

"The Idea and Definition of Value," with John B. Clark *et al.*, *AEA Pubs.*, VIII (March, 1893), 86–94.

"Ideals of Progress," *Sur*, XXVI (June 3, 1911), 387–392.

"Immigration Control: Construction vs. Distribution," *Sur*, XXV (Feb. 18, 1911), 866–867.

"The Importance of Economic Psychology to Teachers," *Sixty-Third Annual Meeting of the American Institute of Instruction* (Boston, 1892), 1–21.

"The Interpretation of Ricardo," *QJE*, VII (April, 1893), 322–353.

Introduction to M. S. Miller, *Songs from the Smoke* (New York, 1914), i–xi.

"Is Christianity Ethics or Religion?" *Ind*, LXX (March 30, 1911), 655–657.

"The Laws of Environmental Influence," *PSM*, LXXIX (Oct., 1911), 396–402.

"The Laws of Social Attraction," *PSM*, LXXIII (Oct., 1908), 354–360.

"Liquidation Taxes," *Annals*, LXXV (Jan., 1918), 165–181.

"Making National Debts National Blessings," *Annals*, LXXXII (March, 1919), 39–51.

"The Making of Economic Literature," *Economic Bulletin*, I (Jan., 1909), 290–300.

"Malthus and Ricardo," *AEA Pubs.*, IV (Sept., 1889), 9–34.

"Mandeville in the Twentieth Century," *AER*, VII (March, 1918), 88–98.

"The Margin of Cultivation," *QJE*, III (April, 1889), 356–358.

"The Mechanism of Mind," *Annals*, LXXI (May, 1917), 202–215.

"The Method of Science: A Reply," *Sci*, XXXIII (April 14, 1911), 578–583.

"The Morality of Force," *NR*, IV (Oct. 16, 1915), 286.

"The Need for New Economic Terms," *QJE*, V (Oct., 1891), 372–374.

"New Adjustments for Women," *Ind*, LXI (Sept. 20, 1906), 674–681.

"The New Jurisprudence," *University of Pennsylvania Law Review*, LXII (Nov., 1914), 1–16.

"A New Statement of the Law of Population," *PSQ*, X (March, 1895), 44–61.

"New Year Resolutions," *Sur*, XXXI (Dec. 27, 1913), 360–362.

"The Organic Concept of Society," *Annals*, V (Nov. 1894), 404–409.

"Our Denominate Measures," *Education*, X (May, 1890), 553–556.

"Overnutrition and Its Social Consequences," *Annals*, X (July, 1897), 33–53.

"Peace Without Force," *Annals*, LXXII (July, 1917), 31–48.

"The Place of University Extension," *University Extension*, III (Feb., 1894), 258–292.

"The Political Significance of Recent Economic Theories," *Annals*, XXXII (July, 1908), 82–94.

"Pragmatism and Social Science," *Journal of Philosophy, Psychology and Scientific Method*, LXXX (Nov., 1911), 273–279.

"The Present Problems in the Economic Interpretation of History," *Annals*, XXIV (Nov., 1904), 540–555.

"President Walker's Theory of Distribution," *QJE*, IV (Oct., 1889), 34–49.

"The Principles of Economic Interference," *Sur*, XXII (April 3, 1909), 14–16.

"Problems of War Finance," *YR*, VII (Oct., 1917), 73–89.

"The Relation of Abstract to Concrete Sciences," *Annals*, V (May, 1895), 942–948.

"The Relation of Economics to Sociology," *Annals*, V (Jan., 1895), 577–583.

"The Relation of Sociology to Economics," with Albion W. Small et al., *AEA Pubs.*, X (March, 1895), 106–117.

"The Relation of Sociology to Psychology," *Annals*, VIII (Nov., 1896), 433–460.

"The Relation of Voluntary to Political Action," *Sur*, XXIX (Jan. 4, 1913), 421–422.

"The Reorganization of Social Work," *Sur*, XXX (July 5, 1913), 468–472.

"Responsibility for the War," *NR*, I (Nov., 1914), 21–22.

Review of *A History of the Theories of Production and Distribution* by Edwin Cannan, *Annals*, IV (Sept., 1893), 317–321.

Review of *Outlines of Economics* by Richard T. Ely, *Annals*, IV (Nov., 1893), 484–486.

Review of *The Present Condition of Economic Science* by Edward Clark Lunt, *PSQ*, III (Dec., 1888), 687–690.

Review of *Principles of Western Civilization* by Benjamin Kidd, *Annals*, XIX (May, 1902), 461–463.

Review of *The Scope and Method of Political Economy* by John Neville Keynes, *Annals*, I (April, 1891), 688–692.

Review of *Sociology in Its Psychological Aspects* by Charles A. Ellwood, *AER*, III (March, 1913), 85–89.

"A Revision of American Policies," *Annals*, LIV (July, 1914), 191–200.

"The Revival of Economic Orthodoxy," *PSM*, LXXXI (Sept., 1912), 246–249.

"The Scope of Political Economy," *YR*, II (Nov., 1893), 264–287.

"Shall Woman Be Tool or Partner?" *Twentieth Century Magazine*, VI (July, 1912), 254–262.

"A Slump in Morality," *NR*, IV (Sept. 11, 1915), 55.

"The Social Basis of Prohibition," *CC*, XX (Sept. 19, 1908), 705–708.

"Social Hymns," *Sur*, XXIX (Dec. 7, 1912), 275.

"Social Reform and Politics," *Sur*, XVIII (April 27, 1912), 173–174.

"Some Explanations Relating to *The Theory of Dynamic Economics*," *QJE*, VII (Jan., 1893), 177–187.

"The Sphere of Voluntary Organization in Social Movements," with Lester F. Ward *et al.*, *Economic Studies*, I (April, 1896), 141–160.

"The Standardization of Family Life," *Annals*, XLVIII (July, 1913), 81–90.

"The Standardization of Life and Its Results," New York *Times*, April 13, 1913, Sect. V, 8.

"Taxation after the War," *Annals*, LXIV (March, 1916), 210–214.

"The Teaching of Economics in the Secondary Schools," *AEA Pubs.*, X (March, 1895), 119–138.

"Territorial Expansion," in *University Lectures* (Philadelphia, 1915), 197–209.

"Theories of Distribution," with Benjamin M. Anderson *et al.*, *AER*, III (March, 1913), Suppl., 89–95.

"Theories of Progress," *AER*, II (March, 1912), 61–68.

"The Theory of Price in Modern Economics," *Ind*, LXVIII (April 7, 1910), 742–746.

"The Theory of Social Forces: An Explanation," *IJE*, VII (July, 1897), 492–496.

"The Tomorrow of Finance," *Annals*, LXXVI (March, 1918), 257–271.

"The Track of Evolution," *Scientific Monthly*, V (Oct., 1917), 350–358.

"Types of Men," *PSM*, LXXX (March, 1912), 273–279.

"University Fellowships," *Sci*, XXXIII (Feb. 10, 1911), 216–217.

"University Training for Business Men," *ER*, XXIX (March, 1905), 217–233.

"The Unnatural Boundaries of European States," *Sur*, XXXIV (April 3, 1915), 24–27, 31–32.

"Wanted: A New Kind of Social Worker," *Sur*, XXIX (Nov. 2, 1912), 116.

"The War and the Stock Market," *Moody's*, XVIII (March, 1915), 113–115.

"Wells' *Recent Economic Changes*," PSQ, V (March, 1890), 84–103.

"Who Is the Good Neighbor?" *CC*, XIX (Feb. 29, 1908), 1642–1646.

"Wish and Will," *Mon*, XXX (Jan., 1920), 130–143.

"The World's Peace in the Making," *World's Work*, XXIII (Dec. 1911), 155–156.

"Young Wives in Industry," *Ind*, LVII (Dec. 1, 1904), 1244–1249.

Articles by Contemporaries about Patten's Thought

Adams, Henry C. Review of *The Economic Basis of Protection*, in *PSQ*, V (Dec., 1890), 710–713.

Anderson, B. M. "Patten's *Reconstruction of Economic Theory*," *PSQ*, XXVIII (March, 1913), 123–139.

Andrews, Charles M. Review of *The Development of English Thought*, in *American Historical Review*, V (Jan., 1900), 330–332.

Ball, Sidney. Review of *The Development of English Thought*, in *Economic Review*, X (Jan. 15, 1900), 114–118.

——. Review of *The Theory of Prosperity*, in *Economic Review*, XII (Oct., 1902), 501–502.

Bastable, C. Review of *The Economic Basis of Protection*, in *EJ*, I (Sept., 1891), 596–599.

Bernard, F. F. Review of *The Social Basis of Religion*, in *AJS*, XVIII (Sept., 1912), 264–265.

Böhm-Bawerk, Eugen. "Aus der neuesten nationalökonomischen Literatur Englands und Nordamerikas," *Jahrbücher*, LII (1889), 672–681.

Bolce, Harold. "Blasting at the Rock of Ages," *Cosmopolitan*, XLVI (May, 1909), 665–676.

Brodnitz, Georg. Review of *The Theory of Prosperity*, in *Jahrbücher*, XXXI (March, 1906), 398–401.

Caldwell, William. "Professor Patten's *Theory of Social Forces*," *IJE*, VII (April, July, 1897), 345–353, 496–497.

Calkins, Gary N. Review of *Heredity and Social Progress*, in *PSQ*, XVIII (Sept., 1903), 539–541.

Carver, Thomas N. Review of *The Social Basis of Religion,* in *AER,* I (Dec., 1911), 790–794.

Clark, John Bates. "Patten's Dynamic Economics," *Annals,* III (July, 1892), 30–44.

———. Review of *The Economic Basis of Protection,* in *Annals,* I (Oct., 1890), 337–342.

———. "The Surplus Gains of Labor," *Annals,* III (March, 1893), 607–617.

Cook, E. Albert. Review of *The Social Basis of Religion,* in *American Journal of Theology,* XVI (April, 1912), 312–315.

Courcelle-Seneuil, M. Review of *The Economic Basis of Protection,* in *Journal des Economistes,* VI (May, 1891), 299–303.

Devine, Edward T. "Neighbors," *Sur,* XLVIII (July 1, 1922), 477–478.

———. "The New Basis of Civilization: Patten," *CC,* XVIII (May 4, 1907), 135–136.

———. Review of *Heredity and Social Progress,* in *CC,* XI (Oct. 3, 1903), 316–318.

Diehl, Karl. Review of *The Development of English Thought,* in *Jahrbücher,* XX (1900), 681–690.

———. Review of *The Educational Value of Political Economy,* in *Jahrbücher,* LVII (1891), 279–280.

Durkheim, Emile. Review of *The Social Basis of Religion,* in *L'Année Sociologique,* XII (1913), 79–80.

Ely, Richard T., *et al.* Discussion of *The Educational Value of Political Economy,* in *AEA Pubs.,* VI (Jan., 1891), 100–115.

———, *et al.* "Memorial to Former President Simon N. Patten," *AER,* XIII (March, 1923), Suppl., 259–293.

Fite, Warner. "Professor Patten's Psychological Doctrines," *JPE,* VII (June, 1899), 384–391.

Gardner, C. S. Review of *The Social Basis of Religion,* in *Review and Expositor,* IX (April, 1912), 280–282.

Gardner, Henry B. Review of *The Theory of Prosperity,* in *YR,* XI (Feb., 1903), 409–412.

Garmo, Charles de. Review of *The Development of English Thought,* in *ER,* XVII (May, 1899), 484–488.

Giddings, Franklin H. "Sociology and the Abstract Sciences," *Annals,* V (March, 1895), 746–753.

———. "Utility, Economics and Sociology," *Annals,* V (Nov., 1894), 398–404.

Gide, Charles. Review of *The Economic Basis of Protection,* in *Revue d'Economie Politique,* V (March, 1891), 410–412.

Goode, J. Paul. Review of *Heredity and Social Progress*, in *Annals*, XXII (Sept., 1903), 366–369.

Greene, William B. Review of *The Social Basis of Religion*, in *Princeton Theological Review*, IX (July, 1911), 471–474.

Hadley, Arthur T. "Recent Tendencies in Economic Literature," *YR*, III (Nov., 1894), 251–260.

——. Review of *The Theory of Dynamic Economics*, in *PSQ*, VII (Sept., 1892), 562–563.

Henderson, C. R. Review of *The Development of English Thought*, in *Dial*, XXVIII (June 1, 1900), 436–437.

——. Review of *The Theory of Social Forces*, in *Dial*, XX (May 11, 1896), 277.

Hickernell, Warren F. "Has the Interest Rate Risen Two Per Cent?" *Moody's*, XIX (Feb., 1916), 61–66.

Hill, C. M. Review of *The Development of English Thought*, in *JPE*, VII (Sept., 1899), 554–563.

Hobson, John A. Review of *The Theory of Dynamic Economics*, in *EJ*, II (Dec., 1892), 687–690.

Hollander, J. H. "Mandeville in the Twentieth Century: A Correction," *AER*, VIII (March, 1918), Suppl., 338–339.

Johnson, Alvin S. "Patten's Theory of Prosperity," *PSQ*, XVII (June, 1902), 313–319.

Judd, Charles H. Review of *Heredity and Social Progress*, in *YR*, XIII (Aug., 1904), 221–222.

Komorzynsji, Johann von. Review of *The Theory of Prosperity*, in *Zeitschrift für Sozialwissenschaft*, VII (1904), 279–280.

Leiserson, William M. Review of *Mud Hollow*, in *Sur*, XLVIII (Aug. 15, 1922), 627.

Leser, Ernst. Review of *The Premises of Political Economy*, in *Jahrbücher*, XIV (1887), 267–274.

Lexis, Wilhelm. Review of *The Theory of Prosperity*, in *Jahrbücher für Gesetzgebung, Verwaltung und Volkswirtschaft im Deutschen Reich*, XXVII (1903), 338–342.

Marrett, R. R. Review of *Heredity and Social Progress*, in *Economic Review*, XIII (Oct. 15, 1903), 498–501.

Marshall, Alfred. "Consumer's Surplus," *Annals*, III (March, 1893), 618–621.

Meyer, Robert. "Die Zunehmende Mannigfaltigkeit der Consumption," *Zeitschrift für Volkswirtschaft, Sozialpolitik und Verwaltung*, II (1893), 385–418.

"The Old Order Changeth," *Outlook*, LXXXVI (Aug. 10, 1907), 765–767.

Pettazzoni, Raffaele. Review of *The Social Basis of Religion,* in *Scientia,* XV (May, 1914), 474–475.

"A Professor on the Rampage," *Na,* XCVI (June 12, 1912), 591–592.

"Professor Patten Tries to 'Modernize' the Hymnal," *Current Opinion,* LXI (Nov., 1916), 337.

Rabbeno, Ugo. *The American Commercial Policy.* Milan, 1893; London, 1895. Ch. xi.

Ramage, B. J. Review of *The Development of English Thought,* in *Sewanee Review,* VII (July, 1899), 366–369.

Review of *The Development of English Thought,* in *Outlook,* LXII (June 3, 1899), 311–312.

Review of *The Development of English Thought,* in *Spectator,* LXXXIII (Sept. 16, 1899), 381–382.

Review of *Heredity and Social Progress,* in *Gunton's Magazine,* XXV (Aug., 1903), 167–170.

Review of *Heredity and Social Progress,* in *Na,* LXXVI (June 11, 1903), 483.

Review of *Mud Hollow,* in "Book Review," New York *Times,* May 28, 1922, 16.

Review of *Mud Hollow,* in "Literary Review," New York *Evening Post,* July 29, 1922, Sect. II, 842.

Review of *Mud Hollow,* in *Times Literary Supplement* (London), XXI (June 1, 1922), 366.

Review of *The Social Basis of Religion,* in *Expository Times,* XXII (June, 1911), 417.

Review of *The Stability of Prices,* in *Jahrbücher,* LV (1890), 98–99.

Review of *The Theory of Prosperity,* in *Gunton's Magazine,* XXIV (Jan., 1903), 76–81.

Review of *The Theory of Prosperity,* in *Ind,* LIV (Oct., 1902), 2365–2367.

Review of *The Theory of Prosperity,* in *Na,* LXXV (July 24, 1902), 74–75.

Rowe, Leo S., *et al.* "Memorial Addresses on the Life and Services of Simon N. Patten," *Annals,* CVII (May, 1923), Suppl., 335–367.

Salter, William A. "Reflections on Professor Patten's Views," *Mon,* XXX (Jan., 1920), 144–152.

——. "Thoughts Suggested by Professor Patten's Recent Article," *Mon,* XXIX (Oct., 1919), 610–615.

Seager, Henry R. "Professor Patten's Theory of Prosperity," *Annals,* XIX (March, 1902), 239–255.

Seligman, Edwin R. A. "Who Is the Twentieth Century Mandeville?" *AER*, VIII (March, 1918), Suppl., 440–449.

Shotwell, James T. Review of *The Social Basis of Religion*, in *PSQ*, XXVII (March, 1912), 152–154.

Simons, Sarah E. Review of *The Theory of Prosperity*, in *AJS*, VIII (July, 1902), 122–129.

Small, Albion W. Review of *The Reconstruction of Economic Theory*, in *AJS*, XVIII (Jan., 1913), 580–583.

——. "Social vs. Societary," *Annals*, V (May, 1895), 948–953.

Smith, Munroe. "Patten's Study of English Thought," *PSQ*, XV (March, 1900), 112–119.

Stickley, Gustav. "Borrowed Plumes," *Craftsman*, XXIII (Jan., 1913), 487–490.

Taussig, Frank W. "Recent Literature on Protection," *QJE*, VII (Jan., 1893), 162–175.

Veblen, Thorstein B. Review of *The Development of English Thought*, in *Annals*, XIV (July, 1899), 125–131.

Vincent, George E. Review of *The New Basis of Civilization*, in *PSQ*, XXII (Dec., 1907), 741–743.

Wallas, G. "United States of Europe," *NR*, IV (Jan. 2, 1915), 24.

Ward, Lester F. Review of *The Theory of Social Forces*, in *AJS*, I (March, 1896), 632–639.

Wenley, R. M. Review of *The Development of English Thought*, in *Sci* (May 9, 1899), 713–715.

Whipple, Guy M. Review of *Heredity and Social Progress*, in *ER*, XXVII (March, 1904), 309–312.

White, Horace. "Wells' *Recent Economic Changes*," *PSQ*, V (June, 1890), 309–326.

Willits, Joseph H. Review of *Mud Hollow*, in *Annals*, CIII (Sept., 1922), 151–153.

Index

Recent books published for the American Historical Association

from the income of the Albert J. Beveridge Memorial Fund

AN AGRICULTURAL HISTORY OF THE GENESEE VALLEY, 1790–1860.
By Neil A. McNall.

STEAM POWER ON THE AMERICAN FARM. *By Reynold M. Wik.*

HORACE GREELEY: NINETEENTH-CENTURY CRUSADER.
By Glyndon G. Van Deusen.

ERA OF THE OATH: NORTHERN LOYALTY TESTS DURING THE
CIVIL WAR AND RECONSTRUCTION. *By Harold M. Hyman.*

HISTORY OF MARSHALL FIELD & CO. *By Robert W. Twyman.*

ROBERT MORRIS: REVOLUTIONARY FINANCIER.
By Clarence L. Ver Steeg.

THE FIRST RAPPROCHEMENT: ENGLAND AND THE
UNITED STATES, 1795–1805. *By Bradford Perkins.*

THE DEVELOPMENT OF AMERICAN PETROLEUM PIPELINES:
A STUDY IN PRIVATE ENTERPRISE AND PUBLIC POLICY, 1862–1906.
By Arthur Menzies Johnson.

COLONISTS FROM SCOTLAND: EMIGRATION TO NORTH AMERICA,
1707–1783. *By Ian Charles Cargill Graham.*

PROFESSORS & PUBLIC ETHICS: STUDIES OF NORTHERN MORAL
PHILOSOPHERS BEFORE THE CIVIL WAR. *By Wilson Smith.*

THE AXIS ALLIANCE AND JAPANESE-AMERICAN RELATIONS, 1941.
By Paul W. Schroeder.

A FRONTIER STATE AT WAR: KANSAS, 1861–1865.
By Albert Castel.

BRITISH INVESTMENTS AND THE AMERICAN MINING FRONTIER,
1860–1901. *By Clark C. Spence.*

RAILS, MINES, AND PROGRESS: SEVEN AMERICAN PROMOTERS
IN MEXICO, 1867–1911. *By David M. Pletcher.*

LAGUARDIA IN CONGRESS. *By Howard Zinn.*